THE CREATIVE EXPERIMENT

By C. M. Bowra

A BOOK OF RUSSIAN VERSE
THE HERITAGE OF SYMBOLISM
FROM VIRGIL TO MILTON
A SECOND BOOK OF RUSSIAN VERSE

THE CREATIVE
EXPERIMENT

BY

C. M. BOWRA

GROVE PRESS, INC.   NEW YORK

Library of Congress Catalog Card Number: 58-5558

The Creative Experiment is published in two editions:
An Evergreen Book (E-80)
A hard bound edition

*Grove Press Books and Evergreen Books
are published by Barney Rosset at Grove Press, Inc.
795 Broadway   New York 3, N. Y.*

PREFACE

This book is a kind of sequel to *The Heritage of Symbolism* published in 1943, and attempts to sketch some main figures and characteristics of the poetry which succeeded that of the post-Symbolists and has played an important part in Europe since 1910. I have, however, adopted a somewhat different method, and discussed, not the complete careers of poets, but what seem to be their most significant works or phases, in the hope that this will make clearer the problems and aims of this movement. As before, I have been inconsistent in my presentation of texts written in foreign languages. I have assumed that few readers will ask for quotations in Modern Greek and Russian, and have given these only in English translations, but that most will know French and be able to manage Spanish with literal versions to help them. I am indebted to the kindness of friends who have helped me, especially to Dr. S. Rachmilevitsch, Mr. I. Berlin, Mr. A. E. Sloman, Miss Helen Gardner, and Professor R. M. Dawkins; to Professor J. Mavrogordato for allowing me to use some of his forthcoming translations of Cavafy; to Mr. J. M. Cohen for similar help with Alberti; and to Mr. Herbert Marshall and the Pilot Press Ltd. for permission to quote from his *Mayakovsky and his Poetry*.

C. M. BOWRA

Oxford
February 1948

CONTENTS

CONTENTS

I

THE CREATIVE EXPERIMENT

In any general survey of the fine arts in the first half of the twentieth century it is impossible to avoid the conclusion that it has in many respects been a time of experiment. Painting, sculpture, architecture and music, which in the nineteenth century had their accepted canons and responded on the whole to standard tastes, have all been rigorously scrutinised and subjected to a variety of new aims and new techniques. The change in poetry has been no less marked. Of course some poets have maintained an older manner and shown what can still be done with it, but the characteristic poetry of the time seems in many ways to have abandoned familiar methods of composition and to aim at new effects through a variety of new manners. The difference between the early Yeats and T. S. Eliot, between Rubén Darío and Lorca, between Mallarmé and Apollinaire, shows how wide a gulf lies between the poetry of the Symbolists and the various modern styles. For poetry the change from the nineteenth to the twentieth century is as great as that from the eighteenth to the nineteenth, and just as the first Romantics were ridiculed and misunderstood largely because they rejected an established style, so the poets of this century have been slow to win the approval of men educated in different manners to different standards of taste. But whereas the Romantics seem to have known almost from the first what they wished to do and what they thought their art to be, the poets of this century have no such confidence. Even if they started with certain common assumptions and were impelled by a common ambition, their variety of practice suggests that their ideas have not been easy to put into effect. They have made many experiments and produced results of very different kinds, and their work raises questions which concern the very nature of poetry.

Like all new movements, the modern movement in poetry

can be regarded historically as a reaction against what preceded it. Such a reaction is inevitable and requires little
comment. As soon as an art reaches the limits of its idiom,
it is doomed to become moribund and to hamper creative
work. What happened to the grand manner of the eighteenth
century happened again at the end of the nineteenth, when
the Romantic movement, after yielding its final flowers in the
special art of the Symbolists, showed that nothing more could
be done with it and that any attempt to continue with it would
mean lifeless imitation. Yeats saw the issue when he turned
from the dream-laden style of *The Shadowy Waters* to the
concentrated, unadorned style of his later books. He realised
that his earlier manner was inadequate to what he now had
to say, for the reason that it had been invented by men whose
creative experiences and ambitions were quite different from
his own. The difficulty was in the first place a matter of
vocabulary. The words which the poets of the nineteenth
century had brought into circulation lost with use their mint
quality and became duller and duller until at last they seemed
to belong to a vanished world. Even if these words had not
been spoiled by use, they would still be incapable of expressing states of mind unknown to the great Romantics and
Symbolists. The first change that poetry demanded was in
language. Old words and phrases must be discarded, new
words introduced, and the whole art of words subjected to
a keen, selective criticism. In most European countries
something of this kind happened. It is almost impossible
now for a man to write with the vocabulary of the early
Yeats or of Darío or of Mallarmé. If he does so, he is
suspected either of distorting his experience through an
inapposite idiom or of being a mere imitator of the great
masters.

The change in vocabulary rises from the need to create
something new, but is not in itself enough to meet this end.
Poets must also reconsider the kind of effect which they produce, the spheres of experience which they think suitable for
poetry, and the degree of liberty to be allowed to the creative
spirit. Of course the nineteenth century with its tremendous
range of creative achievement produced many kinds of poetry.

It was the age not only of Wordsworth and Hugo and Mallarmé, but of Whitman and Browning and Rimbaud. None the less its main and most characteristic tendency was towards a noble, sweet harmony, a poetry in which regular verse and sonorous music impart a special order to experience and give a special pleasure through it. If rebellious poets sought to secure other kinds of effect, they were treated as eccentrics, and their most popular poems were those which approximated most closely to the standard model. On these standards the generation of 1910 had been brought up, and it found some difficulty in abandoning them. For instance, when T. S. Eliot published his first volume, *Prufrock and Other Observations*, in 1916, the average reader found that the only poem which appealed as familiar and friendly was *La Figlia che Piange* which strikes a note reminiscent of Victorian sweetness and ease :

> Stand on the highest pavement of the stair
> Lean on a garden urn —
> Weave, weave the sunlight in your hair —
> Clasp your flowers to you with a pained surprise —
> Fling them to the ground and turn
> With a fugitive resentment in your eyes :
> But weave, weave the sunlight in your hair.

In its choice of words, its regular movement, the quality of its sentiment, this satisfied many readers that it was what poetry ought to be, but they did not feel at all this assurance about the first poem in the same volume, *The Love Song of J. Alfred Prufrock*, with its aggressively unconventional opening :

> Let us go then, you and I,
> When the evening is spread out against the sky
> Like a patient etherised upon a table ;
> Let us go, through certain half-deserted streets,
> The muttering retreats
> Of restless nights in one-night cheap hotels
> And sawdust restaurants with oyster-shells.

It was clear that something had happened to poetry, and many were uneasy about it. But others felt that deliverance had come and that they could now get away from the subjects and spirit of Romanticism and Symbolism to something closer to actual experience.

If modern poetry was born in reaction against an exhausted style, it had still to find its own principles and aims, to decide what it wished to do, positively no less than negatively. It began with a natural assumption that, since poetry had become false through its addiction to conventional manners and subjects, it must again become true to its own nature, rid itself of what did not really belong to it and become purer than before. This sounded well, but raised practical difficulties. The conception of "pure poetry", which has engaged many poets and critics, has not ended in any clear definition of what it is. There is of course a poetry which is purer than some other poetry because it deals more exclusively with what are thought to be poetical states of mind and lacks those prosaic elements which were permitted even by great masters like Hugo and Tennyson. The Symbolists paid much attention to this and excluded anything rhetorical or didactic or ethical on the grounds that it was necessarily unpoetical. But the modern conception of purity is not quite this. It has advanced from where Symbolism stopped and aims at a poetry which is pure in the sense that it gives a special kind of thrill which is regarded as the essential function of poetry and distinguishes it from anything else. Of course all great or real poets from Homer to Hardy provoke this thrill, but not perhaps so consciously or so deliberately as modern taste demands. They are concerned also with other matters, with human interest, with telling a story, with emotions and passions, with the criticism of life and with providing matter for thought. To the strict modern these considerations are irrelevant and even dangerous, because they may deter the poet from his single, indispensable task of providing a special kind of excitement.

This idea is not entirely new. In some ways Nietzsche foreshadowed it when he drew his famous distinction between the Apollonian and the Dionysian elements in poetry. He held that man needs two different kinds of imaginative outlook. On the one hand is the Apollonian world of "dream", typified by the Olympian gods, in which men have an ideal of calm and order and see everything clearly and distinctly. On the other hand there is the Dionysian world of " intoxication ", of excitement and ecstasy, in which there is no calm and no clarity, but a strange sense of power and a narcotic influence which makes a man forget himself and identify himself with nature or the human crowd in its less rational and more instinctive moods. The moderns tend towards the Dionysian outlook. Their idea of the authentic thrill is of something powerful and overwhelming which gives not intellectual light but a sense of more abundant life. In his own way Hopkins believed something of the same kind. He aimed at conveying a sense of powers at work in nature, at communicating what he called " inscape ", that stirring of something in the world whose passage into himself he called " instress ". What mattered for him were certain moments when he felt himself possessed by an influence so extraordinary that it could only be supernatural. For him every word must be charged with power, and he saw that this meant a loss of the regular harmony and classical ease which belonged to his friend Robert Bridges. So too Rimbaud, with the prophetic insight of genius, saw the issue. When he insisted that the poet must practise " un long, immense et raisonné dérèglement de tous les sens ", when he saw a mosque in place of a factory, angels playing drums, or coaches on roads in the sky, when he said that " le poète définerait la quantité d'inconnu s'éveillant en son temps, dans l'âme universelle ", he was moving in the same direction as Nietzsche and Hopkins. He wished to write a poetry which should appeal to much more than a love of harmony and sentiment, to alter the world by the violence of his impact on the imagination and to bring back the lost vitality of the great Greeks.

The modern poets who have discovered these ideas in others or themselves have applied them with some rigour. It is perhaps characteristic of our time that poetry is expected to perform its own essential task and to do nothing else. The same spirit can be seen in other arts, in painting with its insistence on line and colour and design at the expense of representational truth, or in sculpture with its concentration on the pure use of the medium in which it works. In an age of specialism poetry too must specialise, and it has tried to do so. It might be argued that the production of this thrill is not the authentic task of poetry, that harmony and happy ease are in every way as important, that the modern poets, despite their concentration on this end, have on the whole been less successful in attaining it than poets like Dante or Wordsworth who aimed at quite different ends, that this final thrill is an accidental result of poetry and not its essence. In this criticism there is perhaps some truth. There is indeed a poetry in which a sweet harmony is the end, and for many readers it is perfectly satisfying. Lovers of Ovid or Bridges are content almost to dispense with the thrill and to enjoy something quite different. No doubt the modern theory can be assailed, but what matters with a theory in the arts is not whether it is universally true but what it means and does for those who hold it, and it is undeniable that many modern poets believe that the thrill is the end, and that nothing else matters in comparison. They may be wrong before the judgment-seat of absolute truth, but they are right before their own artistic consciences, and that is what counts.

The desire to secure this thrill is combined with something else no less important. When poets insist that the old-fashioned idiom is wrong because it fails to express what they really feel, they assert the need and the value of truth. They must, it seems, tell the truth as they really see it. This is natural and not unexpected ; for no artist, however fantastic, would admit that what he says has not its own kind of truth. But the moderns go further than this and stress a special kind of truth. The truth which they demand is not mere truth or ordinary truth, nor a simple avoidance of falsehood, but the whole truth in the full sense of the phrase, the truth as they see it with their whole natures, when their wits and sensibilities and emotions are all at work. Nor is it just so much of this as can be clearly stated in plain words : it is the full truth, which needs much more than plain words and can be reached only through hints and suggestions and all the means which poetry possesses to convey something in its full value and mystery. The modern poet, who lives in an age of psychological discovery and of an increased awareness of the subtler currents in himself, has a harder task to tell the whole truth than his ancestors had in simpler and less self-conscious times. He is particularly at a disadvantage because the modern means which scientists have invented for psychology, the language which they use and their experimental approach to the subject, are unfitted for poetry. The poet does not analyse himself in this way, nor can he use an abstract language of this kind. His task is not to explain or to analyse, but to portray something just as he sees it, to catch its fleeting hues and its shifting shapes, to make us feel about it what he feels himself, even if neither he nor we are able fully to understand it. In the self modern poetry has a subject which demands the highest standards of truth as they have never been demanded before, and to do its duty by this it must possess a suitable technique.

In general most modern poets try to make poetry as full and as rich as possible in order to secure the maximum of truth and of poetical effect. An experience must be presented in its complexity, without the simplifications and the order which analytical thought gives. Since the originating creative condition is extremely direct and immediate and often very unfamiliar, the poet must not be afraid to state exactly what he feels and to trust that he will be understood. The creative mood may come to him in so strong a flood that it overwhelms and annihilates his habitual ways of thought and refuses to be fitted into any familiar categories. The senses and the mind work so closely together and their interactions are so intricate that the poet cannot distinguish between them and must show how united they are in the moment of creative illumination. We might think that on such occasions the poet's thoughts merely take on a metaphorical dress, but that is to misunderstand him. The truth is rather that his sensations so penetrate his thoughts that the two constitute a single state. What earlier poets do by the more analytical processes of simile and metaphor, most modern poets do by what looks like an illogical process but is really a correct way of saying what strikes them. For instance, when the Spanish poet, Gerardo Diego, writes :

> Habrá un silencio verde
> todo hecho de guitarras destrenzadas. . . .[1]

we might complain that silence may be green but can hardly be made of " unplaited guitars ". Yet that is what is meant. The moment is when guitars have ceased to sound, and the silence which follows is not only almost visible but has so strong a quality that the music, in ceasing, contributes to it, as if a garland were being unplaited. The elements of sight and sound, and even the absence of them, have passed together into the poet's consciousness, and the effect is complete and single.

This desire to express unusual states of mind has given a new emphasis and importance to the use of imagery. All poetry, sooner or later, uses imagery to express those obscure states which cannot be expressed directly or to convey through parallel and simile the real significance of what the poet feels. But so long as he is ready to explain himself, even at the cost of his poetry, the image does not play a part of first importance. It is an element, but no more than an element, in a complex whole. The modern outlook has changed this position, since the poets need images to express the full complexity of their moods and use them more freely to convey the special thrill which they regard as their essential function. It is not enough to say, as the Russian Imagists did, that the image is " the naphthalene which preserves a work from the moths of time ". Its task is quite different, to put as much truth as possible into words. This means that the image plays a more emphatic part in modern poetry and is more closely woven into its texture than it has hitherto been. For instance, the similes which compose most of Shelley's *To a Skylark* are intended to show all the different qualities which he finds in the bird's song, but they are distinguished from it and do no more than illuminate it. Moreover they appear in a regular sequence, and each is kept

[1] There will be a green silence
All made of unplaited guitars.

8

separate from the rest. This is not the way in which modern poets usually work. They tend to make little distinction between an experience and the comparison which it evokes, for the reason that the two are really one. They see the experience as having the qualities of that to which it is compared, and therefore they break down the distinction between them. Moreover, just as in his later plays, Shakespeare sometimes passes in a short space from one image to another, so modern poets change their images with the development of a theme and accumulate them in a single sentence. Each point in an experience may demand its own appropriate image, and there is no need for the different images to belong to a single order of phenomena. For instance, when the Chilean poet, Pablo Neruda, wishes to convey a particular phase of his disgust with life, he produces without preliminary a series of images which suggest the different shades of his feelings, and makes no attempt to compose them into a single picture :

> Hay pájaros de color de azufre y horribles intestinos
> colgando de las puertas de las casas que odio,
> hay dentaduras olvidadas en una cafetera,
> hay espejos
> que debieron haber llorado de vergüenza y espanto,
> hay paraguas en todas partes, y venenos y ombligos.[1]

Each image makes a new point and develops the situation until it emerges in all the richness of its implications.

This use of images is of great importance when the poet describes some purely mental state. Images are more individual and more expressive than the abstract words whose place they take. They give a sufficiently definite outline to states of mind which are perfectly vivid to the poet but for which no standard means of expression is adequate. They tell not only what the poet means intellectually, but all that he feels, the complex of thought and emotion which is his.

[1] There are birds the colour of sulphur and horrible intestines
Hanging from the doors of houses that I loathe,
There are false teeth forgotten in a coffee-pot,
There are mirrors
That must have wept for shame and fright,
There are umbrellas everywhere, and poisons and navels.

(A. Flores)

So the Greek poet, George Seferis, conveys in five lines the sensations which accompany a memory of childhood :

> Your blood froze sometimes, like the moon
> In the inexhaustible night, your blood
> Opened its white wings
> On the black rocks, on the contours of trees and houses,
> With a ray of light from our years of childhood.

Seferis presents something that would otherwise be lost in vague words. He finds an image in perfect harmony with the familiar world and makes it do a special task. Images need not be so coherent as this. At times they have to convey something so complex that no single image is enough, and something like a mixed metaphor is needed because the situation which demands it is also mixed. So when Paul Éluard describes what he feels about his mistress's hair he creates not a picture but a composition of pictorial elements which do not quite cohere into a single design but none the less suggest what he feels :

> Ta chevelure d'oranges dans le vide du monde
> Dans le vide des vitres lourdes de silence
> Et d'ombre où mes mains nues cherchent tous les reflets.

Once poetry has approached these complex themes of the excited consciousness, imagery is indispensable, and there are no limits to what it can do.

This desire to make poetry present existing life means that it enters into spheres of experience which were missed by the narrower vision of the nineteenth century, and attempts a special kind of realism. This is not in the least a scientific realism, an objective record of fact, such as the Parnassians loved, but an imaginative realism which allows no frontiers to the poetic spirit but assumes that it may find its material in any branch of life. The poets of the nineteenth century were on the whole guided by a belief in the Beautiful, and held that some subjects are beautiful in themselves and others not, but the moderns are not very much interested in the Beautiful as such, and do not believe that there is a category of beautiful subjects. What matters is the imaginative appeal of a subject, and there is no means by which this can be forecast in advance. So mysterious indeed are the workings of the creative spirit that it may find its subject in almost any field of experience. And this surely is true. The devotees of Beauty rejected much that Shakespeare or Dante would have accepted without question. What matters to the modern poet is the essential excitement, the exaltation and thrill which he finds, not a preconceived, general notion of what the subjects of poetry are or are not. But this change has perhaps been the hardest for poets to justify to the public. The old conception of beautiful subjects has died hard, and its champions have quite sincerely rejected much of the new poetry because it does not conform to their ideas but deals with matters which are thought to be distasteful or ugly in themselves. The first antagonism to Mayakovsky or Eliot, even to Apollinaire, was based on the conviction that these men wrote about matters unsuitable to poetry, and the only answer is that we should look at their work and decide whether it succeeds as poetry or not. Opinion has now decided that it does, and the doubt has been answered, but in its day it caused much trouble and provoked the poets sometimes to be more truculent than they would otherwise have been and to defy public opinion by showing how disagreeable they could be. Indeed, just because the resistance to the new outlook was so strong, the poets were at times unmannerly and even forgot their own aims in their desire to deal firmly with their critics.

The new conception of poetry is full of ambiguities and even of dangers. Just because it desires something so ardently, it is liable not to think out its conclusions very clearly and to make experiments which we can now see to have been grave mistakes. Since it aims at creating an effect in its readers rather than at direct communication of thoughts, it uses words in a special way by giving a great emphasis to their emotive and associative values. Of course all poetry does this, but the moderns do it more consciously and more ruthlessly than most of their predecessors, and since they believe that this is their first and most important task, it is but a small step to claiming that intelligible meaning does not matter and that words can have a kind of musical significance simply through their sound. Early in this century some simple experiments of this kind were made by the Italian poet, Aldo Palazzeschi, who began a poem about enjoyment with :

> Tri tri tri
> Fru fru fru
> Ihu ihu ihu
> Uhi uhi uhi.

We can see what he is trying to do. The noises are sufficiently evocative to cause no difficulty and to leave us in little doubt about the quality of the poet's feelings. The Russian Futurists picked up this idea and made bolder experiments with a kind of " Jabberwocky ". When Anton Lotov wrote his *Melody of an Easter City*, he somehow succeeded in calling up the noises of the bazaar, at least to those who do not know what they mean :

> Khan khan da dash
> Shu shur i des
> Vilar' yagda
> Suksan kaedeksh
> Mak sa Mak sa
> Yakim den zar
> Vaks bar dan yak
> Zaza
> Siu sech bazd i
> Gar yo zda be
> Men khatt zayde
> Vin da chok me.

So long as *zaumni*, as the Russians called this " trans-sense " language, confines itself to outlandish effects of this kind, no one can take much exception to it, though it is not very exciting. But it has inevitably been applied to matters nearer home, and then its limitations are more obvious. Alexander Kruchenykh went further than Lotov and tried to change the existing Russian language into something which would be, as he claimed, closer to the national genius. " The lily is beautiful," he wrote, " but the word ' lily ' (liliya) is atrocious ; it has been handled a great deal and raped. Therefore I name the lily ' yeouyi ', and the old beauty is restored." He set himself against meaning, wrote a poem in " trans-sense " :

> dir, bull, schchill,
> oubeshchour
> skoom
> vi so boo
> r l ehz

and declared that " in these five lines there is more of the national Russian spirit than in all the poetry of Pushkin ". Perhaps he did not expect to be taken too seriously, but at least he believed that there was some future for words without meaning.

The trouble with " trans-sense " is that, though it is often amusing and sometimes effective, its range is extremely limited. It succeeds only when it deals with irrational, unintelligible sensations, and these form so small a part of poetry that they can almost be discounted. Kruchenykh and his friends were moved by a natural feeling that contemporary words had become stale, but they drew a false conclusion when they decided that words should be divorced altogether from their meaning. For to do this is to deprive poetry of half of its being. Its words are effective because they create a state of mind in which understanding plays a considerable part. Without this element of communication they are nothing but a very inadequate substitute for music, and " trans-sense " cannot hope to succeed as intelligible words do. It is therefore not surprising that the Russian Futurists eventually gave up their search for the " word as such ". Kruchenykh himself took to writing stories in verse and libretti for operas : Kamensky, who in his *Razin* invented noises which sound like Persian but have no meaning, now writes about aeronauts and heroes of Russian history : David Burlyuk, who was in his day a keen advocate of "trans-sense", now complains in quite intelligible stanzas about the miseries of life in New York : even Viktor Khlebnikov, a far more gifted writer than any of these, who began with a mystical belief in the possibility of creating an original, universal language and gave some time to inventing words on what he believed to be philological principles, turned to poems about the ardours and emotions of the Revolution and prepared the way for a new kind of heroic poetry. In its day " trans-sense " may have served a purpose by drawing attention to the value of sound in words, but it soon outlived its usefulness and now has no adherents.

A second risk lies in the claim of modern poetry to express the contemporary consciousness. With such a claim there is no quarrel in principle. It is only right and natural that poets should extract from their own time all that it has to give. But " contemporary " is an ambiguous word. In particular, it may refer not to modern life as a whole but to those qualities in it which distinguish it from the past, and it is but a small step from this to a false view of the contemporary consciousness. An example of this error can be seen in Filippo Marinetti and the Italian Futurists. Marinetti, who published his *Futurist Manifesto* in 1909 and his *Technical Manifesto of Futurist Literature* in 1912, was obsessed by the desire to make literature contemporary in a special sense. He believed that a new art of words, which played havoc with grammar and punctuation, would give a wonderful force to the human spirit, and reflect the dynamic modern world. He felt that poetry was stifled by the past, and proclaimed his " horror of what is old and known " and his " love of the new and unforeseen ". He believed that since we live in an age of machines, we find our self-expression through them and have developed a new kind of mind. For him what matter are such objects as trains, machine-guns, aeroplanes, underground railways and wireless telegraphy. He wishes to reproduce the state of mind which a man has when he loses himself in a machine. This forces him to reject the familiar subjects of poetry and proclaim the " need of spitting every day on the altar of art " and the desire to " exalt aggressive movement, febrile insomnia, the racing pace, the acrobat's somersault, the slap in the face, and the blow of the fist ". He rejects love as sentimentality and glorifies war as " the bloody and necessary test of a people's force " and " the only hygiene of the world ". He sees man as living through machines and being almost a machine himself.

In Marinetti's arguments there is a perverse kind of logic.

At least he faces the need for a new kind of poetry and sees that it must reflect vigorous phases of modern life. But he draws false conclusions because he makes unwarrantable assumptions. There is, for instance, some truth in his claim that the past has become burdensome and imposes literary standards which have ceased to be tenable. But that does not mean that the whole past must be jettisoned or that modern poetry must have no truck with any subject that has been treated before. Just because some love-poetry is sentimental, that does not prove that no love-poetry is possible or tolerable. Marinetti was deluded by his myopic view of what life to-day really is. Now that we have lost our first excitement in the internal combustion engine, machines seldom touch our imagination or stir our emotions. They exist for use, and familiarity with them is so automatic as to be uninspiring. Because he liked noise and speed, Marinetti assumed that these were the essentially modern qualities, and he erred greatly in identifying imaginative or creative strength with physical violence. His cult of war and bloodshed, of crude sensations, is quite different from an enhanced sensibility and produces not an alert awareness but a mental torpor alike in those who inflict it and in those on whom it is inflicted. Marinetti's work shows the narrow limits of his outlook and the falsity of his doctrine. His attempts to describe the Turco-Italian War of 1912 are nothing but bombastic journalism, in which the desire to keep everything at the same pitch of excitement ends in a monotonous rhetoric, without insight or variety or charm. The truth is that Marinetti did not understand either art or life. He liked sensation and noise, and his public meetings were diversified by his ability to cause annoyance and to deal with interruptions. He wished to make words serve his cult of violence, but he failed, because words lose their power when they are put to too great a strain. Later, perhaps, he saw his mistake ; for he gave up pretences to imaginative literature and composed a hand-book of Futurist cookery.

The examples of Futurist excesses show the dangers which lurk in the extreme claims of modern poetry. Even when we pass them over as aberrations of youth, it is still

clear that the modern outlook is faced by considerable problems. Having set its ideal before itself, it has to find what
in practice this demands, and in trying to find the answer to
this poets have tried many new means of writing, and for this
reason their work is experimental. This does not mean that
it is tentative and incomplete. An experiment may succeed
triumphantly. Even the greatest risk may end in some secure
and final result. Poetry has always made such experiments.
Works like the *Divine Comedy* and *Don Juan* are extremely
hazardous experiments in their rejection of current forms and
standards, but they have succeeded beyond criticism and
taken their place as classics. The past too has its failures.
When the Athenian poet, Timotheus, tried to combine the
grand manner of lyrical poetry with a strident realism, his
failure was disastrous. Mallarmé's *Un Coup de Dès* shows how
sadly a great poet can fail when he pushes his theories too far
and tries to write something which consists only of hints. No
doubt modern poetry has many, if less sensational, failures.
Its mere rejection of accepted standards of technique exposes
it to grave risks. Writers with no real inspiration believe that
anything they have to say matters, and produce work which
has no interest at all because it has not even the interest of
careful art. But the bad poetry of an age is no criticism of the
good, and what matters is the quality of the successes won.
These are many and various, and have a special interest because they show how poets have faced the problems of the
new outlook and found solutions to them.

One of the chief problems is how far a poet can go in the
quality of the emotion which he puts into poetry. On the
whole the nineteenth century confined itself to the more satisfying and harmonious emotions, whether of grief or of joy.
While Shelley expressed a divine rapture and exaltation,
Leopardi gave voice to a gloom so unrelieved that it has its
own magnificence. But there are many excited and even
creative states of mind in which this charm is lacking. We
all know moments of pleasure which are not rapturously delightful but complex and in a way disturbing, and we all know
moments of grief or disillusion or distress which are extremely
acute and painful but in no way exalting as truly tragic

emotions are. Such subjects are entitled to a place in poetry
if they yield some genuine excitement. And the question
goes deeper than this. The nineteenth century liked its
poetry, gay or mournful, to give an ultimate sense of harmony. But the moderns have introduced a different quality.
In their search for truth, they see that it is not always necessary
or right for the emotions to pass into a harmonious form, that
they may even end in something discordant and disturbing.
This means that poets draw no exact line between the poetry
of joy and the poetry of grief, and that they admit much which
does not belong absolutely to either but has none the less its
own appeal. No doubt Dante and Shakespeare have anticipated them in this as in other ways, but the moderns have
emphasised the poetry of unresolved tensions and troubling
states of mind. Their work in consequence may often be
lacking in sweetness, but sweetness is not the only test of
poetry. Modern poets have sometimes ventured into distressing and confused corners of experience because they hear
in them the authentic call of the creative spirit.

A singular forerunner of this kind of poetry can be seen in
José Asuncion Silva. He was born at Bogotá, in the South
American republic of Colombia, in 1865, and died by his own
hand in 1898. In this short career, though he was severed
by thousands of miles from Europe, he first developed an
advanced style of Symbolist poetry and then changed from
it to a sharp modern manner. His natural gifts of eye
and ear were remarkable. He learned something from Poe,
something from Tennyson, something from Baudelaire and
Mallarmé. He felt to an almost intolerable degree the discord between himself and his circumstances, and his career
was the reflection of it. His first poetry is Symbolist in its
desire to escape from a hideous world to a realm of beauty,
whether in dreams or in the past or in memories of childhood.
So long as he believed that this search might be rewarded, he
made a noble poetry of it and adapted to finer purposes some
of Poe's ingenious inventions. Like Mallarmé, he dreamed
of a " pure work ", which was perhaps an archetypal pattern
laid up in heaven but was also the inspiration of his actual
work. He tells how he dreamed of writing a perfect poem,

nervous, new and bold, how it should contain both grotesque and tragic elements and reflect its subject in its sounds :

> Ritmos sonoros, ritmos potentes, ritmos graves,
> Unos cual choque de armas, otros cual canto de aves.[1]

It is to tell a fantastic and tragic story of a woman who is adored and dies, and we can hear the voice of Poe that " the death of a beautiful woman is unquestionably the most poetical topic in the world ". Then comes the end, unexpected and ironical :

> Le mostrè mi poema a un crítico estupendo . . .
> Y lo leyó seis veces, y me dijo . . . ¡ No entiendo !²

Silva had seen that his ideal was without meaning for his world and could not be realised. He turned his back on Symbolism and wrote a different kind of poetry.

In his last poems Silva takes an almost malicious pleasure in showing the falsity of romantic notions. The theme of his ideal poem is restated in nine lines : a woman is loved by a man, but before her death he marries someone else, and she dies not of grief but of an abortion. In another poem he shows how a man is always falling in love and identifying himself with the heroes of well-known novels by Lamartine, Dumas, Flaubert and Zola, but none the less his end is prosaic enough :

> Y así pasó la vida entre los sueños
> Y llegó de ella al fin
> Dejando tres chicuelos y una esposa
> Que fué muy infeliz.³

In a third poem Silva destroys the romantic notions of majesty and remote grandeur by his insistence that in one vital respect all men are equal, though hardly in an impressive way. However different their external circumstances may be,

---

[1] Sonorous rhythms, mighty rhythms, rhythms with solemn words,
Some like the shock of battle, some like the song of birds.

[2] I showed my poem to a marvellous critic, who scanned it . . .
And read it seven times, and said, " I do not understand it ".

[3] And so he passed his life in dreaming,
And at his death deserted
Three little children and a widow,
Who was quite broken-hearted.

there is nothing to choose between them when it comes to the sexual act :

> Y si al mismo Juan una Juana
> Se entrega de un modo brutal,
> Y palpita la bestia humana
> En un solo espasmo sexual,
>
> Juan Lanas, el mozo de esquina,
> Es absolutamente igual
> Al Emperador de la China ;
> Los dos son un mismo animal.[1]

Silva abandons his high Romantic or Symbolist beliefs and mocks them as illusions. Life is not at all like that, he says in effect, but much more squalid and depressing.

This poetry is interesting for two reasons. In the first place, it shows why a man of Silva's remarkable sensibility turned against the Symbolist outlook. It is simply that in practice he found it false and at variance with the actual facts of life. His sense of truth compelled him to abandon it and to say what reality meant to him. And because he had to tell the truth, he embarked on quite a new kind of poetry which shirks nothing and delights in unpleasantness. It has wit and irony, but it offers no consolation and resolves no discords. In the second place, Silva justifies this change. He sees that what he now writes is not what people like or expect, but he is convinced that his age needs it. Just as the stomach, he says in *Avant-propos*, becomes dyspeptic with too rich a diet and is forbidden sweet things and prescribed a diet of bitter drops, so with poetry :

> Pobre estómago literario
> Que lo trivial fatiga y cansa,
> No sigas leyendo poemas
> Llenos de lágrimas.

---

[1] If to this Juan a Juana
Like a brute gives herself for mate,
And a single sexual spasm
Makes the human beast palpitate,

Juan Lamas, the boy in the corner,
Is absolutely, all in all,
One with the Emperor of China ;
The two are the same animal.

Deja las comidas que llenan,
Historias, leyendas y dramas
Y todas las sensiblerías
　Semi-románticas.

Y para completar el régimen
Que fortifica y que levanta,
Ensaya una dosis de estas
　Gotas amargas.[1]

Silva regards the question as one of spiritual hygiene, of restoring health to poetry, but he does this because he has found that romance is not enough and that truth has its inexorable claims. The new poetry is not very succulent, but it is healthy. And this surely is the attitude of many who have, without knowing it, followed in his path. They are impelled to write an astringent poetry because they feel that it is in the end more healthy than something in which they do not absolutely believe. This is of course only one aspect of the modern movement, but it exists and is worthy of notice.

When poetry sets out to annex new realms of experience it has to consider its form and its technique. The first revolutionaries were as ruthless in this as in other ways. They rejected both rhyme and regular forms of verse, the first because, as they claimed, all rhymes were exhausted and to repeat old rhymes was inevitably both boring and insincere, and the second because the regularity of a verse would misrepresent the irregular, spasmodic feelings which were theirs. The abandonment of rhyme is nothing new. The Greeks

[1]　Poor literary stomach
Fatigued and tired by the trivial,
By reading poems to itself
　That are full of tears.

Give up the stuffing diet,
Histories, legends and dramas,
And all the semi-romantic
　Sensibilities.

And to complete the regime
That gives strength and relief,
Make trial with a dose of these
　Bitter-tasting drops.

did not use it, nor the Romans until they transformed their art with the triumph of Christianity. Irregular verse is newer than this, but it is at least as old as Rimbaud who used it in *Marine* and *Mouvement* and may have got the idea of it from Judith Gautier's translations from the Chinese, which appeared in 1869. But on the whole the nineteenth century in its lyrical poetry used both regular verses and rhyme because they suited its creative spirit and the kind of regular harmony which it wished to create. They added a touch of sweetness, of order and discipline, such as suited its ideal of art. It is only natural that the moderns should have rebelled against both, not merely because they might be thought to have been used too much, but because the modern conception of poetical experience is of something which does not fall easily into such regular harmonies. The modern poet asks himself whether in using either or both of them he will not destroy much that is essential in his tone and spirit. Yet, on the whole, both have survived, not perhaps quite in their old form, but in forms certainly recognisable. It seems that poets still need them at certain times for certain moods. They may add to the range of rhyme by trying half-rhymes or assonances and to the range of verse-forms by using verses of irregular shape. But the difference is not of kind but of degree, and it throws some light on modern theories of composition.

It would not be entirely untrue to say that the classical conception both of rhymes and of regular verses is that the poet should be able to say what he has to say in any form. It is precisely his adaptation and exploitation of it which show his talent. Just as an architect shows his worth by making full use of the site in which he has to make his building, so the poet shows his worth by making full use of a given form. This was certainly the belief of the Romans when they clung tenaciously to the dactylic hexameter, of the English in the seventeenth and eighteenth centuries with their attachment to the heroic couplet, of the French at the same period with the alexandrine. The Romantics added to the number of possible forms, but they still believed that a regular form was necessary and that lyrical poetry demanded rhyme. In doubting this doctrine poets have been moved by a different conception of the place of technique in verse. They feel that to insist on a fixed form for certain experiences constricts and falsifies them, and that so far from having to make his matter fit his form, the poet should make his form fit his matter. This is less easy than it sounds. It is true that in moments of intense inspiration some poets find that their words fall naturally into the rhythm which is right for them and which cannot be gainsaid. But poetry is not always composed in this way, and a poet may equally find that a certain form of verse almost suggests his subject to him or at least tells him how to treat it. Paul Valéry has said that he composed *Le Cimetière Marin* as an exercise in a certain kind of stanza, which is another way of saying that the tune of the words preceded the actual words. The same may be true of rhyme, and there have been poets for whom the choice of rhymes is an inspiration to the contents of a poem. The problem both of rhymes and of verse-forms is real, and poets have answered it in different ways. If some have allowed themselves complete liberty and exploited the full resources of *vers libre*, others have felt the need for some stricter form and used it. The question is not of a choice between traditional and new methods but of what suits the poet's temperament and subject. So long as his form allows him to make the utmost of what he has to say, it does its work, and no more need be required of it.

An example may help to show what this means. In his *Four Quartets* T. S. Eliot combines different forms of verse. If, on the whole, he uses a supple, sinuous verse of varying length and accent, at times he uses something much more traditional. For instance, in *Little Gidding* he begins with his usual rhythm and freedom :

> Midwinter spring is its own season
> Sempiternal though sodden towards sundown,
> Suspended in time, between pole and tropic.
> When the short day is brightest, with frost and fire,
> The brief sun flames the ice, on pond and ditches,
> In windless cold that is the heart's beat,
> Reflecting in a watery mirror
> A glare that is blindness in the early afternoon.

The quiet, irregular movement reflects Eliot's meditative mood and charged memories. He has to go slowly with such a theme, to let each detail make its proper impression, to adapt the movements of his verse to the movements of his mind. But later in the poem he assays a different task and uses both rhyme and a standard form of verse :

> Who then devised the torment ? Love.
> Love is the unfamiliar Name
> Behind the hands that wove
> The intolerable shirt of flame
> Which human power cannot remove.
> > We only live, only suspire
> > Consumed by either fire or fire.

The sudden moment of illumination concentrates and strengthens his powers and turns him to a grave mood of song. He needs the rhymes and the formality to give full expression to what he now feels. To have presented this experience in free verse would unquestionably have been to spoil it. What Eliot does in this poem illustrates what other modern poets do. They choose their forms to suit their subjects and their moods, not on abstract grounds of art or modernity.

The desire to express experience exactly is extremely important to modern poets, and they see what it demands of them. So far from being careless or reckless in their art, they have an ideal of exactness and precision. So Eliot stresses the need to get every word right :

> The common word exact without vulgarity,
> The formal word precise but not pedantic,
> The complete consort dancing together.

Indeed this desire for precision is all the greater in an age which knows what confusion is and hopes to master its troubles by translating them into a rigorously sincere art. Even so adventurous a poet as Rafael Alberti insists that the greater the confusion of life the greater the need for telling the truth in carefully chosen words :

> Después de este desorden impuesto, de esta prisa,
> De esta urgente gramática necesaria en que vivo,

Vuelva a mí toda virgen la palabra precisa,
Virgen el verbo exacto con el justo adjetivo.[1]

This precision is of a special kind. It is not logical or intellectual. It does not mean that everything which the poet says must be reduced to ordinary categories of thought and pruned of all wild or illogical elements. It is an ideal of truth to emotion, to all that the poet feels, to those darker states of mind bordering on the unconscious which he does not fully understand but knows to be important in his whole condition. Poets try to present complex states with a faithful regard for their emotional and imaginative significance. They must do more than convey ideas : they must re-create certain states for their readers as they have themselves known them. No device which can secure this end may be neglected, and the poet must spare no efforts to make his work as full and suggestive as possible.

This ideal implies that there is no state of mind, however peculiar and undefined, which cannot be suggested in poetry. It means that sometimes a poet, acting with the highest intentions and eager to be scrupulously exact, may say something which is beyond the grasp of his readers. For this reason modern poetry has been much reviled, but it could hardly be otherwise. It is inevitable that such an extension of the frontiers of the imagination should occasionally mean a Cimmerian darkness. But it also means that poets try to express experience not as the mind orders and arranges it in retrospect but as it is really felt with all its contradictions and ambiguities, and this too has led to misrepresentation. This poetry has been accused of being deliberately anti-rational because it speaks of irrational things without attempting to simplify them. But the business of poetry is not to simplify or to explain, but to present. Things should be presented as they are, and to complain that if a poet does this he is an enemy of reason is to say that truth itself is anti-rational. The fact is that poetry is neither rational nor irrational, since

[1] After this disorder laid upon me, this haste,
This urgent grammatical need in which I live,
Every word comes back to me, precise and chaste,
The exact noun comes back with the right adjective.

it is concerned not with the reasoning powers of man but with something else, with the whole range of the human consciousness when it is at work at a certain intensity. It deals with much more than plain statement, and indeed it need not deal with plain statement at all. There are many human moods in which we speak not in the indicative but with imperatives or exclamations, and these are often the material of poetry.

None the less, the moderns are faced by their own problem of the part to be played by the intellect in their actual poetry. In addition to his senses and all the remoter movements of the consciousness the poet needs something which can only be called intellectual. There have been many good poets who have not been intellectual in this sense : they have not given in their verse any evidence or record of hard thought. To this number belong some of the masters of pure song like Catullus and Verlaine. In their art intellectual effort is not necessary, and we do not notice its absence. But there are others in whom the intellectual, analytical, ordering faculty is so strong that it has to have a place in their poetry. This class contains most of the great Greek poets. What gives so special a power to Aeschylus and Sophocles is precisely the impression that hard thought lies behind every word that they say and that they say nothing which they have not judged on its merits as truth. The same may be said of poets so different as Donne and Leopardi and Baudelaire. In each a powerful mind has absorbed the gifts of the senses and the emotions, understood them and judged them before putting them into verse. The result is that in such work the intellectual element has a strictly poetical task. The effort of thought and the adventure and difficulty of finding the truth contribute to the poetical result by making it stronger and more durable, more able to withstand the vagaries of taste and the disintegrating criticism of fact, by giving it a reserve of power which may be lacking in more instinctive and more spontaneous work.

It might be thought that modern poets deny this intellectual element by their emphasis on the exciting effects of poetry. Nor is this untrue of some of them. It is for instance certainly true of such extremists as the Russian advocates of " trans-sense " who deny the intellect any place in poetry.

It is also true of Marinetti's shock tactics, if they belong to poetry. But these are exceptional cases. With other poets the problem is more complicated. It is a question of the degree to which the movements of the considering mind can contribute to the poetical effect by taking part in it, and in answering this question modern poets tend to take one of two courses. Some of them give a great deal of thought to their work but leave it outside the actual poem. This is pre-eminently true of T. S. Eliot, who so purifies his poetry that he omits the thought which has gone to its making and presents only the imaginative results. Even in *Four Quartets*, which has moments which look like dry argument, he practises this method. For the argumentative passages are not really argument. They convey the tone and atmosphere of certain mental activities : they are conclusions which produce a special kind of emotional effect. Eliot relies mainly on impli-cation and suggestion, and does not show the intellectual self at work. On the other hand, some poets keep much of their thought in the finished result and give an additional richness through it, not merely or really because they state the results of their thinking but because they show its strains and stresses, its effect on their emotions and its imaginative significance for them. In different ways this is true of Pasternak and Alberti, whose poetry is indeed fully charged with emotion but in such a way that even the intellect becomes emotional in its rapid changes and apprehensions, its adjustments of itself to varying moods and its complete absorption in them. The outlook of modern poetry demands no single way of treating the intel-lectual element in poetry, but it insists that when the intellect plays a part it must contribute to the poetry and not be a respite from it.

Finally, though modern poets have made a considerable break with the past, they have not lived up to the violent ambitions of their more vociferous advocates in abandoning it altogether. It has in practice been found undesirable and even impossible to dispense with the traditional subjects and means of poetry. Indeed this distaste for the past can now be seen to have been a brief episode in the process of emancipa-tion from immediate precedents. It may have been necessary in the effort of getting rid of a style which suffocated creative work, but the need was exaggerated, and poets quietly returned to tradition with a new eye both for its weaknesses and its strength. The Russian Futurist, Mayakovsky, who in 1912 had cried, " Throw Pushkin overboard ", wrote in 1924 his *Jubilee* in which he saluted Pushkin as a master who transcends the centuries. However advanced Eliot's style may be, he himself claims to be a classicist and insists on the value of the past. Different poets adjust themselves differently to tradition. Some feel that its technique is inadequate for what they have to say, others that with a little arrangement it can be made to yield new and impressive results. The same poet may even at one time feel its claims and at another deny them, as Rafael Alberti does when he composes his first songs in traditional measures and his *Sobre los Ángeles* in a highly modern manner. The decisive factor is the nature of the poet's temperament and experience. He may wish to relate his subject to tradition or to emphasise its novelty. He may feel that the old form gives a new elegance or that it is an intolerable obstruction to the expression of a contemporary consciousness. The issue is decided on its merits in each case, and the result is a poetry in which old and new elements compete for the poet's patronage.

Such are some of the problems which are raised by the modern conception of poetry. They are practical questions which have to be settled not theoretically but in individual cases according to the circumstances. If the new poetry seeks to be as pure as possible and at the same time to be as contemporary as this purity allows, such a goal is sufficiently vague to allow many different means of reaching it. It is not surprising that poets have had to make experiments in their technique when their aim is both so important and so undefined. What is peculiar about these experiments is that they vary greatly from poet to poet. Except in their main aims and outlook, modern poets have much less in common with each other than the Symbolists had. There are far greater differences of manner and effect. Perhaps this is due in part to the absence of dominating figures such as existed in the nineteenth century and did much to impose a single pattern on European poetry. It was almost impossible to avoid altogether the influence of Byron or Hugo or Mallarmé. But more important is the fact that just because it faces a fundamental problem of poetry the modern movement has found different practical applications of a general theory. In its concentration on the essence of poetry it allows a wide range of moods and approaches, and admits quite different philosophies of life. The study of it is all the more instructive because it illustrates the remarkable variety of the creative mind and of its responses to life.

II

CONSTANTINE CAVAFY AND
THE GREEK PAST

The Greek poet, Constantine Cavafy, who was born in 1868 and spent most of his time in Alexandria until his death in 1933, presents a special case, both as a man and as a poet, of one whose situation cut him off from much of contemporary life and from any immediate or easy connection with a civilised past. His case is not unique, and the United States has more than once shown that it cannot always give to its writers a secure sense of an established background, with the result that they have settled in Europe and tried to make themselves at home by re-establishing broken ties with old traditions of race and language. What Henry James and T. S. Eliot did in England, what Stuart Merrill and Francis Vielé-Griffin did in France, are typical cases of what has happened to many men who have left their own country because they did not feel at home in it and sought a more assured background and a greater ease of spirit in London or Paris. With this company Cavafy may be compared. He was a Greek who spoke the mother-tongue but never lived in the mother-country. His life was spent in the polyglot, half-oriental city of Alexandria, whose Islamic and Egyptian traditions meant nothing to him. Cavafy lacked a background more than Henry James did in New York. Nor was he unconscious of this lack. Indeed his poetical performance was his answer to it. But unlike his American compeers and unlike his own countryman, John Papadiamantopoulos, who won fame as a French poet under the name of Jean Moréas, Cavafy made no attempt to find a second home in Europe. He remained in Alexandria and gave his powers to forming a background for his art. He attached himself not to the present but to the past, to a world which he knew only from books but which was so real to him that in it he felt at ease among his own people. With a striking consistency of purpose he sought and found the security which he needed, not in places where the European tradition was still vigorous but in a half-lost and broken past which he made to live by the force of his genius.

This lack of background makes Cavafy's career all the more remarkable for more than one reason. In some ways the most original Greek poet of his generation, he owed nothing in his art to the revival of Greek poetry which began with Dionysios Solomos (1798–1857) and was continued with inventive power and lyrical sweep by Costes Palamas (1859–1942). Whereas they created a new poetry from a combination of Greek folksongs and traditional measures with new themes and forms from France and England, Cavafy used neither Greek nor Western European models. Still less did he owe anything to the East. His manner was his own invention, the reflection of his temperament and his circumstances, guided by a natural instinct for words. Even in his language he went his own way. He wrote neither in καθαρεύουσα, the " refined ", artificial language which educated Greeks inherited from the Byzantines and which has by its lack of contact with living speech been a serious obstacle to good poetry, nor in the " demotic " language of ordinary Greeks, which Palamas exploited with consummate enterprise. Cavafy wrote, as he spoke, in a language which has something in common with both of these and is in fact the idiom of educated Alexandrian Greeks. In it some of the old formality survives, but it is none the less a living tongue despite its strictness and its relatively limited vocabulary. Cavafy at least started with the advantage that he had not to rid himself of an outworn poetical idiom. He could turn to new purposes the language which he spoke and apply it to tasks for which it had hardly ever been used. But this, too, had its dangers. Just because Cavafy was working in an almost virgin field, he had no traditional standards to guide him. So far was he from being burdened by a literary past that he had to make what was really a fresh start. While poets in other countries were busy with creating a new language to replace the stale remnants of romantic idiom, Cavafy had the whole field open before him. He might easily have failed, simply through the apparent easiness of his task and the lack of precedents to guide him, but his sense of words and his critical spirit saved him and showed him what to do.

Though he stands outside the European tradition, and indeed outside any tradition, Cavafy is none the less an important exponent of the modern spirit in poetry for more than one reason. In the first place, he was by nature a realist. What interested him was the actual play of life. Such life as he knew might be limited, but it was undoubtedly real, and he surveyed it with a careful, discriminating, scholarly eye. In it he found a special kind of excitement, as if he were part of it, and saw it vividly as his own experience. This was the spring of his creative strength, the impulse which forced him to transpose what he saw and felt into the finality of words. He felt no call to explore fancies and dreams, but gave to his evocations of the past the solidity and the variety which he found in his own modern surroundings. In the second place, Cavafy's sense of poetry was quite natural and instinctive. As a scholar he had studied the great works of the past but not so that they obscured his vision of what a living poetry ought to be. On the contrary, they taught him its essential, unchanging qualities. He saw that he must secure the greatest possible effect with every word, that what matters above everything is this effect, and that his technique must be subordinated to its requirements. Because he had considerable insight into himself, and through himself into others, he saw that if poetry is to be truthful it must state the whole truth of a case and not reorganise it to suit some distorting " literary " ideal. Finally, he was a modern man in his reserve and his intellectual discipline. His inspiration did not work freely or easily. It had to fight against his highly critical judgment and his distrust of uncontrolled emotions. In him emotions passed into poetry only when his intellect was satisfied of their worth or when his reserve was broken by their appeal to something deep in him. He did not pass slipshod or sentimental work. At first sight his poetry may seem rather dry, but we soon see what reserves of power it has, just because it has been subjected to so strict a criticism. His gifts forbade flights into effortless song, and his poetry is always premeditated and considered, but through this it has a peculiar integrity.

This unusual combination of gifts needed a suitable field

for its expression. Up to a point Cavafy found this in the tavern-life of Alexandria and the special kind of interest which it held for him. But though he wrote some remarkable poems on this, it was not all that he needed, nor did it call out all his gifts. He needed a field of subjects which should enable him to find a deeper significance in the present by relating it to something else. His narrow life limited his creative range and would have left him a minor realistic poet if he had not been guided by his genius to find the extension which he needed. Just because he had no sure background, he had to create one, and with wise judgment he sought it in the traditions of the Greek world in the Eastern Mediterranean. What was for Solomos and Palamas an irrecoverable past was for Cavafy a reality not merely of the imagination but of his own blood and bones. He felt at home in this past, because he knew that ultimately he belonged to it, that he spoke its language, that he shared its sun and air, that his stock was its stock. Nor did he give his main attention to the great age of classical Greece. He did not share the romantic conception of Hellas as a world of gods and heroes, the home of liberty and the cradle of civilisation. Nor had he the Parnassian love of the statuesque and pictorial sides of Greek life with its decorous rites and its domestic sanctities. What interested him most, what made him feel truly at home, was the varied Greek world which once spread from Sicily to Central Asia and embraced many men who were not of Greek race and who spoke the Greek language with Asiatic intonations and faulty syntax. This was the subject of his studies and the theme of his most characteristic poetry. He absorbed it with a scholar's care but not with a scholar's prepossessions. What interested him was not its seclusion but its closeness to the present, the permanent appeal of its confused issues and the living charm of its dramatic paradoxes. If Cavafy became a poet of the whole Hellenistic world, it was because he found in it the roots which he lacked in contemporary Alexandria and a background which explained and illuminated many chapters of human experience.

This discovery enabled Cavafy to solve a problem which troubles many modern poets. The poet needs symbols and myths to give individual form to his indeterminate thoughts. If he shrinks, as he well may, from abstractions because they are too vague and in the end too false, he must have symbols to convey his meaning in its fullness. This has not always been a serious problem. The ancient Greek poets had in their incomparable mythology images and symbols for any situation. Dante had hardly less in the coherent theology of mediaeval Christianity : even the Renaissance and the eighteenth century had in their revived classical myths something which served many useful purposes. But the modern world has no such coherent and recognised system. When Mallarmé set out to compose an entirely symbolical poetry, he found his symbols in his own experience, with the result that many of his readers are unable to catch his full meaning or his exact intonations. Other poets have seen the difficulty and tried to meet it by creating or adopting coherent mythologies. What Yeats found for a time in old Irish legends, what Eliot found for *The Waste Land* in figures and events from anthropology, Cavafy found much less laboriously in the Hellenistic past. His system has advantages which neither Yeats's nor Eliot's has. In the first place, it is really a homogeneous body of material, with its own life and its own plan, and in the second place it is sufficiently familiar to most educated people and has already some meaning for them. Cavafy does not have to train his readers in a knowledge of his stories as Yeats and Eliot have to in theirs, nor does he have to explain what his symbols mean. He appeals to a defined section of the past, takes from it what suits him, and without any real difficulty to himself or his readers applies it to a new purpose. It has an immediacy and a reality which are lacking in Yeats's heroes and heroines and in Eliot's vague figures from the Grail legend. We understand at once who Cavafy's characters are and become interested in them for their own sake ; they have clear personalities and a direct appeal. Just as the poets of the Renaissance were able to use the gods and goddesses of Greece for purposes which everyone understood, so Cavafy uses historical persons of the Greek past for a purpose hardly less clear, though much less standardised and not at all allegorical. His persons are human beings who through something universal in their characters or their situations have the clarity of individual symbols and the reality of living persons. They are concrete universals in the sense that they are at once particulars and representatives of eternal types. By using this kind of myth Cavafy gave to his poetry a remarkable unity and strength.

Cavafy did not at once discover his final way of using this material. His earliest poems, written before 1911, show that he was experimenting with it but still hesitant in making the fullest use of it. At this stage his thoughts are not completely fused into his images, and he gives the impression that he begins with an abstract conception and then chooses some image which will show its significance, but without melting the abstraction and the image into a single whole. For instance, in *Thermopylae* he is concerned with a special type of human nobility. The ideal which he presents means much to him but he approaches it more from an ethical than from an imaginative angle. None the less, he feels its imaginative claims, and to make these clear he compares those whose courage he admires to the men who died at Thermopylae. The result is not a single consistent myth but a situation illustrated by a parallel. This is clear and fine. Such men call for praise, and Cavafy gives it, but in the abstract language of morality without any very intimate or personal touch. His poem has an old-fashioned air as it touches on these high issues :

> Honour to those men who have set the bounds
> Upon their lives and guard Thermopylae,
> Who from their duty never swerve aside,
> Upright and honourable in all they do,
> Yet tender-hearted and compassionate.
> When they are rich, generous, and, when poor,
> They still are generous in little things,
> Giving all succour that is theirs to give,
> And never speaking anything but truth,
> Yet with no bitterness for such as lie.
>
> And greater honour is the due of those
> Who can foresee (and many can foresee)
> That Ephialtes rises in the end
> And at the last the Persians will get through.

The opening and the close, with their vivid images of heroic defence against hopeless odds, have the authentic touch of poetry, but the rest, despite its nobility of tone, is still rather too abstract to ring with all that Cavafy really feels. We miss the concentrated thrill, the intensity of the personal vision. Cavafy is still at a stage where he accommodates his thought to that of other men, and shows his special view chiefly in the image which makes the poem and gives to it its name.

Yet while he was using the past for such effects as this, Cavafy was feeling his way to something more subtle and more profound. His interest in history was so vivid that he learned its lessons with a peculiar attention and saw in many famous episodes examples of recurring human problems. His reaction at first was to draw from some incident what seemed to him its permanent truth and to present this in his own way. So in *Trojans* he sees in the story of the besieged Trojans an example of that human state in which men are destined to destruction and know it, but none the less continue to struggle, and even at moments believe that they will succeed. In *The Ides of March* he picks up the story of the soothsayer's warning to Caesar to beware of the Ides of March and makes it a lesson for all men who enjoy the heights of power. For them, he says, such warnings are always of first importance and must never be neglected, no matter what important business is in hand. In *The God abandons Antony* he gives his own version of the story told by Plutarch, and through him by Shakespeare, of the desertion of Antony by Hercules. For Cavafy such desertions may happen to any man who has enjoyed power and pleasure ; it is not an occasion for regret but a call to courage and to thankfulness for all the brilliant past :

> Listen, your last enjoyment, to the sounds,
> The wonderful instruments of the mystic company,
> And say farewell, farewell to Alexandria you are losing.[1]

In *Ithaca* the story of Odysseus's long-delayed return to his home becomes a lesson on all long searches, and draws the moral that the quest is more important than the goal and gives an experience beyond valuation. The instructive, moral note

[1] Trs. J. Mavrogordato.

is never quite absent from these poems and gives them a certain stiffness and formality. None the less, Cavafy has begun to see that themes from the past have a meaning for the present and can be applied to it. Such poems are more closely welded than *Thermopylae* and have a more individual tone.

At the same time that he was writing these pieces Cavafy had already found a kind of art which suited his special gifts and was to produce his most characteristic work. In this he presents a situation from the past with what looks like perfect objectivity. He passes no comment on it and draws no moral from it. He seems to be interested in it entirely for its own sake, and indeed is so, though naturally his treatment shows a strong personal taste. So in *The First Step* he tells how the poet, Theocritus, chides the young poet, Eumenes, for despairing about achieving greatness and tells him that even to have done what he has, simply to have begun to be a poet, is itself no little thing. No doubt this reflects Cavafy's own views, and the antique dress is perhaps not very necessary. But *The Footsteps* is more accomplished. It tells how Nero's Lares are unquiet in their shrine at hearing a terrible sound on the staircase and fall over each other because of it :

> They understand the meaning of that sound,
> And now they know the footfalls of the Avengers.[1]

Here the situation is conceived as something independent, and the personal touch is kept in much stricter control. What matters is the moment in Nero's life when his doom begins to work against him. The short *King Demetrios* is no less objective and successful. It tells how Demetrios, abandoned by the Macedonians, takes off his golden robes, dresses himself in simple clothes and flies away :

> Doing just like any play actor,
> Who, when the play comes to an end,
> Changes his wear and goes away.[1]

These situations are seen and presented with a keen historical and dramatic sense, but they derive their special power from the fact that such occasions recur and that the clear presentation of a single example calls to mind many parallels when

[1] Trs. J. Mavrogordato.

similar things have happened. Cavafy has begun to use the past as a means to interpret the present and the unchanging ways of men.

This art soon gained in complexity and depth. In *Waiting for the Barbarians*, written before 1911, Cavafy produces a real myth, a story which stands firmly in its own right and yet is rich in universal significance. The scene is set at the end of the ancient world in a city where the Barbarian conquerors are expected. So far from being frightened the people of the city make elaborate preparations to welcome them. The Senate is not sitting because there is no need for it to make laws when the Barbarians will make them. The Emperor is on his throne at the city-gate, with his crown on, waiting to receive the Leader and make an honorific address to him. The local officials have put on their finery for the occasion :

> Why have our two consuls gone out, both of them and the Praetors,
> Today with their red togas on, with their embroidered togas ?
> Why are they wearing bracelets, and all those amethysts too,
> And all those rings on their fingers with splendid flashing emeralds?
> Why should they be carrying today their precious walking-sticks,
> With silver knobs and golden tops so wonderfully carved ?
>> Because the Barbarians will arrive to-day ;
>> Things of this sort dazzle the Barbarians.[1]

The orators are not present because the Barbarians are bored with speeches. So the scene is set in all its paradoxical feelings and brilliant colours. But Cavafy is not content with this. His climax comes with an unexpected thrust :

> Why should this uneasiness begin all of a sudden,
> And confusion ? How serious people's faces have become.
> Why are all the streets and squares emptying so quickly,
> And everyone turning home again so full of thought ?
>> Because night has fallen and the Barbarians have not come,
>> And some people have arrived from the frontier,
>> They said there are no Barbarians any more.
>
> And now what will become of us without Barbarians ?
> These people were some sort of solution.[1]

---

[1] Trs. J. Mavrogordato.

With this deliberately flat conclusion, this highly conscious anti-climax, the scene ends. The human drama is finished, and no comment is passed on it. The last words are emphatically conversational and show the emptiness which everyone feels at this end to the excitement.

In this poem Cavafy presents a theme which had a certain popularity in his time. The Russian poet, Valery Bryusov, wrote *The Coming Huns*, in which he welcomed the onrush of the Barbarian conquerors into a weary world in need of new blood and new life. In a not dissimilar spirit Stefan George wrote *Der Brand des Tempels*, in which he dramatised the strange appeal that a merciless conqueror has for a people whose most holy relics he destroys. Both poems are set in the past but reflect modern anxieties and hopes. Both Bryusov and George felt that their own age was sick and might be healed through some vast cataclysm which would overwhelm the civilisation of centuries. Cavafy's approaches the subject in a different spirit. He understands why people feel like this and creates a situation where this feeling can be seen in its most advanced form. But he himself stands outside it. It is not the reflection of his own desires but something which he knows in other men and finds interesting for its own sake. He is ironical and playful in his approach to it. The whole fine occasion shows the extraordinary character of men, their ability to throw themselves into causes which are, on a wider view, entirely inimical to their interests, and their pleasure in any gay show or spectacle. There is a gentle malice in Cavafy's description of the clothes of the consuls and the praetors, their jewels and their walking-sticks. And this ironical presentation of what may well have been a familiar occasion at the time of the Barbarian invasions ends with a special stroke of paradox. It is strange enough that men should wish such a thing to happen, but it is more strange that it should fail and that men should feel flat and empty without it. This is Cavafy's comment not merely on the contemporary desire that the world should be refashioned through some fearful change but on the wilfulness of history which frustrates men's wishes and shows how curious political emotions are.

The cunning and depth of this art can be seen from a poem written in 1912, *Alexandrian Kings*, which tells of a festival in the time of Cleopatra when her children go to the sports-ground. It is a great public occasion. The soldiers are out in the streets, and the children are proclaimed as kings. Into the description of the occasion Cavafy throws his eager, anti-quarian sense of an historic situation :

> Alexander — him they called the King
> Of Armenia, Media and the Parthians.
> Ptolemy — they called him King
> Of Cilicia, Syria and Phoenicia.
> A little forward stood Caesarion,
> Dressed in pink-coloured silk,
> Upon his breast a bunch of hyacinths,
> His belt a double row of sapphires and amethysts ;
> His shoes were laced with white ribbons
> Embroidered with rose-coloured pearls.
> They acclaimed him more than the little ones,
> They acclaimed him by the name of King of Kings.

This is the main theme, and it carries a contrast and a com-ment with it. The Alexandrian populace greatly enjoys the show. The day is warm, the sports-ground a triumph of artistic achievement, the courtiers magnificently dressed :

> Caesarion was all grace and beauty
> (Cleopatra's son, of the blood of the Lagids).

No wonder that the Alexandrians run to the festival, applaud-ing in Greek and Egyptian and Hebrew. They are enchanted by the spectacle, but they are not deceived by it :

> The Alexandrians understood of course
> That this was nothing but words and play-acting.

That is all. It is a consummate effect, a wonderful evocation of a distant episode, very much as it must have been, with no judgment or conclusion stated. The poem stands complete and flawless in this special kind of art which Cavafy has invented.

The charm of this poem comes largely from the extra-ordinary imprint of truth on it. So, we think, it must have happened. We wish it to be true, because the subject is one which inevitably attracts us. In the past history of his own Alexandria Cavafy found a time which has a universal interest. Cleopatra is a heroine of whom anyone might be proud, but Cavafy says little about her and concentrates his attention on her small sons, Caesarion, whom she had by Julius Caesar, and Alexander and Ptolemy, whom she had by Antony. The subject, which is interesting enough in itself, gains a new depth through the children, who have their own pathos, not merely because later Octavian killed Caesarion and made Alexander walk in his triumph, but because there is something undeniably distressing in the use of the children to further their parents' political aims. And behind the pathos Cavafy sees an ironical paradox. The Alexandrian crowds, who greatly enjoy the spectacle, are not deceived by it. It is in the end useless, despite all the efforts made to secure its success. Such are the vagaries and contradictions of the human heart. The whole scene, presented at different levels, stands before us. And just because it has this complex character, it is much more than a chapter of history. The human situation which it illustrates is as real to-day as in the time of Cleopatra, and Cavafy's skilful evocation of the past reveals his sharp insight into the present and his wise understanding of the cross-currents in the human soul.

The art of *Alexandrian Kings* can be appreciated more fully if we look at Plutarch's Life of Antony where Cavafy found his subject. Plutarch, who was no mean teller of an historical tale, records that Antony and Cleopatra staged a great festival in the sports-ground. They sat on golden thrones on a silver dais, and Cleopatra was proclaimed Queen of Egypt, Cyprus, Lydia and Lower Syria, while her children also were given resounding titles. Alexander was dressed like a Persian king, Ptolemy like a Macedonian. The main outlines of the scene are faithfully kept by Cavafy, but his whole emphasis is different. Plutarch makes Antony and Cleopatra the chief actors in it : Cavafy does not mention Antony and hardly mentions Cleopatra. Plutarch tells the story to show how Antony was corrupted by the East and adopted its presumptuous ways : Cavafy is not interested in that but in the parts played by the children and the crowd. Plutarch describes the clothing of the children to emphasise the preposterous claims made by Antony for oriental kingdoms : Cavafy changes the details and makes them an element in the glittering pathetic show. Plutarch suggests that Antony compelled the Alexandrians to go to the sports-ground : Cavafy indicates that they went gaily and gladly. The story which Plutarch tells to illustrate a single point of behaviour is given an entirely new character in its combination of pathos and irony and its objective treatment of a fascinating occasion.

Alexandrian Kings anticipates some important features of Cavafy's mature art, and especially his ability to extract something of universal interest from historical records. He understood this mixed world of the last Ptolemies, half-Greek and half-Egyptian, and saw in it a prototype of the society in which he lived. Though in his early poems he drew material from the masterpieces of Greek literature and gave his own interpretation of the fall of Troy, the death of Achilles, the death of Sarpedon, he soon left this well-trodden field and concentrated on the Hellenistic, Greco-Roman and Byzantine ages, with their more confused issues and stranger characters. His imaginative curiosity drew him to men and societies in which race or religion or politics created unusual paradoxes, and it was this element that made him write of ambiguous figures like Nero and Julian, Ptolemies and Seleucids, Hellenising Jews and early Christians, sculptors and painters of the later Roman Empire, Byzantine rulers like the Comneni and Cantacuzenes, and princes on the fringe of the Hellenistic world. The great age of Hellas, with its superb simplicity and directness, was no subject for his subtle taste. He preferred something with sharper conflicts in its inner being and more unexpected crises in its actions. This was what appealed to him with his uncertain background and mixed affinities and challenged him to express it in verse. He was interested not in the great lessons of history but in its smaller episodes, in which he saw more human interest than in the triumphs of heroes. The world of the past must come alive for him, and he confined himself to those sections of it which could be interpreted by the present and in their turn help to interpret it.

This poetry is singularly economical and unadorned. Though in some of his early poems Cavafy is not above aiming at a rich effect, he soon found that his special class of symbols drawn from the past was all that he needed. His object was to make his scenes as significant and as telling as possible in themselves. His poems are highly dramatic and objective, and their style is fitted to this. It is concentrated, almost dry. It states facts and situations with a remarkable paucity of words and with no attempt to underline any inner meaning. Yet because of this restraint this poetry has a peculiar quality. It is not in the least lyrical, but it is always dramatic. Cavafy takes great pains to see that every situation appeals at once through its own interest and never allows his words to come between his readers and their immediate comprehension of his subjects. His style effaces itself before his themes, but though we may hardly notice the style or the rhythm, they are managed with uncommon skill. Cavafy puts into his words a power which makes them do in their own sphere what only poetry can do. They reflect the passions, the hesitations, the pretensions, the excitements, the doubts of his characters. The simple words move naturally in response to the varied moods which he presents, but their simplicity is a triumph of art, in which everything superfluous or merely decorative has been pruned away, and we are presented with only the essential facts expressed in words which catch their shifting hues and shades. The more we read this poetry the more we see how powerful it is. The situations speak for themselves not merely to the historical curiosity but to deeper and warmer human feelings. The revived figures of this mixed past come to life with the appeal of human beings, simplified and reduced by high art to their essential qualities.

This language which disappears so modestly into its subjects has its own interest for the scholar. Though Cavafy wrote in his own variant of " refined " speech, he did not scruple to make use of the possibilities which the varieties of modern Greek allow to a writer. If, on the one hand, the advocates of the old austere style regard him as unnecessarily colloquial, the advocates of the " demotic " think that he insults the living language by making so little use of its rich vocabulary. Cavafy keeps a perilous mean between two extreme positions, and his reputation in Greece has suffered from it. None the less, in his own way, he conducts subtle manœuvres in the intricate terrain of spoken Greek. He will at times introduce a truly commonplace word in order to secure a special kind of effect, as he does when in *Waiting for the Barbarians* he refers to " walking-sticks " by a word that comes from shops and streets and speaks of " some sort of solution ", or when in *Alexandrian Kings* he says that the Alexandrians " knew of course what it was worth ". Conversely, at times he will introduce, almost in inverted commas, phrases which smack of late classical rhetoric or Byzantine Greek or the language of the Church. Such variations in his language do more than catch the exact tone of an occasion in words suited to its time or place : they stress the variations in Cavafy's own feelings and approach to his subject. They give just that fall or rise which shows the richness of the human situation and the different responses which it may evoke in a single moment.

Though Cavafy treated a wide range of subjects, he liked particularly anything in which there was an element of paradox or contradiction or which showed a discord in men themselves or between their hopes and their actual circumstances. His response to such situations varied greatly, and though there is often an element of irony in it, an acceptance of an unresolved conflict, this is not the central quality of his work. It is less the ironies of life that engage him than its riddles. For him human beings were indeed unaccountable, and he liked to explore their inexplicable contradictions. With careful skill he would probe a subject until he found in it some final, insoluble conflict, and then he would present this in an individual dramatic crisis. The conflict was his subject, and he took care to see that his dramatisation of it was true to human nature. He hardly ever tells a story. His concern is with the core of a situation, with the human factors at work in it, and with the riddles that it raises. The excitement in his work is not so much about what is going to happen as why it happens and why the characters think and feel as they do. He examines the curious, contradictory and ambiguous activities of the human soul, not indeed in its dark splendours and fearful humiliations, but in its smaller and yet hardly less exciting conflicts, with a deep conviction that here is something worthy of close attention and sympathetic understanding and in its way as thrilling as more heroic and magnificent outbursts of the spirit.

Cavafy's situations vary considerably in the kind of conflicts which they reveal, just as contradictions in the human self arise from many causes and evoke many kinds of response. They may, for instance, come from a fundamental discord in a man's own nature, between his beliefs and his behaviour, or between two sets of convictions which are really contradictory and yet exist without much trouble in the same man. In *Of the Jews* A.D. 50 Cavafy sketches a young Jewish artist who has been deeply touched by the appeal of Greek civilisation. He is a painter and a poet, a runner and thrower of the discus, " as beautiful as Endymion ", but he comes from a family dear to the synagogue, and believes that his best days are those when he leaves the search for sensation and the Greek devotion to the body :

> And I become what I should wish
> Always to be : a son of Hebrews, of the holy Hebrews.

The desire is perfectly sincere, and yet it is not carried out :

> But he did not remain anything of the kind ;
> The Cult of Pleasure and the Art of Alexandria
> Found in him a most devoted servant.

The type which Cavafy sketches is common and can still be met in countries like Egypt and India which have been in close contact with the West and have produced an educated class which is not completely at home in either East or West, but is torn between the habits of its origin and what it has learned from abroad. Nor is the contradiction confined to this type. It can be seen in any man who feels equally the claims of austerity and pleasure, of the soul and the body. Cavafy finds his theme in such a man and does not attempt to explain it. It has its own appeal, and that is enough.

Such conflicts take a special form when religious beliefs make exacting demands and are at variance with other, more human, feelings. Just as in his Hellenising Jew Cavafy shows the conflict between devotion and pleasure, so in *Priest of the Temple of Serapis* he shows the conflict between the religious convictions of a convert and his natural filial love. The young man who speaks has lost his father, to whom he was deeply attached, and from this the situation emerges. The son is a devout Christian who observes the rules of the Church in every action and word and turns away with horror from all who deny Christ, but he is the victim of an irreconcilable discord. He loved his father and grieves for him :

> But now I grieve,
> O Christ, and make lamentation for my father,
> Who was — I shudder when I speak of it —
> Priest at the most accursed Serapion.

This has its own pathos, and there is no solution to it. Such is the price which men often pay when they embrace with complete sincerity an exacting creed and yet are unable to sacrifice completely to it other things which they still feel to be sacred. The hardest of sacrifices is that of the affections which a man knows in his heart to be holy, and in his young Christian Cavafy portrays the lineaments and the struggles of this ageless type.

A different kind of contradiction is that between a man's assumptions and his circumstances. He may plan and hope and act as if one thing were true, whereas in fact the truth is different and often hostile. This special irony of circumstance was a favourite theme with Thomas Hardy who turned it often to high tragic purposes and showed the pitiful helplessness of man in his illusions before the relentless determination of doom. In such contrasts we often feel that circumstances are working their will and deliberately blinding man to what is coming. The ancient Greeks made full use of this theme, of the fate which a man hopes to avoid and is confident that he will, until suddenly it strikes him and he knows that all his efforts to escape from it have been futile. Cavafy casts this experience into *Nero's Term*. After the murders of his mother and his wife Nero visited Greece, and visited the Delphic Oracle, which told him " to beware three and seventy years ".

Like others who think that oracles are clearer than they really are, Nero believes that this must refer to his own term of life, which will be seventy-three years, and assumes that, as he is still a young man, he has many years before him. He puts anxieties away and looks back on his time in Greece,

> In the theatres, in the gardens, in the sports-grounds,
> The hours of evening in the towns of Achaea . . .
> And, best of all, the delight of naked bodies . . .

That is his illusion, his ignorance of his doom. It is the year before his death, and soon Galba is to seize his throne and drive him to kill himself. And so Cavafy changes at once from the illusion to the fact, and shows the march of this doom:

> So Nero. Galba secretly in Spain
> Gathers his army together and prepares it,
> The old man of the three and seventy years.

Behind Nero, behind the mechanism of the oracle, we see the gap between illusion and reality, the discord between what men think or hope and the hard facts which forbid it.

The contrast between illusion and fact need not always have this tragic or serious quality, and such is the range of Cavafy's irony that he sometimes reverses the situation and shows how the deluded opinions of men add glory and glamour to a situation. In *One of their Gods* he picks up a theme from the Greek world which bears an amusing resemblance to the chapter in the *Acts of the Apostles* where at Lystra Paul and Barnabas are taken for Mercury and Jupiter. A young figure comes to Seleukeia in the evening, tall and handsome:

> With the joy of incorruptibility in his eyes,
> With his black and perfumed hair.[1]

The passers-by look at him and ask each other who he is and where he comes from; a few notice that he disappears into the quarter of the town which comes to life at night with its orgies:

> They would wonder which it could be of Them
> And for what disreputable sensuality
> He had come into the streets of Seleukeia
> From those majestical, All-holy Mansions.[1]

---

[1] Trs. J. Mavrogordato.

So Cavafy presents his vision of what the Greeks meant when they thought that a god was among them, and no doubt his interpretation is right. But it is more than that. In his understanding of the appeal of physical beauty Cavafy may indeed mark the ironies of human illusion, but he knows that the source of it is admiration for so fine a physical specimen. And this illusion somehow gives dignity to the unknown stranger and to his beauty. Despite his dubious quest, he has an Olympian glory, and goes on his own business without caring what others think of him.

Cavafy's curiosity about the wayward movements of the human spirit is presented with much more than a purely intellectual interest. He passes beyond curiosity to a more excited and more enraptured state, infuses each poem with its own spirit and appeals to many emotions. His range is not at all narrow, and he covers a wide series of effects from gentle humour to an almost tragic seriousness. As he studies the past and sees its affinity with the present, he treats it with the varied responses which we give to the living scene. He often shows his own kind of quiet humour, of indulgent tolerance for the frailties of the human race, especially when he deals with it in the mass and watches the emotions of the crowd. Just as in *Alexandrian Kings* he interprets what the multitude feels about a glittering occasion, so in *In a District of Asia Minor* he shows the fundamental indifference of the ruled to their rulers. No doubt he had observed this in Egypt, but he had ample precedent for it in the Hellenistic East. The defeat of Antony by Octavius at Actium has been regarded as one of the decisive battles of the world, and to Virgil and Horace it was indeed the victory of the upright spirit of Rome over the corrupting influences of the East led by the lascivious, drunken Antony and the " Egyptian woman ", Cleopatra. But Cavafy knew that this view was not held by everyone at the time, and his poem gives a different, more cynical picture. His situation is immediately after the battle, when the news of Antony's defeat comes as a startling surprise to some Greeks of Asia Minor who have been so confident of his victory that they have prepared a laudatory inscription in his honour. But though they are astounded at the news, they are not in the least troubled or distressed. Antony means nothing to them, and their only desire is to placate whoever is going to be their ruler. They see at once that with the change of a few words the text can be made perfectly appropriate to Octavius. They have merely to alter

> Who has delivered the Romans
> From the disastrous Octavius

to

> Who has delivered the Romans
> From the disastrous Antony,

and then all the flights of panegyric will suit the new ruler. Cavafy gravely sets out the obsequious praise with its emphasis that the conqueror is the champion of the Greeks, who honours their customs and speaks their language, and then the poem is brought abruptly to an end in a way which shows how little the high-flown words really mean :

> And so on and so on. It all fits splendidly.

Cavafy is reported to have said of this poem that to towns like this " it was completely indifferent whether the ruler of the world was called Antony or Octavian ", and his poem shows how he interprets this. He smiles at the simple cynicism of the whole manœuvre, but he does not condemn or despise it. Behind it he sees the natural instincts of men to preserve themselves and to treat their rulers as nuisances which must be humoured.

Cavafy is not always so indulgent to his subjects. There are some men and women whom he seems to have disliked, and for them he reserves sharper weapons, as he dexterously exposes their weaknesses and pretences. His dislike is kept well in hand, but it is discernible and gives a sharper quality to his poetry. He was, for instance, much interested in the curious character of the Emperor Julian, but it is quite clear that he did not admire him. Indeed, so far from seeing anything attractive in this last futile champion of the pagan gods, Cavafy looks at him through the eyes of the Christians who opposed him and did everything to belittle him. In *Julian seeing Negligence* he makes some character condemn Julian's

48

idea of setting up a new church. In *Julian in Nicomedia* he shows how, before he became Emperor, the future enemy of Christianity was ready, in the interests of his own safety, to attend Christian services with an air of pious devotion. In *Julian and the Citizens of Antioch* he shows how the people of Antioch refused to surrender to Julian's demands,

> To his airy chatter about the false gods,
> To his annoying chatter about himself
> To his childish fear of the theatre ;
> His graceless prudery ; his ridiculous beard.[1]

In *Understood Not* he takes the side of the bishops in their controversy with the emperor about Christianised versions of the classics and a Homeric version of the Psalms. And finally, in *On the Outskirts of Antioch* he gives, again from the Christian point of view, the story of a quarrel between Julian and the Christians of Antioch over the burial of the martyr Babylas in the precincts of Apollo. The Christians indeed triumph since Apollo's precinct and statue are burned, to Julian's great chagrin. There was something about Julian which Cavafy disliked, and his poems about him are less indulgent than those about other, less formidable, figures. Perhaps Cavafy felt that Julian, with his asceticism and pedantry, denied the essential pleasures of life and was for that reason to be condemned.

This disapproving attitude is not at all emphatic. No actual words of condemnation are said, but the themes are chosen and presented in a way which leaves little doubt about Cavafy's feelings. One of his victims is the Byzantine princess, Anna Comnena, who wrote in her *Alexiad* a life of her father, the Emperor Alexius I Comnenus, and prefixed to it an account of her grief for her husband, Nicephorus Bryennius, who died in 1137. With this Cavafy's *Anna Comnena* begins. He shows what excesses of grief she claims to feel, how she " dims her eyes with rivers of tears ", how her grief " burns her to the bones and marrow and cleaving of her soul ". But this display of grief is not so simple or so natural as it sounds. Anna's husband had joined her in rebelling against her brother at her father's death and trying to seize the crown for

---

[1] Trs. J. Mavrogordato.

herself. Her deepest, sharpest grief is not for the loss of her husband but for the failure of her ambitions :

> It is more like the truth that only one sorrow,
> One mortal sorrow, this ambitious woman knew ;
> Only one deep hurt she had
> (Even if she never confesses it) this haughty Greek,
> That she never managed, with all her cleverness,
> To seize the Empire ; but it was taken
> Almost out of her hands by the insolent John.[1]

John, whom his mother called " insolent ", had in fact saved the empire for himself by taking the ring from the dead hand of his father and establishing his own claim with it. For an ambitious woman like Anna, Cavafy has not much mercy. He does not actually condemn her, but his skilful juxtaposition of her high-flown words of grief and her actual feelings gives his poem a keen edge. He recognises her gifts, but knows that her dominating passion is ambition.

In his ironical survey of human actions Cavafy often shows real compassion and sympathetic understanding. He does not demand that his various subjects should be conceived on a grand scale and sees pathos in quite simple situations. For instance, in a poem with the curious title *Melancholy of Jason, son of Cleander, poet in Syria Commagene*, A.D. 595 he touches on an obscure little subject and shows how much it means to him. The poem is extremely short :

> The old age of my body and my beauty
> Is a wound from a terrible knife.
> I have no endurance of any sort.
> To you I fly for help, Art of Poetry,
> Who know something about medicines,
> Attempts to numb grief in fantasy and speech.
>
> It is a wound from a terrible knife, —
> Bring your medicines, Art of Poetry,
> That my wound, for a time, may not be felt.

The title is almost as important as the text. Cavafy sets his scene at a time when the Byzantine hold on Asia Minor was

[1] Trs. J. Mavrogordato.

precarious owing to the incursion of the Avars, and fine literature can hardly have existed. But even in this threatened and
uncertain world poetry keeps its wonderful power of healing
wounds. The universal theme is set in a carefully chosen
setting just to show how universal it is, and the power of
the poem comes from Cavafy's gentle response to the
situation, from the warmth and humanity with which he
approaches it.

Cavafy is too restrained an artist to allow his pathos to flow
freely and so lose half its appeal. He tends to restrain it, to
dilute it, to combine it with some appeal to other emotions,
and to make it an element in a complex result. For instance, in
A Craftsman of Bowls he begins with a topic near his heart,
the pleasure which an artist takes in his work. This craftsman
has made a mixing-bowl of pure silver and adorned it with
flowers and thyme and streams. In the centre is the figure
of a naked and handsome young man, and to this the craftsman has given all his attention and all his powers, trying to
make it as truthful and exact as he can. But this young man
is only a memory :

> Great has been my difficulty because
> Full fifteen years have passed since the day
> When he fell, a soldier, in the rout of Magnesia.

Cavafy's silversmith is both a man and an artist, and the two
sides of his nature are almost at war. As an artist he finds it
hard to portray the figure of a young man who has been dead
for fifteen years, but as a man he insists on it and holds to it.
So Cavafy shows the difficulties of the artist who will be satisfied only by the highest performance, and this refines the
pathos which might otherwise come too easily and miss some
of its effect.

In *Aristoboulos* Cavafy exploits pathos with more cunning.
He begins with a scene of mourning in the house of Herod.
The king will not be comforted because Aristoboulos has been
drowned when playing with his friends. The news will make
all the Greeks in Syria, and especially the poets and sculptors,
mourn, since they greatly admired his looks. In this apparently general grief a sinister note is heard. Aristoboulos'

mother, Alexandra, takes part in the mourning, but when she is alone her mood changes :

> She moans and raves and reviles and curses.
> How they have tricked her ! How they have cheated her !
> How in the end they have got what they desired !
> They have laid waste the Asmonean house.
> How has the wicked King succeeded,
> The treacherous, the low, the criminal !

Aristoboulos has in fact been murdered by Herod, and much of the grief at the court is feigned. Even the mother's grief for her son is less than her hatred for his and her enemies. She cannot endure to think of the joy which Herod's mother, Cyprus, and his sister, Salome, will feel :

> How they will triumph now and rejoice in secret,
> The wicked women, Cyprus and Salome,
> The low-class women, Cyprus and Salome.

Alexandra knows that she is powerless and compelled to acquiesce in the lies spread about Aristoboulos' death. She cannot tell the people what has really happened, and that is her sharpest blow. So the poem begins with a false air of pathos and moves to new depths in which grief is lost in hatred, and pathos in drama. Cavafy resists the temptation to secure a simple effect and shows how complicated such a situation is and what passions it awakes in its participants.

No less skilful in its mixture of motives and emotions is *The Sickness of Kleitos*. It begins with what looks like a pathetic situation. The young Kleitos, who is well-bred and knows Greek well, is dangerously ill with fever, and his condition is the more serious because he was struck down at a time when he was extremely exhausted and depressed by the failure of a love-affair. No wonder that his parents are afraid. Such is the beginning, and we do not expect much to happen, knowing Cavafy's interest in young men and their fortunes. But he develops it with a true instinct for surprise. Kleitos' old nurse trembles for his life. In her anxiety she remembers an idol whom she used to serve in her childhood before she joined a Christian household and became herself a Christian. She takes cake and wine and honey to the idol and sings what she can remember of his hymns, and then comes the end :

> But the silly woman
> Does not understand how little the black god cares
> Whether a Christian recovers or not.

The pathos of the sick young man is left behind and replaced by a different pathos, more complex and more profound, of his old nurse, whose desire to save him makes her forsake her adopted religion and even so to no avail. The situation expands and develops and invites a greater variety of response than its opening suggests.

Cavafy's sympathetic understanding of human weakness and failure did not blind him to human strength. He, who in his early poems had praised the virtues of endurance and confidence, kept his regard for them, enlarged his vision of them, and paid them tributes of respect. He had, as many Greeks have, a real love and admiration for the courage which accepts hard facts without complaint and sets to work to make the best of a bad situation. He knew that one of the most sinister obstacles which prominent men have to face is the dishonesty of underlings and toadies who hide the truth from them, and he admired a man who could see through this and rise to the drastic call of an occasion. This lies behind his short poem *Manuel Comnenus*, about the Byzantine Emperor who reigned from 1146 to 1180 and was one of the most formidable soldiers of his age, compared by Gibbon to Richard Cœur de Lion. Cavafy takes this reputation for granted, and his poem tells of the last years of the Emperor. He begins in his most engaging way :

> The King and Emperor Manuel Comnenus
> On a melancholy morning of September
> Saw that his death was near.

Manuel calls for his paid astrologers, who, being courtiers, tell him that he has many years to live, but he knows that this is the kind of thing they always say, and makes his own decision :

> From the cells of the monastery he orders
> Ecclesiastical raiment to be brought to him,
> And puts it on, and is glad that now he shows
> The solemn air of a priest or holy man.

But Cavafy is not quite content even with this effect. He increases the significance of the Emperor's action by passing a comment on it in the manner of the time :

> Blessed are all they who believe
> And like King Manuel end their days
> Dressed in the solemn raiment of their faith.

This puts the action in its right setting and shows what the Emperor's choice meant to his contemporaries. The comment completes the poem by suggesting that the emperor who is brave enough to defy his astrologers is still a soldier and puts on his monkish garb as he would his armour for battle.

This respect for human courage and character is perhaps Cavafy's most characteristic note. He valued human strength all the more because he knew to what ailments the spirit of man is heir. It is therefore not surprising that some of his finest and richest poems are concerned with the triumph of men over circumstances. He did not allow his admirations to obscure or to simplify his vision of the actual occasions of which he wrote, but through their complexities he shows how the will and the creative instinct rise above adverse conditions. He saw that this can happen in unexpected and in otherwise undistinguished fields, and that even writers may be examples of it. In his *Darius* he dramatised such a possibility. The scene is in Pontus in the reign of Mithridates VI, the Great, just before the Romans declared war on him. His poet, Phernazes, is writing an epic on Darius, from whom Mithridates claims to be descended. He pursues his task conscientiously and tries to understand Darius's character and motives :

> But here
> He needs philosophy. He must analyse
> The feelings that Darius would have had :
> Perhaps arrogance and intoxication ? No, rather
> An understanding of the vanity of greatness.
> Deeply the poet meditates the matter.

At this point a servant breaks in to say that the Romans have declared war and Mithridates' army has crossed the frontier.

The poet is appalled. What interest can the king have now in this poem ?

> In the middle of war, think of it, Greek poetry !

He is worried. He has hoped to make a great thing of his poem and to confound his envious critics with it :

> What a delay, what a delay to his plans !

Nor is the delay the worst thing about it. The danger is really serious. Amisos is not a very strong town, and the Romans are formidable enemies. Can the Cappadocians defeat them ? He can only ask the gods to help and defend Asia. Still, even in this crisis the human spirit asserts itself. The poet continues to pursue his thoughts about his poem and solves his special problem :

> None the less in all that trouble and disturbance
> The poetical idea comes and goes insistently —
> Most likely, certainly, arrogance and intoxication,
> Arrogance and intoxication Darius would have had.

There is something noble and admirable in the way in which despite himself the poet is not defeated by his circumstances but goes on with his work.

Cavafy, living in Egypt, had few patriotic enthusiasms, but he was proud of his Greek traditions and of the part which his remote ancestors had played in spreading Hellenic civilisation to remote corners of the world. In *200 B.C.* he gives definite shape to this feeling. He sets his action at a time when the successors of Alexander still ruled from Macedonia to the Hindu-Kush, and vast Asiatic populations felt the magical appeal of Hellenic ways. He again takes his theme from Plutarch, who tells how Alexander, after his victory over the Persians at the Granicus in 334 B.C., sent the spoils to Greece with the inscription " Alexander, son of Philip, and the Greeks, without the Lacedaemonians ", because the Lacedaemonians had refused to join his confederacy and had thereby missed all its glories. Cavafy presents the issue through a man of a later generation who understands what the words mean for history. He imagines what the Lacedaemonians felt when they saw these words. No doubt, they were not affected by them, since they did not like to be ordered about and would not accept any leader but one of their own kings. He understands their position and recognises that theirs is a possible attitude. But then he recalls what they missed, what Alexander and the other Greeks did without them, the glorious achievements of the army at the Granicus, at the Issus, at Arbela, where the Persian host was swept away. He sees what magnificent results have followed :

> And from that wonderful expedition of all the Greeks
> The victorious, the renowned,
> The illustrious, the famous,
> As no expedition has ever been,
> The incomparable, we have risen
> A great new Hellenic world.

Of this achievement he is indeed proud, but especially because it is the work not so much of the mainland Greeks as of Greeks from many countries of Africa and Asia.

> We, from Alexandria, from Antioch,
> From Seleucia, and the countless
> Other Greeks from Egypt and Syria,
> In Media and in Persia, and all the others,
> With our far-flung domination,
> With the various influence of wise adaptation.
> And our Common Hellenic Speech
> We brought to the middle of Bactria, to the Indians.
> Now let us talk about the Lacedaemonians !

This is almost the myth of Cavafy's own belief in the Greeks. The world created by the armies and the successors of Alexander is for him far more important than the narrow, proud society of Sparta, and he is glad to express his pride in belonging to this company and this tradition. He sees, with justice, that in the history of the world the Hellenisation of the East was far grander than any achievement of the small Spartan state, and he pays his tribute to the men, drawn from many lands and doubtfully of Greek descent, who worked this extraordinary miracle.

Religion, no less than politics, provides examples of a

heroic and triumphant spirit. If at times Cavafy showed his keen understanding of the old Olympian faith, at other times he paid his tributes to Christianity. What caught his imagination was the access of confidence and strength which it brings, and in more than one poem on its early days he shows how Christians, despite their inner contradictions, still remain faithful to their cause. In *A Great Procession of Priests and Laymen* he gives a precise form to this enduring spirit and its strange strength. It is in Antioch after the death of Julian the Apostate. Christians are again allowed to practise their rites, and there is a great procession through the streets. A young man in white raiment carries the cross with uplifted hands :

> Our strength and our hope, the Holy Cross.

The heathen, who recently were so arrogant, have withdrawn, and the Cross goes on :

> To every quarter
> Wherever the Christians dwell in godliness
> It brings comfort and joy.
> They come, the devout, to the doors of their dwellings
> And full of joy worship it,
> The strength, the salvation of the world, the Cross.

This is the language and the spirit of the time, and it rings with truth. It is indeed a special occasion ; for the persecutor is dead, and the Christian cause has triumphed :

> The unclean, the abominable
> Julian reigns no more.
> Let us pray for the devout Jovian.

The historical occasion is perfectly chosen — the moment of deliverance from the oppressor and of hope in his successor who has granted freedom of worship. The poem tells the triumph of faith and with perfect candour shows it in its pride and its intolerance and withal in its tremendous confidence and sense of a special calling. Cavafy was drawn to such a display of strength and set it out with truth and power.

In his re-creation of the past Cavafy gives his own special vision of life, and it is surprising how positive and even normal it is. We might expect that, with his peculiar circumstances and character, he might have dwelt on morbid and defeated moods and have passed gloomy comments on the futility of existence. Such charges have been laid against his poems of modern life with their insistence on the strange vagaries of sexual appetite. But through the past he found a different and more confident self. The dignity of history gave him freedom from his immediate cares and enabled him to exercise his full gifts. This concern with the past was not an escape from life, but a fuller interest in it, a way to see perennial issues in their right perspective and their real importance. By identifying himself with figures of history and seeing their lives, so far as he could, from their own points of view, Cavafy both extended his own personality and gained a sharper insight into that of others. If he began by treating the past as a source of illustrations for the present, he came to see that both past and present have the same abiding qualities and that human nature presents much the same problems and paradoxes at all periods. He pierced through the local and ephemeral qualities of a situation to its permanent character and created not a record of history but an imaginative criticism of life. His range is by no means narrow, and though he confined himself to the Mediterranean world of the Greco-Roman and Byzantine ages, this did not hamper his gifts or restrict his scope. On the contrary he was wise to keep himself to it for more than one reason. In the first place, this was the past in which he felt at home. He was its child : he understood its character through the people that he knew and the air that he breathed. He was thus able to give to it that special searching insight which was indispensable if he was to make poetry out of it. It had for him not the glamour of the distant scene but the solidity of reality, of men whose ways and speech he understood. And in the second place Cavafy's world has its own unity and harmony. If he had strayed outside it to other regions and other civilisations he would have impaired its consistent and convincing character. As it is, despite its great variety of human types and situations, it has its own homogeneous reality and the special appeal which belongs to a single department of experience organised and interpreted by a single creative mind. The different poems supplement and complete one another and succeed in creating a special life for this section of history.

This achievement is all the more remarkable because it is in any analysis a triumph of poetry. There are no lapses, no irregularities or uncertainties. Each poem does its own task as well as it can be done. This poetry of course is of a special kind, and in this Cavafy's originality lies. A poet of the previous generation would have flung greater riches into these evocations of the past and no doubt would have secured successes which were beyond Cavafy's desire or reach. We can imagine how a great Romantic would have treated Caesarion or Nero or Julian or any other of Cavafy's figures. But the gain in visionary sweep would have detracted from the reality of the presentation, and this is indispensable to Cavafy's art. In order to secure this reality, and because it was in this direction that his unusual gifts lay, Cavafy risks no stunning effects. His is a quiet poetry, strictly truthful and circumstantial and realistic, concerned above all to present human nature as it is and to make its presentation entirely convincing not merely to the imagination but to the intelligence. This quiet air, which looks so easy to maintain and must have in fact demanded the greatest self-control and critical judgment, is Cavafy's special triumph. It is poetry because it enchants and remains in the memory, because every word of it, however unassuming, matters, and because every detail contributes something to the final effect, every variation of tone enriches the dramatic interest and the human appeal. By restricting his style Cavafy was able to secure a remarkable variety of tone, to give to each episode not only its dominating atmosphere but the variations and complexities within it. A more elaborate style and a less controlled imagination would have destroyed Cavafy's subtle and special charm. The texture of his verse, so carefully meditated and achieved, is precisely the right medium for the kind of effects which he wished to produce. By some fortunate inspiration he rid himself early of ambitions for a grand style and conceived the idea that his poetry could be written with a control and moderation which should yet allow full play to his own kind of subject. That he had difficulties about this can be seen from certain traces of rhetoric and of the grand manner in his first verses, but with a true sense of what poetry needed in his time, he purified his style and found what was in its own way a counterpart to the styles which poets in other countries were fashioning for themselves.

If one of the chief problems of modern poetry has been to combine a purely poetical thrill with a full sense of the complexity of the modern consciousness, there can be no doubt that Cavafy, who began to work before the problem had become clear in many parts of Europe, found his own successful solution to it. His thrill is not indeed the dynamic excitement which Apollinaire or Lorca gives, nor is his complexity that of Pasternak or Eliot, but he gives a genuine thrill and his is a real complexity. Of course in some ways his task was easier than that of poets caught in the established tradition of Western Europe. He had to surmount fewer conventions and a less entrenched view of what poetry ought to be. Nor does he explore those obscure activities of the semi-consciousness which other poets have found so rich in possibilities and prospects. He knew his limits and perfected his art within them. By his dramatic handling of his material he was able to enter into many strange corners of the human soul, and so firm was his grasp on the essentials of reality that he seems always to deal with something of fundamental importance. He might so easily have fallen into paradox for its own sake and concentrated on amusing eccentricities. But he did not do this. He was always sane and in touch with actual life, because he was concerned not with the vagaries of human nature but with its mystery.

III

ORDER AND ADVENTURE IN
GUILLAUME APOLLINAIRE

It is the fate of some writers to gather such a legend about
their lives and personalities that it turns attention away from
what they have actually done and obscures their real worth.
For such a result they themselves are not always responsible.
Obedient to their powerful instincts and blind to the conventions which inhibit ordinary men, they go blithely on their
way, only to find that their superficial eccentricities excite
more interest than their real achievements and that their true
merits are imperfectly understood. Wilhelm Apollinaris de
Kostrovitzki, known to the world as Guillaume Apollinaire,
was such a man. In his lifetime he was almost a legendary
figure, and even now many are more interested in his legend
than in his work. His origins were mysterious. His mother
was a Russian or Polish woman of the *demi-monde* and was
either unwilling or unable to say who his father was, though
she hinted that he was a prince of the Church, and in later
years Apollinaire's friends accepted the myth and paid tributes
to it by giving him the attributes of a cardinal in their portraits
of him. The higher criticism has raised grave doubts about
this piece of hagiology, but it is characteristic of Apollinaire
that his beginnings were wrapped in mystery. The legend
which began with such auspices received new chapters as he
pursued his independent path through life. There are many
stories about his eccentric dress, his odd behaviour, his practical jokes, his preposterous whims, his mania for collecting
beautiful or rare objects, his vast bulk, and his heroic and
fabulous greed. It was typical of his destiny that when in 1911
the *Mona Lisa* disappeared from the Louvre, he was quite
wrongly accused of stealing it. A Bohemian acquaintance of
his, Guy Pernet, used to steal figurines from museums for
pleasure and gave one to Apollinaire, who kept it on his
mantelpiece ; so the police were not wholly unjustified in

arresting him, though he never anticipated such an event and was deeply distressed and dismayed by it. It was tragically in tune with his life that, when on 11th November 1918, he lay dead in Paris, those who came to pay the last honours to his body heard the crowds crying " À bas Guillaume ! " and could not help imagining that these cries for vengeance on the Kaiser were somehow directed against their dead friend. Apollinaire's legend encompassed him from birth to death. He accepted it cheerfully, did not trouble to disown it, and at times made his own contributions to it.

It even affected his work. A conservative reader might at first sight feel that Apollinaire's two volumes of verse, *Alcools* (1913) and *Calligrammes* (1918), bear too many signs of smart modernity and of the sophisticated, urban jauntiness which invaded poetry about 1910. Apollinaire was sufficiently a child of nature and of his time to enjoy the thrill of shocking the respectable, and sometimes he went out of his way to pretend that he was more outrageous than he really was. Vastly different though his own gifts were from Marinetti's, he coquetted for a short period with Italian Futurism and aped some of its affectations. Just as Marinetti wished to destroy syntax, to get rid of adjectives " because the naked substantive keeps its essential colour " and to replace existing systems of punctuation by mathematical and musical signs, so in *L'Anti-tradition futuriste* (1913) Apollinaire laid emphasis on " mots en liberté ", on the virtues of onomatopoeia and puns, and condemned adjectives, punctuation, regular typography and verse-forms. He even assimilated something of Marinetti's hatred of sentiment and the past, when he dismissed " la douleur poétique " and scorned the literary tradition as represented by

Les frères Siamois d'Annunzio et Rostand
Dante Shakespeare Tolstoi Goethe.

His manifesto achieved a notoriety, which Marinetti might have envied, because it contained " le mot de Cambronne ", which had hitherto been regarded as unprintable. It is not surprising that his grave elders did not treat him quite seriously.

When he condemned punctuation, Apollinaire acted on a tenable theory. He did not want any new system of musical or mathematical signs. He had for some time ceased to use punctuation and had no intention of returning to it. His defence was to claim the precedent of old religious texts and to assert that his unpunctuated verses forced men to read them in a level monotonous voice as one reads psalms or canticles. He also argued, with more cogency, that the punctuation of a poem means nothing to a reader who follows its sense and rhythms and needs no extraneous help to make him understand it. His foible, if such it was, was not intended to create mystery or ambiguity. His most fantastic thoughts fell into clear and grammatical sentences, and, if we wish to put in the stops, there is no doubt where they should go. The first stanza of *La Chanson du Mal-Aimé* may perhaps frighten the inexperienced reader by its unpunctuated nakedness :

> Un soir de demi-brune à Londres
> Un voyou qui ressemblait à
> Mon amour vint à ma rencontre
> Et le regard qu'il me jeta
> Me fit baisser les yeux de honte.

But if we read this aloud, the difficulties disappear. The structure is perfectly straightforward, and the sense is as clear as if Apollinaire had printed it in the ordinary way :

> Un soir de demi-brune à Londres
> Un voyou, qui ressemblait à
> Mon amour, vint à ma rencontre,
> Et le regard qu'il me jeta
> Me fit baisser les yeux de honte.

It was perhaps tiresome of Apollinaire to omit punctuation, but its absence in no way affects the essential clarity of his verse.

In *Calligrammes* Apollinaire started a new source of misunderstanding by presenting some poems in pictorial forms, making the typography follow the outline of a smoking cigar or a necktie or a watch or a fountain or rain, rather as Greek poets in Alexandria had presented poems in the shape of an

altar or an egg or a shepherd's pipe. Apollinaire did this in
the first place because he wrote these poems on post-cards,
many of them from the front in the First World War, and
hoped to amuse and cheer his friends by them. When he
published them later, it was no doubt because he felt that his
designs had a certain charm and elegance and recalled the
conditions in which he composed them. The drift of rain in
five wavy vertical lines, the curving rise of water from a
fountain, the smoke curling from a pipe, have considerable
grace and show that Apollinaire knew what purity of line is.
If we take the trouble to reduce these designs to ordinary
script and to punctuate them, the result is surprisingly normal.
Jet d'Eau, for instance, is constructed with regular lines and
rhymes :

> Tous les souvenirs de naguère,
> O mes amis partis en guerre,
> Jaillissent vers le firmament,
> Et vos regards en l'eau dormant
> Meurent mélancoliquement.

This has the ease and limpidity of classical French verse, and
we cannot denounce Apollinaire as Dryden denounced
MacFlecknoe :

> Choose for the command
> Some peaceful province in Acrostic land,
> Where thou may'st wings display or altars raise,
> And torture one poor word a thousand ways.

Apollinaire had his airs and fancies, but they are superficial,
and it is easy to penetrate behind them to the real poetry.

Apollinaire's originality may in part be explained by reference to the art of painting with which he had an intimate
acquaintance. Just as the Symbolists owed much of their
mysterious magnificence to the example of music and sought
to reproduce some of its effects in words, so Apollinaire found
his inspiration and his example in painting. The change from
the one art to the other is a commentary on the difference
between the outlooks of two generations. The Symbolists
admired music because it suggests those impalpable powers
which they believed to exist in an ideal world : Apollinaire
preferred the visible world as painters see it. His love for

painting was intensified by personal ties and admirations. Early in the century he formed close friendships with Picasso and Picabia, fell easily into their ways of thought and not only absorbed their theories but amplified and clarified them. When the Cubists held their first exhibition in 1911, Apollinaire introduced their work to the public in his *Peintres Cubistes*, where with sympathetic insight and dialectical ability he sketched the aims and qualities of Picasso, Braque, Metzinger, Marie Laurençin, Picabia and others. His criticism shows how well he understood the general movement of the arts in his time. He saw that painting was trying to be purer, that these artists " ont pour but secret de faire la peinture pure ", that " la peinture se purifie, en Occident, avec cette logique idéale que les peintres anciens ont transmise aux nouveaux comme s'ils donnaient la vie . . . et c'est tout ". But though he understood this " ideal logic " and saw where it led, he was not an advocate of purely abstract painting. He had enough respect for the past to believe that art must be related to actual objects, and he attributed the same trust to his painters : " La plupart des nouveaux peintres font bien de la mathématique ; mais ils n'ont pas abandonné la nature, qu'ils interrogent patiemment à cette fin qu'elle leur enseigne la route de la vie ".

His associations with painters and his first-hand knowledge of new movements like Cubism encouraged Apollinaire to do in poetry what his friends did in line and colour, and to create a purer art of words than was practised by his contemporaries. His sense of the value of words was as keen as a painter's eye for colours and design, and, without in any way confusing the different conditions of the two arts, he wished to give to poetry not only a greater purity, such as he thought the Cubists gave to painting, but also that " fourth dimension ", that spiritual or metaphysical quality, which he found in Picasso. He deplored the limitations of the impersonal, realistic art of the Parnassians which was still dominant in his first creative years. In it he missed something vitally important, something which he was determined to bring into his own work. He was neither a mystic nor a scientist : what moved him was the imaginative appeal of life, the enchantment which it laid on him, the hints that it gave of unsounded depths and unsolved mysteries. He felt that existing poetry was too cautious, too careful, too obedient to rules and conventions. To this belief he always held, and right at the end of his life in *La jolie Rousse* he made himself clear on the issue. It was the old quarrel between tradition and invention, between order and adventure :

> Entre nous et pour nous mes amis
> Je juge cette longue querelle de la tradition et de l'invention
> De l'Ordre de l'Aventure.

He asks indulgence for himself and his kind, and offers as his justification his belief that there is a vast field of experience where poetry has never ventured and where he himself can make enthralling discoveries :

> Nous voulons nous donner de vastes et d'étranges domaines
> Où le mystère en fleurs s'offre à qui veut le cueillir.

This was his fourth dimension, the element which he found absent even from Greek art. He believed that poetry, like painting, must perform its proper task and justify his trust that " les grands poètes et les grands artistes ont pour fonction sociale de renouveler sans cesse l'apparence que revêt la nature aux yeux des hommes ".

When Apollinaire wished to force upon men a new vision of the world, he realised that he must make a fresh start and abandon some of the traditional methods of handling experience. Feeling that the old assumptions of painters and poets were wrong, he sought a freshness and a simplicity of outlook which might at first sight seem at variance with his keen intelligence and his taste for advanced techniques. But in this he was perfectly genuine. It was because he was so intelligent that he looked for artists with an entirely fresh vision from which he could himself profit. This accounts for his admiration for some primitive kinds of art like Negro sculpture and the paintings of Theodore Rousseau, " le douanier ". In the first he saw how a complete sincerity and an unquestioning outlook can produce works of art, which, however inadequate they might seem by the standards of his time, have a special directness of appeal : in the second he realised how a man's eyes, when not trained in an academic discipline, can see aspects of things which are invisible to the masters of the schools. Nor was this appeal purely artistic. In Apollinaire's nature there was a strong element of simplicity and naturalness. He had something of the eternal *gamin*, of the unbroken schoolboy, who enjoys things for the first time and sees them quite differently from his more sophisticated elders. In his technique and his theories Apollinaire had a mature and critical mind, but in his approach to experience he had the gift of perpetual boyhood. The combination is unusual and explains much in his work.

Apollinaire's unerring eye for the right means to a given end can be seen from his use of metres. At a time when *vers libre* was widely vaunted, he kept his head and used both old and new metres, allowing his subject to dictate the rhythm which was best suited to it. The result is that he is a master of most forms from classical alexandrines to long unrhymed lines of varying rhythm. In each case we can almost see why he chooses a form and why, having begun with it, he changes to another. When he writes in impeccable alexandrines, he speaks solemnly with an air of dignity and needs the resources of authority behind him. In shorter metres, especially in a regular five-lined stanza in which the third and fifth lines rhyme with the first, he conveys the play of his mind as it turns round a subject and looks at it from different angles. At times he even bursts into lyrical song, as in the ravishingly melancholy *Le Pont Mirabeau*, and, more artfully, in *Les Saisons* where a haunting refrain breaks the realism and solemnity of the heavier, more formal verses. When he felt the need for free verse, he indulged it inventively. He began, as most of his contemporaries did, with restricting himself to short lines and aiming at a quiet, soothing effect, and this gives much of its peculiar charm to *La Maison des Morts*, where the well-controlled lines are suited to this fancy of dead men coming to life and help to emphasise that their activities are extremely ordinary. But in the thrill of battle Apollinaire found a new use for free verse and saw that he must apply it differently to reflect the chaotic variety of the battlefield, its splendours and its squalors, its alternations of deadly hazard and commonplace routine. With great long lines that leap into space and yet keep all their litheness and suppleness Apollinaire catches many facets of war. His broken manner of progression suits its shocks and surprises. His catalogues are indeed catalogues, almost of unrelated items, and as such refuse to fit into any regular form. His free verses reflect the variety of his experience and give to it its proper weight and movement. It is a triumph of his virtuosity, of his ear and command of rhythmical effects. War has this spasmodic character, and free verse of this adventurous kind is well able to express it.

Apollinaire's vocabulary shows the same care and delicacy as his choice of rhythms. He did not invent new words or revive obsolete ones. If at times he uses words of Greek origin like " pyraustes ", " argyraspides ", or " dendrophores ", it is exceptional and no doubt rises from his love of recondite information. Normally he writes with exceptional ease and clarity, goes straight to the point and has the rare gift of saying all that he wants so succinctly that it seems impossible to say it otherwise. But the wonder of this ease is that it is so full of poetry. The plain statements are charged with intense significance : there is no suspicion of artificial simplicity. Apollinaire may set out a situation in the quietest way possible and yet make it remarkably exciting, as in the opening lines of *Annie*, which seems to have been written when one of his loves had gone to America :

> Sur la côte du Texas
> Entre Mobile et Galveston il y a
> Un grand jardin tout plein des roses
> Il contient aussi une villa
> Qui est une grande rose.

Nothing could be simpler. The words are the commonest words from the speech of every day. But they are none the less so fresh and lively that the attention is immediately arrested and held. Apollinaire's eye relates what he sees to speech without any appearance of effort. Every word does its work at the same level of power and ease. Again, when in *A la Santé* he describes his entry into prison :

> Avant d'entrer dans ma cellule
> Il a fallu me mettre nu
> Et quelle voix sinistre ulule
> Guillaume qu'es tu devenu,

there is the same miraculous impression of ease. The action is called up in the shortest possible space, and the effect of horror appears in the adjective " sinistre " and the verb " ulule " with the suggestions of some cruel, menacing oracle, while the unadorned question in the fourth line is exactly right for a man who finds himself in an unexpectedly hideous situation and is appalled and horrified by it.

Such an equipment for metre and for language was needed by Apollinaire in the task which he set himself. He adapted and improved the traditional means of French poetry for his own special vision of life. He was a true successor to Rimbaud in his unquestioning acceptance of poetry as a life-giving force and in his conviction that artistic success depends on an adventurous exploitation of the sensibility. Gifted as he was with eyes that missed nothing, he was no mere recorder of visual impressions. His pleasure in what he saw awoke in him many thoughts and fancies and made him start on flights of imagination which gave a new and deeper meaning to common things and events. As he himself says in *Les Fiançailles* :

> Les fleurs à mes yeux redeviennent des flammes
> Je médite divinement
> Et je souris des êtres que je n'ai pas créés.

His special gift was for visual evocation. Thoughts turned in his mind into pictures, and the pictures developed new themes which added greatly to the richness of the whole effect. In *Zone* Apollinaire shows that this pictorial gift was something which he had preserved from childhood. He recalls his boyhood and his uncritical religious devotion and especially his literal trust in the Ascension. After some sincere words about what Christ means to him, he develops the theme of the Ascension with a child's simple vision of what such an event means in the physical world. For the young Apollinaire the ascended Christ was like an airman or a bird, at whom the devils gape with envy, while angels and prophets fly round him:

> Icare Énoch Élie Apollonius de Thyane
> Flottent autour du premier aéroplane.

This strange creature of the air is joined by all the birds of the sky, from crows and owls to the kolibri and the fabulous roc. The scene, composed by Apollinaire in the plenitude of his powers, has the quality of a fairy-tale, so brilliantly is it seen and presented. But behind it we can discern the experience of childhood which creates its visions from simple materials with an absolute trust in them. This gift Apollinaire kept and put to great uses.

Apollinaire found no difficulty in expressing his thoughts and feelings by appropriate images. He was quick to notice resemblances between one thing and another and turn such relations to immediate profit. The boy who had thought of the ascending Christ as a bird or an aeroplane grew into a man who was never at a loss to make his meaning vivid through some unexpected and apt comparison. In his earlier poems this gift sometimes leads to strange results. Apollinaire seems not always to have cared what an image was so long as it was surprising and reasonably appropriate, and, partly inspired by a desire to shock, he allowed himself an occasional indulgence which detracts from the gravity of his work. His Merlin, looking at the evening sky, says:

> La lumière est ma mère ô lumière sanglante
> Les nuages coulaient comme un flux menstruel.

His hermit prays:

> O Seigneur flagellez les nuées du coucher
> Qui vous tendent au ciel de si jolis culs roses.

He himself described an evening in Paris:

> Les becs de gaz pissaient leur flamme au clair de lune,

or his own quiet state:

> A la fin les mensonges ne me font plus peur
> C'est la lune qui cuit comme un œuf sur le plat.

Such images were not of the kind to which the Parnassians and Symbolists had accustomed the reading public, and it is easy to dismiss them as youthful excesses. But even in these we can see how Apollinaire remains faithful to his impressions and uses strange comparisons to express an unusual sensation or point of view. In the first case it is, after all, the corrupt old magician who speaks and finds a sinister pleasure in the blood-red clouds. In the second the image reflects the dark unconscious movements of the hermit's mind which turns easily to thoughts of flagellation. The third conveys the sight, sound and colour of the gas-jets, and the fourth suggests not only Apollinaire's quiet state but his implicit contempt for it. The images are not beautiful in a conventional sense, but they are chosen with care and insight and must not be dismissed as wilful eccentricities.

Far more often Apollinaire chooses images which delight the inner eye and add greatly to the significance of his poetry. There is something humorous and yet more than humorous in his disgust at a display of trite opinions :

> Or ces pensées mortes depuis des millénaires
> Avaient le fade goût des grands mammouths gelées.

The stale taste of frozen mammoths hits off perfectly the pomposity and emptiness of platitudes. The apprehension of advancing age has a new and delicate pathos in

> Jeunesse adieu jasmin du temps.

The pleasure in light coming through an open window is brilliantly and faithfully caught :

> La fenêtre s'ouvre comme une orange
> Le beau fruit de la lumière.

The retreat into memories of first love, with its sense of security and seclusion, comes out in

> J'ai hiverné dans mon passé.

The night in the trenches before an attack becomes a hideous counterpart to the night when a husband waits for his wife's child to be born :

> Nuit qui criait comme une femme qui accouche
> Nuit des hommes seulement.

While he waits for his beloved to come, his soul is like a ship escorted by submarines in war-time and guarded as if it were infinitely precious :

> Que de sous-marins dans mon âme
> Naviguent et vont l'attendant
> Le superbe navire où clame
> Le chœur de ton regard ardent.

His attempts to remember his beloved when he is separated from her are like the efforts of a spy to find all about a fortress in a short time :

> Pâle espionne de l'Amour
> Ma mémoire à peine fidèle
> N'eut pour observer cette belle
> Forteresse qu'une heure un jour.

The images are delightful for their own sake, but by their remarkable truth and relevance they add greatly to the richness of Apollinaire's effects and lift his sensations and thoughts to a purely poetical brilliance.

The advantage of this gift is that it allows a poet to say what relations he finds between disparate things and how they really strike him. His imagery responds closely to his actual sensations and to the thoughts which they provoke. Apollinaire's mastery of it can be seen from a little masterpiece, *La blanche Neige* :

> Les anges les anges dans le ciel
> L'un est vêtu en officier
> L'un est vêtu en cuisinier
> Et les autres chantent
>
> Bel officier couleur du ciel
> Le doux printemps longtemps après Noël
> Te médaillera d'un beau soleil
> D'un beau soleil
>
> Le cuisinier plume les oies
> Ah ! tombe neige
> Tombe et que n'ai-je
> Ma bien-aimée entre mes bras.

We can easily reconstruct the bare and unessential bones of this poem. It is a winter's day with some remnants of blue sky, and then the snow begins to fall. From this Apollinaire builds his myth. He imagines angels in the sky, the one blue like an officer, the other white like a cook. The officer will be rewarded later when the fine weather comes : the cook plucks a goose, and the falling snow is its plucked feathers. The imagery is precise and coherent, and it does more than illuminate the visible impression. The thought of the spring ahead is conveyed in the delightful image of the medal to come, and the sudden, exciting moment of snow falling becomes more familiar and more friendly through the image of the plucked goose. Then, as the snow falls, the tone changes, and the poet forgets his myth and wishes that his love were in his arms again.

This use of fancy is capable of considerable extension, and sometimes Apollinaire pursues an image through a whole poem and gets the utmost out of it for the interpretation of something which has caught his imagination. In *Les Sapins*, for instance, he commemorates fir-trees by the Rhine. For him they have a special, human quality, though this varies with the seasons and invites different comparisons. When he first sees them they have a mysterious, pontifical air, which is well in place in the home of German fairy-tales :

> Les sapins en bonnets pointus
> De longues robes revêtus
> > Comme des astrologues
> Saluent leurs frères abattus
> Les bateaux qui sur le Rhin voguent
>
> Dans les sept arts endoctrinés
> Pars les vieux sapins leurs aînés
> > Qui sont de grands poètes
> Ils se savent prédestinés
> A briller plus que les planètes.

As the poet watches the fir-trees and marks their look of wisdom and experience, he thinks of the future that awaits them, the glorious starry future when they will become Christmas-trees. But before this they have their special life as singers and magicians :

> Les sapins beaux magiciens
> Chantent des noëls anciens

Au vent des soirs d'automne
Ou bien graves magiciens
Incantent le ciel quand il tonne.

In winter they are covered with white cherubs, in summer
they are like rabbits or old ladies. When the mountain is in
travail, they bring healing herbs and

De temps en temps sous l'ouragan
Un vieux sapin geint et se couche.

In the changing appearance of the fir-trees Apollinaire finds
rich material for thought, and his delight in them kindles his
fancy to show what they mean to him and what relations he
establishes with them.

It is a small step from imagery to myth, from conveying
one aspect of a situation to portraying a whole situation in a
mythical tale which emphasises its essential character. By
throwing into the objective form of a story something which
he knows in himself, Apollinaire suggests that it has a much
wider significance. Wherever he found his myths, he set so
new a character on them that their origins are of little importance. Once, for instance, he drew on the Arthurian cycle, and
wrote *Merlin et la vieille Femme*, in which the ostensible subject is Merlin's love for Vivian and the effect which this has
on him when he remembers it by an accident in old age. The
story becomes the myth of the creative life. We may need
love and win it, but more powerful than love is the sudden
violent memory of it, the chance return of an apparently lost
moment in a flood of inspiring beauty. Again in *Salomé* he
takes up a favourite theme of the 'nineties and gives it a new
meaning. His Salomé's love for the Baptist is beyond
brutality and perversion, but when he is killed it is an
occasion for weird ecstatic joy, and the poem ends in a frenzy
of dancing. This, too, is a myth of artistic creation. The
artist loves his subject and in a sense destroys it when he
gives it a permanent form, but the destruction is an occasion
for wild delight and triumph. There is something fierce and
reckless and insane in all true creation, something which the
mad dance of Salomé expresses. In *La Maison des Morts*
Apollinaire tells with studied quiet how the dead come to life

and pursue the ordinary activities of the living. They dance and sing and make love and promise eternal devotion, then say good-bye and return to their graves. Behind this lies the idea that what still endears the dead to us are the most simple things, the ordinary moments passed, the affections and hopes shared with them. Love survives the separation of death, and love of the dead is specially pure and exalting because it is sustained by elementary loyalties. Apollinaire transposes these profound truths into his poem, and the whole tone of it, the tranquil movement, and its insistence on the charm of common occupations, stress his message. His myth gives a new appeal and a new significance to his thoughts. Indeed all Apollinaire's myths have their own existence and their own appeal as stories — so full are they of delicate observations and life — but their special strength is that through the interest which they arouse they call to wider and less noticed issues which are his fundamental concern.

In these poems, as in all Apollinaire's work, there are many startling effects. He seems to have written in a frenzy of creative energy, and a first reading does not suggest that he took much care about construction. No great effort is needed to understand him, but his details are so provocative that we may think that Apollinaire was no great architect in building a poem. Actually he was more careful than is often admitted. He built his verses into fine patterns and shaped quite long poems out of them, so that even when he seems to be at his most ecstatic he is really in control of his material and imposes a noble order on it. A resplendent example of this skill is *La Chanson du Mal-Aimé* which is composed in seven parts of different lengths and contains fifty-nine five-lined stanzas of regular form. It is much more than a lament for lost love : it covers the whole range of the poet's feelings in his crisis, and each part develops a different aspect of the complex situation. But Apollinaire uses a special, new technique. While the first, third, fifth and seventh sections give, as it were, the direct story of his love, the second, fourth and sixth sections, which are much shorter, provide imaginative comments on it and relate its themes to wider issues by developing their implications and almost creating separate poems, as Apollinaire advances from his present catastrophe to brilliant fancies which half console him for his loss.

The first, third, fifth and seventh sections tell the story of this lost love, beginning at the point where the poet really realises what the loss means, and begins to see its importance for him at the moment when he recovers from his dull stupor at the first shock. He begins by telling how this truth comes to him in London and how he contrasts his abandoned state with that of famous figures renowned for the loyalty of the women who loved them. He gives the poetry of a man trying to rid himself of a haunting memory, of an affection which still has a hold on him :

> Adieux faux amour confondu
> Avec la femme qui s'éloigne
> Avec celle que j'ai perdue
> L'année dernière en Allemagne
> Et que je ne reverrai plus.

The third section shows how, for the moment, Apollinaire recovers from this defeated condition and shows signs of fight. He finds that he is still faithful to his lost love and unwilling to abandon it. He will therefore find some consolation in singing of it and in defying the destiny which has robbed him of it : he compares himself to the worshippers of perished gods and to those human beings who prolong their devotion to their loved ones after death :

> L'amour est mort j'en suis tremblant
> J'adore de belles idoles
> Les souvenirs lui ressemblant
> Comme la femme de Mausole
> Je reste fidèle et dolent.

This defiant mood is short-lived, and in the fifth section Apollinaire returns to his regrets which are now sharper and more vivid as he remembers more clearly the time when his love was returned :

> Ses regards laissaient une traîne
> D'étoiles dans les soirs tremblants.

He even hopes that his beloved will come back to him, and he is ready to welcome her. He does not wish to forget her, and his longing for her makes him regret all the more his forsaken condition. He is so full of regrets and memories that he can speak of himself only with coarse contempt :

> Et moi j'ai le cœur aussi gros
> Qu'un cul de dame damascène.

In the seventh and last section Apollinaire comes back to reality and faces the hard facts. He feels like the prince who wished to drown himself and failed, and now he walks in Paris without the heart to die. His wound is not healed, but he feels life again around him and accepts its claims :

> Soirs de Paris ivres du gin
> Flambant de l'électricité
> Les tramways feux verts sur l'échine
> Musiquent au long des portées
> De rails leur folie de machines.

Each of these sections shows a different aspect of the poet's self in this time of loss. Each gives its special poetry to a different mood, and while keeping strictly true to the actual condition succeeds in casting a special light on it.

Between these sections Apollinaire sets others which give a wider vision to his subject. Each is introduced with some care. At the end of the first section his memories turn to a day in April when he sang of his love, and from this he moves to the second section which recaptures the blissful mood of the spring and conjures up the rapturous days when success seemed certain :

> Viens ma tendresse est la régente
> De la floraison qui paraît
> La nature est belle et touchante
> Pan sifflote dans la forêt
> Les grenouilles humides chantent.

This, coming after the intimate account of the loss of love, shows both how great his loss had been and what joy he still finds in its memory. The radiant verses take us back to the full delight of this vanished spring and provide a brilliant contrast with the regrets that precede and follow them. So, too, the third section, with its proclamation of defiant loyalty, ends by Apollinaire comparing himself to the Cossacks who are violently loyal to their homes and their religion. Then the fourth section takes up the idea and shows what the Cossacks are like by giving an imaginary letter which they write to the Sultan, who has demanded their allegiance. Perhaps Apollinaire had in mind Repin's picture in which Cossacks, bursting with life and liquor, greet with boisterous laughter the composition of an extremely rude letter to their self-appointed lord. They are figures of defiant proud resistance, and Apollinaire resembles them in his resistance to the destiny which has tried to humble him. For the moment he is as wild and reckless as they are, and transforms his regrets into bellicose abuse. Finally, the fifth section ends with a mention of the seven swords which have pierced his heart, and in the sixth section he turns his sorrows over and shows how each is a sword. With a strange, mediaeval charm he dwells on the name and character of each sword. He has passed beyond his sorrows to a world of mystical allusions where weapons are forged with almost divine powers. They stand for the memories which he cherishes, for the different kinds of delight and charm which he found in his beloved, and that is why he compares them in turn to a winter sky, a rainbow, a goblet, a green and golden stream, a cypress, a tomb, a glorious metal and a dead rose. In this section, as in the second and the fourth, Apollinaire passes beyond his immediate situation to something wider and more significant. This is his way of displaying the extent of his loss.

In this balance and contrast of parts Apollinaire gives a great richness and an architectural beauty to his poem. He is at pains to set his complex emotions in order and to show that he understands their conflicts and paradoxes. He sees the situation from several angles and knows it both from near and from far. The result is that his poem on lost love is much more than a lament in its range and its variety of moods. It changes lightly from dark despair to moments of rapturous remembrance, from realistic descriptions of a foggy evening in London to soaring flights of fancy. Yet, despite its variety, it is a unity cunningly constructed not merely through the

balance and interconnection of its parts but through certain
themes which run through it and guide its movement. Two
are of special importance, and Apollinaire emphasises them by
repeating the one three times and the other twice, always in
places which stress their meaning. The first proclaims his
belief in love :

> Voie lactée ô sœur lumineuse
> Des blancs ruisseaux de Chanaan
> Et des corps blancs des amoureuses
> Nageurs morts suivrons-nous d'ahan
> Ton cours vers d'autres nébuleuses.

The starry splendour of love is something which Apollinaire
cannot refuse to himself, and that is why he must dwell on his
loss and see what it means. Hardly less important is another
theme, the theme of song :

> Moi qui sais des lais pour les reines
> Les complaintes de mes années
> Des hymnes d'esclave aux murènes
> La romance du mal-aimé
> Et des chansons pour les sirènes.

Apollinaire needs song to counter his grief. It is the voice
of his complaints, of his sense of destruction, of his feeling
that he has been lured to disaster. The two themes pass
through the poem and help to set its tone and to hold it
together.

In *La Chanson du Mal-Aimé* Apollinaire's youthful gifts
found their finest form. There is not a line in it which is not
indubitably poetry and does not shine with a peculiar radiance.
Though Apollinaire does not explain the situation and often
passes unexpectedly from one image or idea to another, there
is no real obscurity. Each image and each idea stands out so
clearly that we know at once what it means to him. The
words are all perfectly familiar, except when Apollinaire wishes
them to be unusual, and even then they cause no trouble.
There is a great concentration of power in the short sentences,
and each achieves its own kind of effect. Indeed there seem
to be few effects which Apollinaire cannot achieve. He is

equally successful with plain statements of fact like

> Un soir de demi-brune à Londres,

and of feeling like

> Mon cœur et ma tête se vident
> Tout le ciel s'écoule par eux,

and with adventurous parallels and images, like

> Qu'un ciel d'oubli s'ouvre à mes vœux,

or

> Dans ses yeux nageaient les sirènes,

or

> Malheur dieu pâle aux yeux d'ivoire.

He passes with imperceptible ease from fact to fancy, from plain emotional statement to a vivid transformation of his feelings into some bold image, as in

> Je suivis ce mauvais garçon
> Qui sifflotait mains dans les poches
> Nous semblions entre les maisons
> Onde ouverte de la mer Rouge
> Lui les Hébreux moi Pharaon.

or

> Mais en vérité je l'attends
> Avec mon cœur avec mon âme
> Et sur le pont des Reviens-t'-en
> Si jamais revient cette femme
> Je lui dirai je suis content.

His comparisons of himself to characters so varied as the burghers of Calais or the prince-regent of Bavaria may astonish us, but they fit with perfect ease into his varied, vivid pattern. Into this poem Apollinaire flung the riches of his reading and his observation, and it remains a consummate masterpiece in which a regular, carefully considered form encloses an experience deeply felt and seen with the full resources of a powerful imagination.

With a technique so adaptable and so well controlled Apollinaire could say what he wished without sacrificing anything essential. He had abundant material at his disposal and could afford even to squander it in perishable communications like letters and post-cards to his friends. The man who could write from the front in 1915 :

> Je t'écris de dessous la tente
> Tandis que meurt ce jour d'été
> Où floraison éblouissante
> Dans le ciel à peine bleuté
> Une canonnade éclatante
> Se fane avant d'avoir été,

was not one to keep all his best work for print. Apollinaire's poetry was his immediate and instinctive reaction to life. He had an extraordinary gift for making the most of his circumstances and extracting some positive profit from them. Everything that he saw made some impression on him, and he was the last man in the world to be influenced by established notions of what is worth seeing and knowing. So his poetry, which seems disparate and heterogeneous, is the true reflection of his life. When he went to Germany he was inspired not by the romantic German past or the familiar mystery of the German landscape, but by the pathos of a prostitute in Cologne, the animals of the Gipsies on the banks of the Rhine, the quarrel of two old Jews on their way to the synagogue, children playing in the cemetery, and the hoot of owls in the wind over the water. In his many references to France and to Paris he is equally faithful to his own sensations and memories, and records with scrupulous exactness the moments which have meant most to him, the workmen and the typists walking to their labours in the morning, the polyps under the water in the Mediterranean, the noise of bells ringing in a railway station, an old peasant driving his ox slowly through a fog and singing a song of unfaithful love, the gas-jets hissing by moonlight, the beauty of Parisian nights in September on the empty quays, the acrobats performing in the street on 14th July. Apollinaire's poetry is crowded with observation of things which struck him and remained with him because of some beauty or humanity in them. Through his poetry we enjoy his vivid awareness of life and his remarkable gift for seeing the significance of what would escape most men's attention.

These experiences, which came naturally to Apollinaire, are not presented objectively as matters for curiosity and scientific interest, but because they have some special appeal for him and open doors to unexpected places. Some quite trivial event will through his interpretation of it become charged with emotion and significance. The little poem *Souvenirs* shows how his sensibility absorbed the world around him and chose for emphasis small, common and superficially trivial scenes. He feels the contrasts which give new perspectives to familiar activities, and marks how men and women, engaged in the common round of life, become symbols of its mystery and its paradoxes, like the man who sings while he shaves himself :

> Un monsieur en bras de chemise
> Se rase près de la fenêtre
> En chantant un petit air qu'il ne sait pas
> > très bien
> Ça fait tout un opéra.

So too Apollinaire finds in real circumstances signs and symbols of wider realities. In *L'Émigrant du Landor Road* he describes the visit of a man to a tailor's shop where the clothes are displayed on dummies in the window. A suit is taken off one of them, and he buys it, and this quiet little action is the means to catch the enormous pathos and misery of a man who leaves his home for strange lands. The dummies are symbols of what he leaves behind and show the failure and emptiness of his life :

> Au dehors les années
> Regardaient la vitrine
> Les mannequins victimes
> Et passaient enchaînées.

Against this background Apollinaire sets the emigrant's voyage over the unfamiliar sea, and the trivial end which awaits him after it. Apollinaire's moments of vision illuminate much more than the main themes of a poem and relate them to wider and more mysterious issues.

The same sense of mystery and of unexplored horizons gives a special power to many small and relatively unimportant moments. With a deceptive clarity Apollinaire makes statements which are perfectly plain and direct but full of meaning and emotion. His language with its evocative power is quite different from the precise descriptions practised by the Parnassians. For instance, in *Le Lévrier de Magnus* Leconte de Lisle wrote :

> Écoute, c'est le vent dans la tour écroulée
> Où le hibou hulule et qu'il habite seul,
> C'est le Rhin qui murmure et fuit dans la vallée.

This calls up the scene to the eye and the ear, but not with so suggestive and immediate a magic as Apollinaire's single line, which of course owes something to it :

> Le vent du Rhin hulule avec tous les hiboux.

It is part of Apollinaire's art to pack his lines with significance without reducing in any way their clarity. The mystery and the melancholy of autumn are suggested by two figures walking in the dusk :

> Oh ! l'automne l'automne a fait mourir l'été
> Dans le brouillard s'en vont deux silhouettes grises.

The rough caress of ocean winds is felt from their touch on the seafaring emigrant :

> Les vents de l'Océan en soufflant leurs menaces
> Laissaient dans ses cheveux de longs baisers mouillés.

The songs which he hears in the country remind him of the greater, unheard song of Paris :

> Et j'écoutai longtemps tous ces chants et ces cris
> Qu'éveillait dans la nuit la chanson de Paris.

Apollinaire knew how to make his words suggest much more than they actually say, and echo with many unanswered questions.

When the creative fit was on him, Apollinaire applied his gifts without any great effort or premeditation. His instrument was so well in control that it responded to any subject that stirred him. An example of this immediate reaction can be seen from what he wrote when he was arrested for the alleged theft of the *Mona Lisa*. On the morning of 7th September 1911 the police came to his lodging, arrested him and locked him up. He was thrown into great mental anguish. He could not understand what the arrest meant and was deeply distressed by the senseless indignities which he was made to suffer. His clothes were stripped off him : he was flung into a cell where the electric light could not be extinguished and prevented him from sleeping : on the wall was written the name of a former occupant, with the addition that he had been held on a charge of murder. Apollinaire felt that he had been cruelly spirited out of his familiar, friendly world into some kind of hell from which he could not escape and where he could expect neither reason nor justice. But in circumstances where a more deliberate artist would have been too over-whelmed with misery to be able to write, Apollinaire composed *A la Santé*, in which six short poems maintain all his style and elegance as he laments his fate. If we compare these with what Verlaine wrote in prison, we see how much closer Apollinaire was to ordinary life, how intimately his surroundings affected him and what significance he found in the routine of prison. The stripping of his clothes, the daylight coming past the bars, the sound of footsteps overhead, the daily walk in the yard, a fly on the wall, and the noises from the world outside, all touch him with a poignant intimacy and stress the horror of his isolation. There is no rhetoric in this poetry. Apollinaire notes what happens and shows what meanings it has for him.

Deep though Apollinaire's distress was, it did not prevent him from writing with his usual balance or from discovering moments of illumination in his plight. The daily walk of prisoners emphasised his helplessness, and he saw himself as a chained bear :

> Dans une fosse comme un ours
> Chaque matin je me promène
> Tournons tournons toujours toujours
> Le ciel est bleu comme une chaîne
> Dans une fosse comme un ours
> Chaque matin je me promène.

Verlaine, too, noticed the blue sky from his cell, but, haunted by guilt and remorse, saw it with different eyes, as the home of peace and calm which contrasted with his own troubled soul. Apollinaire, feeling himself the victim of inexplicable injuries, sees in it a blue chain, an apt symbol of his own oppression. Again, both poets sought refuge and consolation in prayer, but, while Verlaine thought that imprisonment was an expiation for his sins, Apollinaire calls simply and sadly for help :

> Que deviendrai-je ô Dieu qui connais ma douleur
> Toi qui me l'as donnée
> Prends en pitié mes yeux sans larmes ma pâleur
> Le bruit de ma chaise enchaînée
>
> Et tous ces pauvres cœurs battant dans la prison
> L'Amour qui m'accompagne
> Prends en pitié surtout ma débile raison
> Et ce désespoir qui la gagne.

Apollinaire's feelings are naturally and acutely human. He has received a terrible shock and struggles to keep his sanity, and he thinks not only about himself but about all who suffer like him. The six poems are too agonised to allow flights of fancy, but they have an extraordinary intensity in their simple presentation of his emotions. There is a powerful concentration in such lines as tell of the slow passage of time in the cell,

> Que lentement passent les heures
> Comme passe un enterrement,

or of Apollinaire's final triumph over his fear of madness, when he asserts himself and trusts in his sanity :

> Nous sommes seuls dans ma cellule
> Belle clarté Chère raison.

These poems show what a master of his craft Apollinaire was, how immediately it responded to an agony which would have made other men silent or hysterical.

Prison was only a short interlude in a full and energetic life in which Apollinaire made most of what Paris had to offer him. He is almost the only poet of the world which was lost for ever in 1914 who was fully conscious of what enjoyments and prospects life held for him. He has no quarrel with society or the universe, no dark sense of guilt or inadequacy. His superb vitality, his uncommonly tender and affectionate nature might lead him to fall in love, as it often did, with women not really suited to him. But after passing the regular stages of ecstatic joy, self-distrust, and melancholy at his final failure, he emerged the same charming, delightful, cheerful poet, bent on making the most of life and extracting the most from it. His art developed, his inspiration showed no signs of running dry. If not always fortunate in his loves, he was always fortunate in his friends, who inspired both his creative powers and his abiding affections. Then, in his thirty-fourth year he was flung into the ordeal of war. He was not a French citizen, but France was his only home, and he loved it with passionate devotion. He faced the challenge with a courage which was all the greater because he had no illusions about the dangers that lay ahead, and said : " Mes amis, je sens le Temps en marche . . . Levons-nous, ô amis, devant la mort qui nous appelle." He bore with characteristic good humour the discomforts and humiliations of military life, liked his companions, and was proud of his horse and his guns. He fought on the Western Front and was inspired by it to write many remarkable poems which showed new sides of his genius. In a sense he enjoyed the experience and was quite honest when he wrote :

> Ah Dieu ! que la guerre est jolie
> Avec ses chants ses longs loisirs.

Apollinaire was happy largely because he believed that he was acting rightly. His life had now a clear aim which gave direction and purpose to it. His love of France supplied him with a mission which gave importance to everything that he did. He felt that the soldiers who, like him, stood in defence of France were a divine sign of her destiny :

> Nous sommes l'Arc-en-terre
> Signe plus pur que l'Arc-en-ciel,

that old symbols of patriotism, like the bas-reliefs on the Arc de Triomphe, had suddenly become alive with a new majesty and beauty :

> Le glaive antique de la Marseillaise de Rude
> S'est changé en constellation.

In such a cause he believed that a poet had a special part to play, and that through his verse he must foretell the finer world which lay beyond the carnage, and celebrate the devotion which would create it :

> Prends mes vers ô ma France Avenir Multitude
> Chantez ce que je chante un chant pur le prélude
> Des chants sacrés que la beauté de notre temps
> Saura vous inspirer plus purs plus éclatants
> Que ceux que je m'efforce à moduler ce soir
> En l'Honneur de l'Honneur la beauté du Devoir.

In his long months at the front Apollinaire was sustained by an inner vision of France, of the ideals for which he fought and of the life which he knew and loved and wished to make richer and more abundant.

The vast disarray of the battlefield did not distress him, but with a lively eye for unnoticed details he found much to charm and delight him. He felt the appeal of the rockets which made the front like a show of fireworks, of the shells which whistled through the air with a sinister menace of death, of the shadowy forms lit by camp-fires, of the strange troglodytic life in dug-outs, of trees blackened and blasted by bombardment. He enjoyed the delightful contrasts made by the song of birds, the unexpected growth of flowers, the coming of dawn and dusk, the rising of the stars. He knew how to put down his sensations with a remarkable economy and point, like the thrill of shell-fire :

> L'air est plein d'un terrible alcool,

or signal-rockets in the sky :

> Ce sont des dames qui dansent avec leur regard pour yeux bras
> et cœurs,

or the dull echo of guns :

> Les canons tonnent dans la nuit
> On dirait des vagues tempête
> Des cœurs où pointe un grand ennui
> Ennui qui toujours se répète,

or rats devouring dead bodies :

> Mais le rat pénétre dans le cadavre et y demeure,

or a bird singing :

> Écoute il chante tendrement
> Je ne sais pas sur quelle branche
> Et partout il va me charmant
> Nuit et jour semaine et dimanche.

In the strange, crowded stage of war there was little that escaped Apollinaire's notice or in which he did not find some charm or excitement.

His experience at the front helped Apollinaire to advance his technique and use imagery in a new way suited to his new surroundings. War creates a dual personality in those who take part in it. On the one hand, it is always and insistently present. There is no escape from the abnormal conditions which it imposes on its victims. On the other hand, in it the soldier's thoughts turn inevitably to what is normal and familiar, to his affections and his loves at home. In this double condition his thoughts are shot simultaneously by vivid recollections of home and by an awareness no less vivid of his present state : the themes of the one life are inextricably mingled with the themes of the other. Apollinaire understood this dual state ; for it was his own. No one appreciated more keenly the life which he had left behind him in Paris or the strange, unnatural existence which war forced on him. Sometimes he portrays it quite simply, as in *Simultanéités*, where a German prisoner enters the French lines with all his thoughts on his mistress, or in *Un Oiseau chante*, where Apollinaire hears a bird singing and imagines that is the soul of his Madeleine awakening. From such simple beginnings he moves to more elaborate effects. The sight of the prisoner makes the poet think of his own love and speak of it in the language of war :

> Notre amour est une lueur
> Qu'un projecteur du cœur dirige
> Vers l'ardeur égale du cœur
> Qui sur le haut Phare s'érige.

The bird becomes a symbol for the love which every soldier has, and the poet above all :

Oiseau bleu comme le cœur bleu
De mon amour au cœur céleste
Ton chant si doux répète-le
A la mitrailleuse funeste

Qui claque à l'horizon et puis
Sont-ce les astres que l'on sème
Ainsi vont les jours et les nuits
Amour comme est le cœur même.

By this use of imagery Apollinaire identifies one set of experiences in his divided self with another and shows how the scene of war penetrates his thoughts of love and is transformed by them into something more significant.

This method opened the way to new successes. The violence of battle is identified with the violence of love, and in *Chef de Section* Apollinaire uses the language of the attack to stress the power of his passion :

Ma bouche aura des ardeurs de géhenne
Ma bouche te sera un enfer de douceur et de séduction
Les anges de ma bouche trôneront dans ton cœur
Les soldats de ma bouche te prendront d'assaut.

This is the way in which the poet who is also a soldier turns his experiences to profit. It is more than a metaphor : it is the reflection of a dual state of mind. In *Le Vigneron champenois* the same kind of comparison shows how war makes human beings become part of the natural scene and absorb some of its forces into themselves. In a vine-growing country Apollinaire sees the grapes growing and is caught by the fancy that his soldiers are like bottles of wine and that he himself is the vine-grower :

Bonjour soldats bouteilles champenoises où le sang fermente
Vous resterez quelques jours et puis remonterez en ligne
Échelonnés ainsi que sont les ceps de vigne
J'envoie mes bouteilles partout comme les obus d'une
    charmante artillerie.

In the vine-scented air the poet feels that he, his men and their surroundings are united in some hidden harmony. In the conception of life and strength held in the narrow limits of a bottle he finds an appropriate image for his soldiers who with a similar strength are going out to their work. In *Océan de Terre* Apollinaire dramatises a feeling known to soldiers, that they are lost in some vast, alien element. He compares this to the sea, and indulges in the fancy that he builds a house under the tides among the creatures of the deep. Yet even this dwelling is not entirely safe ; for strange monsters may threaten it :

> Les avions pondent des œufs
> Attention on va jeter l'ancre.

So the duality of existence persists even in the most self-contained dreams, and the image hints how difficult it is to escape from the inexorable menaces of war.

His pleasure in the visible scene and the opportunities which it gave him to elaborate his fancies did not prevent Apollinaire from understanding the human dramas which took place on the battlefield or from feeling the pathos of lives condemned to suffering or death. Though he called his companions a necklace hung round his beloved France, he saw their human claims. He was touched by the swift irony of death which carries off four soldiers while they exchange reminiscences. He notices the daily round in the trenches with its human drama, the man blinded by gas, the captain who waits for news by wireless from America, the soldier who saws planks for coffins, the German prisoner holding his helmet in his hands, the songs before an attack. For this existence with its moments of childlike joy, its intense absorption in the present moment, its helplessness in the face of deprivation and of doom, Apollinaire felt a deep compassion. His soldiers were part of himself, and he bore their sufferings with them in the mud and the cold. Perhaps the most touching of such pieces in *Les Soupirs du Servant de Dakar*, which tells of an African soldier who finds himself in the meaningless, unfamiliar world of the Western Front. He thinks of his home in an African village, of its songs, dances, love-making, and long talks, of his father, who fought against the Ashanti, his mother, who was a sorceress, his sister " with breasts hard as shells ", of the unintelligible process by which he became a soldier, of the desert and its splendid skies. The whole story is told in simple language as befits its subject. We see the confusion of the African as he wonders what it all means :

> Pourquoi ne pas danser et discourir
> Manger et puis dormir.

Apollinaire's tenderness responded to the pathos of war and made him portray it with touching gentleness.

In this war he was himself a victim. On 17th March 1916, a fragment of shell hit him on his steel helmet and wounded him in the head. His skull was trepanned, and though a first operation seemed likely to leave him paralysed, a second averted this danger and gave him two more years of life. There can be little doubt that his wound permanently impaired his health and made him an easy prey to the savage influenza which killed him two days before the armistice in 1918. In his bad physical state he felt a sense of desolation, a secret conviction that now he could never realise his gifts or fulfil his hopes of creative achievement. It is of this that he speaks in *Tristesse d'une Étoile* :

> C'est pourquoi de mes maux ce n'était pas le pire
> Ce trou presque mortel et qui s'est étoilé
> Mais le secret malheur qui nourrit mon délire
> Est bien plus grand qu'aucune âme ait jamais celé
>
> Et je porte avec moi cette ardente souffrance
> Comme le ver luisant tient son corps enflammé
> Comme au cœur du soldat il palpite la France
> Et comme au cœur du lys le pollen parfumé.

He cherished his sufferings because they gave him a new insight into existence and a new sense of its value, but he felt that he was doomed and could not do all that had once been within his reach, and that much of what he had done was of no great worth.

To many of his contemporaries Apollinaire seemed a comedian or an imposter, " le flâneur des deux rives ". They did not even realise that his pranks and poses were the natural reflection of his ebullient boyishness. Others, who came nearer to the truth about his personality, regarded him as a wild revolutionary in art, the champion of ridiculous causes and the exponent of an absurd kind of poetry. But Apollinaire is remarkable because at a time when artistic ideals were being challenged, he kept his common sense and saw what was useful to him in the new ideas and what was not. It is true that his later work sometimes shows a more advanced and more adventurous technique than his earlier, and this might lead us to suppose that he was slow to absorb the new methods and might, if he had lived, have been in the front rank of experimenters. But this is to be doubted. The language of *La jolie Rousse*, written in the last months of his life, has a delightful lightness and limpidity : his *Tristesse d'une Étoile* is a triumph in his most classical manner. One of the remarkable things about Apollinaire is that his technique developed but did not change fundamentally. He began by knowing how much he liked and needed in the new methods, and applied his principles throughout his career. He was drawn to the new ideas because he saw that they were well fitted to express certain ecstatic moments which he knew, but these were not his only moments, and for other moods he had different manners. So his career provides a practical criticism of some ideas which were powerful when he grew to maturity and which reached their greatest influence after his death. More than any other poet of his generation he showed how the technique of poetry is inseparable from its matter, and that a poet must take care to choose a form which enables him to say exactly what he means in all its range and its subtlety.

What Apollinaire gives in his poetry is not in the least narrow or affected or esoteric. Of all poets in this century he is perhaps the closest to natural man in his straightforward love of simple things and his delighted acceptance of what life has to offer. Whether he writes about love or war or Parisian life, he shares the tastes of other men, and his special claim is that he interprets their feelings with the intensity of genius and so transforms experience into something new and extraordinarily exciting. But behind his extremely human tastes he had a guiding philosophy and an inspiring vision. He believed that life could be vastly enriched and extended and intensified through a new use of words, and to this he gave much attention in his last years. He saw that poetry is a power to transform even the dullest activities of the mind, to waken the consciousness to a more vivid awareness, and to make everything more exciting and more fascinating. This was what he himself did. He did not collect his experiences on any preconceived plan or falsify his presentation of them by making them conform to conventional ways of thinking. He really said what he felt and expressed exactly what passed through his lively sensibility into his receptive and creative mind. He knew that the human soul is rich in unexplored possibilities and that there is no limit to the new poetry which can be extracted from it if only the poet will express his feelings and fancies in their original fullness. He was able to do this himself because he was a master of words, who had a most uncommon sense of their worth and associations and could subordinate them to varied and enchanted rhythms. So his poetry reflects with perfect truth and persuasive power his ebullient, courageous, tender and imaginative self.

IV

THE FUTURISM OF
VLADIMIR MAYAKOVSKY

In the years immediately before 1914 the Russian Symbolist movement, which had done so much to revive poetry at the beginning of the century, was beginning to show signs of decline. It is true that its greatest exponent, Alexander Blok, had still some of his finest work in front of him, but for the moment he seemed to be sunk in anarchic despair. Indeed the conditions which had created and fostered Symbolism had changed. It had flourished among men whose hopes had been frustrated by the years of reaction after the Revolution of 1905 and who turned to a mystical cult of Beauty in their disgust with the actual world. Such a poetry did not appeal to younger men who refused to accept defeat or to believe that mystical aestheticism was an adequate substitute for an interest in actual life. There were some who rejected Symbolism and sought a new kind of poetry. They wished to be free of intellectual and spiritual restraints, to express themselves with truth and candour, to convey their rich experiences to others, to be positive and dynamic and modern. About 1908 the first rumblings of revolt could be heard. A group of young men, impressed by the achievements in painting of Impressionists and Cubists and making little distinction between Cézanne and Matisse or between Van Gogh and Picasso, wished to revolutionise poetry on what they believed to be similar lines and to make it more vivid and more contemporary. If their desire was for " free art as the foundation of life ", they were not yet very precise about practical aims. Their chief ambition was to be rid of rules and precedents, and they justified this by the argument that art is a more vivid form of life. They claimed that if words could be freed from their hackneyed associations, they would have a new magical power. Since most of them practised painting before poetry, they applied to words the doctrine of " non-representational " art which had already been tried so sensationally in line and colour. On this circle Marinetti undoubtedly made an impression, and to him and his methods Russian Futurism owed some of its first notoriety. But it was not his creation. It had come into existence almost before his first Manifesto, and would have continued to exist if it had never heard of him. But he provided the Russian Futurists with a name and some useful ideas and phrases, fortified their desire to be rid of the past, and taught them some tricks of advertisement and controversy.

In its beginnings Russian Futurism attracted men of diverse gifts and was a label for more than one poet who was discontented with the literary ideals of the time. What the first Futurists desired was to create a new poetry which should be concerned with actual contemporary life. In December 1912 a manifesto appeared over the signatures of David Burlyuk, Alexander Kruchenykh, Vladimir Mayakovsky and Viktor Khlebnikov, called *A Slap in the Face of Public Taste*. For the moment the four authors had found a common programme and delivered it with all the confidence of youth and with all youth's delight in shocking its elders. It is still of considerable interest :

To readers Our New First and Unexpected.

We alone are the *Face of our Time*. Time's trumpet blares in our art of words.

The past is stifling. The Academy and Pushkin are more unintelligible than hieroglyphs.

Throw Pushkin, Dostoevsky, Tolstoy, etc. overboard from the steamer of modernity.

He who will not forget his first love will not recognize his last.

Who is fool enough to give his last love to Balmont's scented whore ?

Would it reflect the manly spirit of to-day ?

Who is coward enough to be afraid of tearing the paper armour off warrior Bryusov's frock-coat ? Is there in it any dawn of unknown beauties ?

Wash your hands which are filthy with the dirty slime of books scribbled by countless Leonid Andreevs.

All these Maxim Gorkys, Bloks, Sologubs, Remizovs, Averchenkos, Chernys, Kuzmins, etc. etc. — all they want is a villa by the river. That is how fate rewards tailors.

From the height of skyscrapers we look down on their insignificance.

We demand respect for the poet's right :

1. to enlarge the vocabulary with arbitrary and derivative words—neologisms ;
2. to uncompromising hatred for the language used hitherto ;
3. to tear with horror from their proud heads the crowns of worthless fame made of bath-room brushes ;
4. to stand upon the rock of the word " We " in a sea of cat-calls and indignation.

And if *our* lines show the dirty traces of your " common sense " and " good taste ", yet the first lightnings of a New Dawn of Beauty in the Self-Sufficient Word are already trembling upon them.

The debt to Marinetti is obvious. The manifesto rejects the past ; it claims to be the authentic voice of modernity and stridently asserts its virility ; it condemns old " sentimental " themes such as love and romance as Balmont and Bryusov treated them ; it hints at a glorification of mechanical inventions in its references to steamers and skyscrapers. Above all it recalls Marinetti in its cock-sure impudence and its arrogant assumption that its adherents alone have the right to be called poets.

These claims, despite their airs and affectations, were based on something real. The Russian Futurists were militantly discontented with their time and especially with its imaginative literature. They felt that its poetry, instead of making life more vivid and more various, was a kind of dope. Behind their criticism of the arts lay a criticism of society. Unlike Marinetti, whose Futurism was a craving for sensation and found an outlet in violence for its own sake, the Russians were rebels who believed that their social system daunted and deadened the soul. Their irony was a cover for the powerful uneasiness which they felt when they compared their own ideal of a free and imaginative life with the opportunities offered by existing conditions. Russian Futurism was revolutionary in more than one sense. Its hostility to mystical poetry was a special manifestation of that hostility to religion which Lenin showed when he followed Marx and said that it was " the opium of the people " : its disrespect for the past was but another aspect of the revolutionary contempt for the romantic and sentimental conservatism which the Tsarist system offered as an alternative to reform : its sense of hidden energy and its desire to let this loose on the world were natural to a generation which had known too many restraints and disappointments and found that its patience was exhausted. When Marinetti visited Russia and found himself harassed and disowned by the Russian Futurists, whom he regarded as his disciples, it was because his politics horrified them. They could not believe that they owed anything to a man who held such views. In them the revolutionary spirit which had been curbed by political reaction since 1905 found a special manifestation. They showed it chiefly in their theories and practice of art, because they were artists and art was their first concern. But politics was never far from their thoughts, and their political views gave a direction to their poetry.

Of the four signatories to *A Slap in the Face*, three, Burlyuk, Kruchenykh and Khlebnikov, were primarily interested in the creation of a new vocabulary for poetry and gave most of their attention to it. The fourth, Vladimir Mayakovsky, was not troubled by such theoretical considerations. He was drawn to Futurism for more than one reason. In the first place he liked its revolutionary character. From the beginning he was a rebel. He joined the Bolshevik party in 1908, when he was fifteen years old, and before he was twenty he had been arrested three times for subversive activities. In 1909 he met Burlyuk who made a poet of him. As he himself says : " Read my stuff to Burlyuk. Said a friend of mine wrote it. David stopped. Looked me up and down, yapped ' You wrote it yourself ! You are a genius ! ' This grandiose and unmerited title overjoyed me. Became immersed in poetry. That evening suddenly I became a poet." Mayakovsky felt that Futurism was his form of art because it wished to get rid of the past and to create a new kind of life. His revolutionary feelings may have been emotional and instinctive, but they were the mainspring of his being. He had a real sympathy for the oppressed masses and had, under the name of " Comrade Constantine ", worked among them. The Revolution of 1905 had broken into his boyhood and convinced him that " Socialism can disentangle facts and systematise the world ". His circumstances, especially after his father's death in 1906, were poor, and he knew the humiliations and the sufferings of the dispossessed. But stronger than these motives was something less easily defined. In his youth Mayakovsky had a passion for personal liberty rather as Pushkin had it. It was the passion of the artist to be at all costs himself, to be free of any control, external or internal, which interfered with the full development and expression of his personality. What he desired so strongly for himself, he demanded for others. It is characteristic of him that, when he attended an art school, he " stood up for the badgered ones ". From the start Mayakovsky was a rebel because he wished to be free and felt this desire as a dynamic, exalting inspiration. His strong personality was determined to find a full field for its endeavours and to treat the world in his own way. In Mayakovsky the creative principle which made him a poet was derived from the enormous powers which he felt in himself and desired to exercise.

These powers were of a special kind, and Mayakovsky was an unusual figure in Russian literature for more than one reason. In the first place, despite a childhood spent in the Caucasus, he was pre-eminently a townsman. He drew his inspiration from Moscow and Petersburg, from the human beings whom he saw there and especially from the impoverished class to which he himself belonged. And secondly, he was not a scholar or even, in the narrow sense, a cultivated man. His conception of poetry owed nothing to the great masters of the past, and he seems to have passed through almost no period of literary apprenticeship. These two circumstances made him exceptional from the start. He had his own outlook, his own idea of what poetry is. His creative gift lay in a remarkably original sense of words. He had an excellent ear which enabled him to produce new harmonies of his own and to dispense with traditional rhythms. He had a good eye for the scenes of urban life, which provided him with a new kind of imagery. His powerful emotions, inhibited and strengthened by years of repression, made him a formidable figure even among his friends and clamoured for expression in verse. Not only did his revolutionary temperament despise the limitations imposed by " good taste ", but his nature lacked subtlety and delicacy. He was not interested in fleeting effects or finer shades. But he made up for these deficiencies by an astonishing vitality and vigour. What he felt he felt strongly, and though he often seems crude and brutal, that is largely because he never shrinks from facing the facts or from saying what he really feels. He had in him something primitive with both its advantages and its disadvantages, and he was well fitted to be the poet of the great changes which were to take place in Russia and of which he was the prophet and the advocate. It is as if in him the great, subdued forces of the Russian people found a significant voice for its abundant vitality and its simple outlook on life.

In the winter of 1913–1914 the Futurists conducted a tour of Russian towns and read their works to large, if not always appreciative, audiences. This suited Mayakovsky excellently. With his commanding height, his good looks, his resonant voice, and his gift for ready, if rude, repartee, he was a brilliant performer at public gatherings which had to be cowed if they would not be cajoled. He recited verses in public and through this gave an important direction to his art. From the beginning he possessed a natural rhetoric, a gift for forcible, violent language. Now he adapted his language and his metre to suit the requirements of recitation. His vocabulary, as befitted a Futurist, was experimental and unusual. But he did not write " trans-sense " as some of his colleagues did. His language was based on conversation, even on slang. It was a more vigorous and more pointed version of what ordinary people spoke. It took full advantage of any licences which spoken Russian allows in the treatment of syntax or the formation of new words. If Mayakovsky felt that pre-positions were unnecessary, he did without them ; if he pre-ferred them to adverbs, he used them. He invented many new compounds and even new words, but Russian is more generous than English to inventors, and Mayakovsky's inventions are not so recondite as to be unintelligible. He exploited his own mannerisms, quotations from popular songs and parodies of well-known poems, puns and plays upon words, emphatic repetitions and evocative onomatopoeic noises. With such devices his language is emphatically his own, explosive and expressive. He gave great care to composition and reached his final version of a poem only after several drafts, but in the result there is no sign of labour. All runs with perfect ease as if Mayakovsky were speaking spontaneously.

In recitation metre was no less important. Marinetti had abandoned metre for a staccato prose, and Mayakovsky's fellow Futurist, Khlebnikov, kept a regular verse-structure and rhymes which sometimes interfere with the naturalness of his effect. Mayakovsky found a compromise between the two methods, by keeping a verse-form and rhyme but harmonising them with the natural flow of words. Early in his career he invented a system which combined the freedom of *vers libre* with the harmony added by rhyme. Instead of using regular stanzas of fixed shapes he made the sentence his unit and used rhymes to emphasise the ends of the subordinate clauses and of the whole sentence. An example will show how he worked :

> There's not a single gray hair in my soul ;
> With nice old men I have nothing to do !
> The world shakes with my voice's roll,
> And I walk handsome
> And twenty-two.

This is a single sentence and a single metrical unit, and the clauses of the sentence fall into the parts of the metrical scheme. The rhymes bring the whole together without spoiling its conversational flow. At the same time Mayakovsky knew the value of surprise in poetry and secured remarkable effects by peculiar rhymes. His way had been prepared by the Symbolists, but he went much further. He does in Russian what Browning sometimes does in English but on a larger scale and with less regard for exact correspondence of sounds. Sometimes he uses *la rime riche*, sometimes complex assonances, sometimes mere echoes. The effect of his rhymes is not comic except when he means it to be. They help to maintain his conversational tone and keep the audience waiting to see what will come next. They are an instrument of recitation, of rhetoric, and give a remarkable air of novelty to Mayakovsky's verse.

Before the Revolution of 1917 Mayakovsky's poetry followed a natural line of development. He exploited and improved the means which he had invented when he first found himself to be a poet. His poetry is entirely personal and displays the paradoxes and contradictions which we might expect from a man of his ebullient personality and restricted circumstances. It was only natural that at times he should be stridently self-assertive and self-confident, and at other times relapse into self-mockery and self-abasement. His confidence in his own powers was tempered by his knowledge that the age was hostile to him and that his chances of making a mark were small. Just as his fellow Futurists drew attention to themselves by painting pictures on their faces, so Mayakovsky wore an enormous tie, and found that it made an effect. His poetry has something of the same spirit. One of his first poems, published in 1913, is called *I* and speaks with candour about himself. His so-called tragedy, *Vladimir Mayakovsky*, was acted at the Luna Park Theatre in 1913 with Mayakovsky in the chief part and was an attempt to portray him as a fanciful hero in conflict with typical figures of his time. In *Spine-Flute* (1915) his personal feelings are again the chief subject, and in *Man* (1916) he composed a drama about himself in the manner of the Gospel story, in which the different sections are called " Mayakovsky's Nativity ", " Mayakovsky's Life ", " Mayakovsky's Passions ", " Mayakovsky's Ascension ", " Mayakovsky in Heaven ", and " Mayakovsky in the Ages ". The self-assertion in these poems was partly a tactical move but more urgently a spiritual need. Mayakovsky had to unburden his feelings, to release his conflicting emotions, to take the world into his confidence. He was a powerful elemental being who knew that extraordinary powers were at work in him and that he must let them speak.

In these poems Mayakovsky fused his warring elements into a single result. His self-assertion and his self-pity, his caustic satire and his strange lyrical quality, are inextricably entangled not only in the same poem but often in the same line. The combination and quality of his gifts can be seen from *A Cloud in Trousers* (1915). The poem is planned in four parts, which deal successively with love, art, society and religion. But of course the treatment of these subjects is very much Mayakovsky's own and has a highly personal touch. Beginning with an unhappy love-affair he delivers his attacks on most aspects of the world which concern him and creates a special kind of poetry, crowded with images, violent in its expression, and yet undeniably melodious and striking and at times even touching. It shows what Mayakovsky felt at an important crisis of his career. The outbreak of war and the failure of a love-affair brought many powers in him to work and produced the most characteristic and remarkable of his early poems. It is not surprising that when Mayakovsky read the poem to Gorky, Gorky was impressed by it and said that it was written " with genuine words ". In it Mayakovsky fulfilled his first ambition of what poetry ought to be.

A Cloud in Trousers is in the first place remarkably candid and intimate. Mayakovsky has no false modesty, and sets out his emotions exactly as they are. To this candour his art makes a special contribution. Though he habitually uses violent metaphors and hyperboles, he is always in effect true to what he feels. His violence reflects his real self and is not a means of rhetoric, and once we recognise this, we see how acute an observer Mayakovsky is of himself. He sees the absurd disparity between his physical strength and his pathetic helplessness in love, and sets the facts out in their paradox :

> No one would recognize in me
> This muscular mass
> That groans
> At a touch.
> What can this great clod want
> So desiringly ?
> Ah, but a clod can want so much ! [1]

---

[1] Trs. Herbert Marshall.

He describes all the pangs of waiting for his beloved to come, and the effect which the striking of the clock has on him :

> Twelve o'clock has struck
> Like a head that falls from the block.

He shows how his nerves keep " jerking and jumping ", how the night oozes through the room, and then at last she comes :

> Suddenly the door
> Ground its jaws in the gloom,
> As if the hotel's own teeth didn't meet.[1]

The account of the conversation which follows, when he realises that the woman will have nothing to do with him and is going to marry someone else, is not only perfectly convincing as fact but has this same violent intimacy. He accepts his defeat in a curiously reasonable way :

> I saw one thing only
> You were a Gioconda
> That had to be stolen !
> And they stole you.[1]

He tries to be calm, but his calmness soon breaks down, and he bursts into hysteria as he rings up his mother and tries to tell her what has happened. As poetry of love the first section of *A Cloud in Trousers* is notable for its realism and its agonising candour.

This intimacy is presented through a remarkable variety of effects. At first sight some are so surprising that we may fail to see how true they actually are, how well they reflect an extremely agitated and troubled mind in which the fancy is set to work by uncontrollable emotions. For instance, the third part contains an account of a stormy sky in which the poet sees signs and portents of political brutality. He does not spare the details of the comparison between the sky and the forces of reaction :

> From behind stormclouds thunder emerged, ferociously,
> Blew its colossal nose with a reverberating bark,
> And the skyface for a second twitched rapaciously
> In the grim grimace of an iron Bismarck.[1]

---

[1] Trs. Herbert Marshall.

Now that is not really in the least strained. To the poet's haunted fancy, full of fears of persecution and injustice, it is only too natural that the sky should take on this character and behave in this way. Against this he sets his hopes of revolution, and for the moment knows that they are useless. So, with perfect aptness, he continues his comparison of the sky with political events :

> In the sky, red as the Marseillaise,
> Shuddering in its death-throes, the sunset died.[1]

Then the imagery continues. Night comes like the Tatar conqueror Mamai or the police-agent Azev — and eyes cannot pierce through it, so thick and black is it. The whole sequence is developed with a real feeling for the rise and fall of the emotional effect. It shows how Mayakovsky drew his imagery from his actual experience, and, through his great powers of fancy and emotional drive, was able to make it highly relevant to his lovelorn state.

Perhaps the most striking quality of *A Cloud in Trousers* is the way in which Mayakovsky brings off the most reckless experiments. At times he unleashes his fancies, lets them chase a theme which seems to have little relevance to his immediate subject, and yet bring it home successfully. His way of showing how violent his feelings are is that no comparison is too strong for them and that his nature is so primitive and primaeval that it can only be measured correctly against violent natural forces. Thus he takes up the notion that his heart is aflame with love, — but this flame is a conflagration, and he makes the most of the parallel. His words rush forth from him, " like whores from a burning brothel ". He tries to jump out for safety :

> Let me escape from my ribs for a start.
> I jump ! I jump ! I jump ! I jump !
> I crashed back.
> You can't jump out of your heart ![1]

This is of course a trope, but a trope conceived so genuinely that it performs a special function. It shows that Mayakovsky

[1] Trs. Herbert Marshall.

is on the edge of hysteria and that the image which forms in his brain affects him so powerfully that he almost believes in it and must think in terms of it. He himself shows what happens. His words are beyond his control, the inevitable issue of his condition :

> As children from a burning building fly,
> Scorched figures and words
> Surge from my cranium.
> Thus in fear
> Clutching at the sky
> Stretched out
> The burning hands of the Lusitania.[1]

In 1913 this was certainly a new kind of poetry, but it is, for all its strangeness, perfectly sincere and true. This is what Mayakovsky felt, and his art is perfectly adjusted to his feelings.

A Cloud in Trousers shows the anguish and hysteria of a powerful personality when he finds circumstances beyond his control and attacking him in all the activities which he thinks important. Through it there breathes an angry spirit of revolt. But anger was not Mayakovsky's only weapon. He was a master of controversy in more than one form. Most characteristic perhaps is an ironical exaggeration which makes his opponent's case look absurd. By seeming to treat it with politeness and reason Mayakovsky grossly misrepresents it. He rejected with passionate disgust the religious orthodoxy of his time, but he did not allow his indignation to get the better of him or to make him heavy-handed. His method can be seen from *Listen*, where he tilts against the theological argument from design and the belief that the starry skies are evidence for the existence of God :

> Listen !
> Just because the stars light up their fires,
> Does it mean that someone insists on it ?
> Does it mean that they answer someone's desires ?
> Does it mean that someone gives the name of pearls to
>   that spit ?
> And toiling and moiling

---

[1] Trs. Herbert Marshall.

In storms of the midday dust
Does he force his way up to God,
Does he fear he is late,
Lament,
And kiss God's sinewy hand,
And demand
That a star be compelled to exist ?
Does he swear
That this starless torment he will not stand ?
After that
He goes round alarmed,
Though quiet to look at.
He says to someone :
" Now, is that nothing to you ?
Are you not afraid ?
True ? "
Listen !
Because the stars light up their fires,
Does it mean that someone insists on it,
Does it mean that someone must have it so,
That every evening
Over the roofs
One star at least must be kindled and glow ?

This is an anti-sentimental and anti-religious poem, but its propagandist purpose is partly concealed by its humorous irony. The opponent's case is deliberately travestied, and the success of the poem depends largely on the contrast between the apparently absurd fancies of the religious believer and the matter-of-fact way in which Mayakovsky deals with them. By this means he asserts his sanity and common sense and yet keeps his poem at a level of amusing fancy.

In such a poem there is an element of caricature. Mayakovsky was an excellent draughtsman and drew remarkably good and amusing caricatures. He would seize on some salient feature and exaggerate it until it dominates the whole design, and in particular he would find some grotesque detail which suits a character and yet makes it absurd, as in his anti-Tsarist caricatures of 1916 he satirised the Imperial monopoly of vodka by depicting the Tsar and Tsaritsa as sitting on their thrones holding large bottles instead of sceptre and orb. The strength of such caricature is that by fanciful exaggeration it draws attention to truths which elude other means of description. There are contradictions and absurdities in human nature which can be shown at their true worth only if they are transferred to some unreal, symbolical order of things. But Mayakovsky's art of caricature in words has a special quality simply through the poetry which he gives to it. He creates his imaginary settings with so keen an eye for their fitness and so vivid a sense of their implications that his words pass beyond caricature to an imaginative criticism of life. Through the delight and excitement of his words he does much more than show up the faults of what he attacks : he makes us share his contempt or anger or disgust for it.

The spirit of caricature can be combined with strong and powerful feelings. Mayakovsky could be a deadly critic of social institutions, especially when they denied those rights and instincts of the natural man which he understood so well in himself. His *Hymn to a Judge* (1915) shows how he can use a fantastic setting for a just and ferocious attack on certain types of men. In it galley-slaves sing of their Peruvian paradise which was once a delightful home for natural man, with its bananas and pine-apples, its wine, its birds and its dances. This is ruined by the advent of a judge :

> The judge's eyes were a pair of tin-cans
> A-gleam in a garbage hole.

The judge's eye, " austere as Lent ", makes even the tail of an orange-blue peacock fade, while the colibri, who fly on the prairies, are caught by him and have their down and feathers shaved off. The volcanoes no longer flame as they rise from the valleys ; for the judge has put up a notice : " This valley for non-smokers ". Of course Mayakovsky's verses are forbidden as " another intoxicating drink ". The result is that Peru has no birds and no people. It has become a wilderness, where

> Hideously walled in the vault of the laws
> The dismal judges live on.

The poem is written with passion, even with hatred for those who destroy the joy of life for some inhuman, abstract discipline, but Mayakovsky's violence is well in control and his anger only sharpens his criticism and makes his imagery more effective.

At times Mayakovsky turned this art of caricature against himself and his own circumstances. In the discord between his aims and his hopes, between his political ambitions and the world as it was, he saw much matter for irony and mockery. As the war went on, he saw the gap growing between himself and his countrymen and felt that he was indeed a ridiculous misfit in such a world. He set out his feelings in *Russia*, which begins by showing how outlandish he thinks himself to be :

> Here I go,
> An ostrich from over the sea,
> With stanzas and metre and rhythm for feathers.

He cannot belong to this snow-bound country, and dreams of another, a scorched, southern land, with sands and oases. But his life is what it is, and he turns with childlike misery to his mother who is unable to comfort him. So he lives on in the unfriendly north: in the long streets, with the cold and the rain, he must pass the whole year, and he closes with a sigh :

> Perhaps I shall vanish,
> Stranger from over the sea,
> In the fury of all Decembers.

The image of the ostrich fits his situation ; and his presentation of it, with its fancy and its humour and its pathos, shows exactly what he feels.

In this poetry there is an authentic force of fancy and of imagination. Mayakovsky has a peculiar gift for seeing relations and identities between things which are not commonly associated. He has his own way of interpreting experience and he expresses it with a special force and a modern aptness. He is contemptuous of the old kinds of metaphor and simile and finds new examples in the life of the streets and the bars which are his home. He likes his images to make an immediate, almost shocking effect, to strike home at once with force and to overwhelm the reader into accepting them as true. So he tells how stupid speech wounds him :

> On the pavement
> Of my well-trodden soul

> The footsteps of lunatics
> Plants heels of harsh words.

He says that his verses must be " sharp and necessary as tooth-picks ", and he shows his contempt for his public if it expects anything else from him :

> Your thought,
> Dreaming on a softened brain,
> Like a sodden lackey on a greasy couch.

Nor does he wish his poetry to seem other than it is :

> I once again glorify
> Men bed-ridden like a hospital
> And women worn out like proverbs.

In this spirit he flung his various strange images into his poetry. His comparisons are not elegant but exact and forceful. There is no lack of power when he speaks of himself as " alone like the last eye of a man who goes among the blind ", or of " the chameleon of the time ", or of " the Caesarian operation of war ", or of correct poetical language as " like the pulse of a corpse ", or of figures passing in a foggy evening :

> One after another the giants go,
> Mastodon after mastodon,

or of the thaw in a city :

> The street-ice falls in, like a syphilitic's nose.

He likes to express horror, because he feels it. But he is capable of other less frightening effects, as when he says in love :

> I simply beg for your body,
> As Christians beg :
> " Give us this day
> Our daily bread ",

and

> Your body
> I shall cherish and love,
> As a soldier cut down by war,
> Useless,
> Nobody's,
> Cherishes his single leg.

Mayakovsky's images are unprecedented, but they do what he demands of them and give a perfectly correct impression of his feelings.

In this poetry Mayakovsky is extremely self-centred. He could hardly be otherwise, since he is defending his precious gift of poetry and all that it means to him against an unfriendly world. Even when he falls in love, he speaks chiefly of his misery, and tenderness or affection seldom competes with his desire for conquest and possession. And this, too, is to be expected. Mayakovsky's poetry rises out of his conviction that he possesses special powers to create and transform, and for this reason he writes about himself. But this self-absorption is not matched by an equal self-confidence. At times he suggests that he is not his own master but the plaything of uncontrollable powers which will break him if he is not careful. He seems to have felt this specially about love. He knew all too well what it meant, and he was uneasy about a passion which so undermined his self-confidence and made him the prey of incalculable forces. He gave expression to this fear in a remarkable poem, *To myself the beloved are these lines dedicated by the author*. The situation is that four women have fallen in love with him, and he rejects their advances, not for reasons we might expect, but because he feels that to yield would be an act so enormous and so monstrous that it must not happen. The poem moves through a resplendent series of fanciful hyperboles, but they cloak a real emotion, — the poet's desire not to surrender himself because he feels that if he does, strange powers will be unleashed and shake the world. To avoid any imputation of solemnity he states the problem with humorous exaggeration and draws grotesque parallels :

> If I were
> As small
> As the great ocean,
> I should rise upon waves tiptoe,
> And wheedle the moon with my tide.
> But, being loved, where can I go,
> Being as big as I am ?
> In such a small sky
> Such a love cannot hide.

He is afraid that once he lets himself go the order of his life will be destroyed. But he feels that he is something outside nature, and that it is not for him to give way :

> If only
> In all its power
> I let loose an enormous voice,
> Comets would stretch out their flaming hands
> And hurl themselves down in desire.
> I would gnaw the nights with the light of my eyes,
> If only I were
> As dim as the sun.
> I should never feel pressed
> With my brightness to water
> Earth's withered breast.
> I should go
> Dragging my lover with me.
> In what nights
> Delirious and suffering
> What Goliaths should I breed
> So enormous
> And good for nothing !

The whole poem moves at a level of delightful absurdity, but it is built on a real fear, and this playfulness is Mayakovsky's escape from it.

This sense of great powers in himself, and of their conflict with the world, dictated most of Mayakovsky's early poetry. For him the creative principle lay in this central, primitive strength which he found in himself. His conviction that he must at all costs preserve it and exercise it forbade him to yield to anything which demanded the submission of his will or his intelligence. This created difficulties for him in his approach to his art. It made him a rebel in literature because only by being true to his own unusual poetical instinct could he be himself, and his gifts were not those of other men. He resisted the claims of others to impose their literary standards on him and could not disguise his contempt for them and their way of life. In *Brother Writers* (1916) he denounces the conventional poets of the time. He begins by proclaiming his contempt for their lives and habits :

> It's plain I shall never get used
> To sitting at the " Bristol ",
> To drinking tea
> And telling lies by the line.
> I shall upset the glasses,
> Climb on the table.
> Listen to me,
> Literary brothers of mine !
> You sit
> With your eyes sunk in tea ;
> Scribbling has worn your plush elbows bare.
> Lift up your eyes from unemptied glasses and see !
> Shake your ears out of your hair !

In his contempt for his brother-poets Mayakovsky advances by a natural process to something very like contempt for the literary life in any form. He reminds his fellows that when Villon had finished writing he used to be a burglar, and he taunts them with not seeing how interesting life is. He rejects their old sentimental subjects such as " pages, palaces, love and lilacs " and says that if such men are really poets then he must spit on all art. To such activities he prefers any active life :

> Better open a shop,
> Go on the Stock Exchange,
> Make my sides swell with fat wallets ;
> With a drunken song
> In a tavern latrine
> I shall vomit my soul.

Of course this represents the natural contempt of a young poet for his old-fashioned fellow practitioners, who do not know how important their art really is. But at the same time it shows how Mayakovsky's powerful instincts carried him beyond poetry into something else. In him the desire to create had no certain goal, and at times he questioned his calling.

Mayakovsky's private and eagerly defended citadel had, sooner or later, to come to terms with the outside world. He himself desired a solution, provided it gave him what he wanted. He was well aware that he was not alone in his miseries and frustrations and that others, in their own ways, shared his discontents. He felt a bond with such people and believed that men like them and him, the despised and the outcasts, were the truly innocent children of the world :

> We,
> Convicts in a lepers' colony,
> Where gold and filth have run free,
> We are cleaner than Venice's azure sky,
> Washed both by sun and sea.

He saw in the hopes of revolution a cure to the corrupt state of affairs no less than a fulfilment for himself. In *A Cloud in Trousers* he found a consolation for his emotional troubles in the thought of a wrath to come, and his insight was not far wrong when he prophesied :

> There, where man's vision
> Is cut short by the hungry heads between,
> In the crown of thorns of revolution
> I foresee nineteen-sixteen.

To this he was drawn both by his desire to be free from his own hateful circumstances and by his real sympathy for the mass of Russian humanity. His Futuristic delight in machines made him the prophet of a mechanised age :

> We ourselves are the prophets of burning hymns,
> The din of factories and workshops.

He compared his own visions more than favourably with the magical illusions which Mephistopheles produces for Faust or with the strange fantasies of Nietzsche's Zarathustra. He did not work out the details : he was sure that life would be more vigorous and more wonderful. He believed that his task was to inflame the crowds to action until they were wilder than those who captured the Bastille. In him the consciousness of creative powers turned naturally into revolutionary fervour, but it was to be a revolution in which he himself took a prominent part and which would satisfy his dynamic view of life.

The realisation of these hopes seemed for a while to be hindered by the First World War. In its first years Maya-kovsky wrote some of his best and most intimate poetry. But it was not without a struggle. For a time, on his own admis-

sion, he " lost all interest in art ", and though at first he " took
the war excitedly " and " thought of it in its decorative and
noisy aspects ", he soon felt " disgust and hatred for it ".
His finest feelings were outraged. He felt deeply for the
Russian people and saw no justification for the vast slaughter.
He was moved to pity for the millions of all countries who
suffered from it :

> The peoples die
> On a stone in a hole.

He felt that half the world was drunk, and that the other half
was crying out in agony. Behind the marching-songs of the
soldiers he heard the weeping of mothers and children. His
War and the Universe (1916) shows how deeply he was distressed. He, who believed in the unity of mankind, saw all
the nations of the world fighting each other for causes which
meant nothing to them and were indeed beyond their comprehension. He dwelt, with fascinated horror, on this new
gladiatorial show which needed another Nero to enjoy it :

> To-day
> The whole world
> Is a Coliseum,
> And the waves of every sea
> Are the velvet hung over it.

He believed that the war was the work of imperialist Capitalism, and he warned the countries of Europe that it would
destroy all that they most treasured. He spoke with bitter
irony of the delight that men take in war :

> It is good to burn and ravish
> To the music of machine-guns.

He felt that love and happiness had vanished, and he asked
bitterly if there was a single happy man in the world, and
answered that perhaps there was one such — in Brazil.

The war called out Mayakovsky's most human and most
tender qualities. He showed that underneath his irony and
his display he hid a love for his fellow men. Though he was
appalled by the carnage and the cant, he did not surrender to
despair. He characteristically looked for a solution and found

it in the new comradeship which the victims of war had learned through their common agony, and he proclaimed that before long this would lead to revolution. He believed that great natural forces were all on his side, that the Rhine and the Danube, China and Persia, would help his cause. He discovered that his own creative qualities were somehow those of the common people in many lands, and he was eager that the whole world should join him in abandoning war and promoting human brotherhood. This wild hope finally broke down Mayakovsky's defences and turned him from a self-centred into a public-minded poet. Here was a cause which responded to his conviction that the artist should be a man of action and made him at last feel that he was not a misunderstood oddity but a man who felt as the mass of other men felt. The war not only confirmed and justified him in his revolutionary views, but gave him a new insight and sympathy. He believed that mankind was changing :

> A people is born,
> A people of to-day,
> Gentler and better than God Himself.

This conviction and this hope united his different gifts and showed him what to do. His central flame was now single and shed its light on a prospect of a world free and active as Mayakovsky had known himself to be in his creative hours. Just as Blok saw in the Revolution the transformation of ordinary men into a nation of artists, so Mayakovsky foresaw an unleashing of enormous powers and the creation of a new humanity.

In 1917 Mayakovsky's hopes were realised. As an old Bolshevik he was not content with the government of Kerensky and said, " for me it was clear that the Socialists must inevitably replace it ", and when the October Revolution came, he was free from any doubts or hesitations : " To accept or not to accept ? For me, as for the other Moscow Futurists, this question never arose. It is my revolution." Where the Symbolists, Blok and Bely, saw a purification of the world through blood, the Futurists, Khlebnikov and Mayakovsky, saw a wonderful door opened to vast possibilities of creation. The wild creative force which was the most important thing in their lives and the justification for their Futurism was suddenly released from restraints and inspired to call up visions of what lay in store for millions of men freed from the shackles of centuries. Hitherto both poets had written complicated and difficult verse as the true reflection of their conflicts and their troubles. Now in a moment their conflicts seemed to be solved, and their genius darted forth in untrammelled song. In *Liberty for All* Khlebnikov sings his song of the triumphant proletariat :

> In a stormwind, single undying,
> All, all are for Liberty there !
> On swans' wings the People are flying
> To lift flags of work in the air.
>
> Liberty flames on their faces —
> Fire set beside it is cold.
> Who cares for old shapes in earth's places ?
> New words shall their hunger unfold.
>
> We march with songs that are burning,
> Together to Liberty, on !
> Though we die, we shall rise, and returning
> Life shall revive what has gone.
>
> We move on a journey enchanted,
> And the loud marching rhythm we heed.
> If the gods are in irons, undaunted
> We shall see that the gods are freed !

The mood is the mood of 1917, though underneath it we can detect Khlebnikov's special conviction that the Russian people have found a new strength because the Revolution is a return to natural simplicity. That is why he accepts the destruction of much that exists : he thinks that the encumbrances of civilisation will be replaced by a more vital form of life. When he speaks of freeing the gods, he is not using myth or metaphor : it is the powers of nature, the old Slavonic gods, who will be brought back again to power.

Mayakovsky shared this exultant confidence and gave his own version of it in *Our March*. He, too, saw the great surge

of marching crowds and felt the call of vast new adventures :
he, too, burst into rapturous, Utopian song :

> Tramp squares with rebellious treading !
> Up, heads ! As proud peaks be seen !
> In the second flood we are spreading
> Every city on earth will be clean.
>
> Pied days plod.
> Slowly the years' waggons come.
> Speed's our god.
> Hearts are beating a drum.
>
> What gold is than ours diviner ?
> Can the waspy bullets sting ?
> Than our songs no weapons are finer.
> Our gold is in hearts that ring.
>
> Green let the grass grow,
> Covering days past.
> Rainbow, gleam, glow.
> Let galloping years travel fast.
>
> The stars are too bored to bother ;
> Without them our singing shall blow.
> Oh, ask, Great Bear, our mother,
> That alive to the stars we go !
>
> Drink of delight ! Drink ! Shout !
> Veins with the spring-flood thrumming.
> Hearts, up ! Strike out !
> Our breasts are brass cymbals drumming.

Mayakovsky's poem is not pantheistic like Khlebnikov's, but
it has the same sense of great events afoot, of enormous powers
liberated, and of vast prospects in the immediate future. His
old contempt for the past has produced a fierce desire to
transform the present into something swift and marvellous :
his Futurist's love of speed has turned from machines to
human beings : his irreligion has become a spur to drive
mankind on to the conquest of the physical universe. *Our
March* is a peak in Mayakovsky's career. In it all his lyrical
spirit is at work in harmonious unison. It is his finest and

almost his final word on the dynamic urgency which he felt in himself and in mankind, his purest expression of the creative force which made him both a poet and revolutionary.

At this period Mayakovsky found a perfect field for his varied talents, for his new power of song, for his fantastic humour, for his satire and caricature. The new world called for his help against its enemies, and he gave it freely. The result, among much else, was *Mystery-Bouffe*, which appeared in 1918 and then in an expanded form in 1921. Mayakovsky called it "a heroic, epic and satiric representation of our epoch". It is cast in the form of a play and was actually acted, though it did not have much of a success on the stage. It was rightly hailed as a new departure in Russian literature. It is in fact a kind of Aristophanic fantasy, though Mayakovsky might not have appreciated the comparison. It is Aristophanic in its mixture of boisterous, knock-about fun and lyrical delicacy, in its great assortment of characters who vary from typical workmen and contemporary figures, like Clemenceau and Lloyd George, to machines and things, in its clean-cut distinction between the good and the bad characters, who are the Unclean and the Clean, the workers and the capitalists. It takes place in fantastic circumstances. After a deluge has destroyed the earth, the play opens at the North Pole, changes in turn to an ark which the survivors of mankind build, to Hell and Paradise, to Chaos which the Unclean subdue and reduce to order, and finally to the Promised Land on earth, the Communists' paradise of material plenty. The action is equally fantastic. After being duped by the Clean into establishing a monarchy, in which the Negus of Abyssinia eats all the food available on the ark, and a democracy in which the rich take everything and leave the workers nothing but paper receipts, the workers visit Hell and leave the Clean there, visit Paradise which they find very unsatisfying since there is nothing but clouds to eat, make their way through Chaos and enter the new golden age when machines provide plenty for everyone. It is a myth of the struggles and triumph of Communism and bears as little relation to reality as Aristophanes' *Birds*. But it is a wonderful feat of creative imagination from the first scene, where

Eskimos fish in holes in the ice and are disturbed by the arrival of various European and other figures, to the last scene with its city of skyscrapers and factories, of trams and motor-cars, of gardens planted with stars and moons and surmounted by the sun.

Mystery-Bouffe is by no means a mere fantasy of ideas. It has a peculiar dramatic quality. There are excellent passages of comic dialogue and intrigue as when Lloyd George at the North Pole is mistaken for a walrus, or the Negus is thrown overboard from the ark, or the inhabitants of Heaven are fussed by the arrival of a lot of unexpected guests, or the devils complain of the dullness of their life. The characters, though sketched in broad lines, have at least the vitality of farce. Methuselah, who arranges a very unsubstantial repast for his visitors ; the Menshevik conciliator, who always tries to com-pose disputes by showing that the parties really agree; the Woman, who offers her favours to whatever party happens for the moment to be triumphant and settles finally in Hell, are Aristophanic in their trueness to type. Though there is a slight thread of allegory in the persistent theme of the hunger which dogs the Unclean, it is not at all troublesome but gives an extra point to the struggles which the Unclean endure to gain some sort of happiness and freedom. The final scene has great variety and vitality. There is a delightful moment when the workers refuse to believe that the earth is theirs to be enjoyed and cling to their old notion that they will have to pay for it until the Things apologise for the trouble they have caused, owing to unjust masters, in the past, and promise a new and better order :

> Roar in the factories, moving the wheels,
> Rush over the rails, coursing the fields,
> Now the world makes holiday,
> Now the night shines as the day.
> Now until the end of time
> Yours are we, workmen . . .[1]

There is a nice touch of farce when a Farm Hand puts his hand on the earth and becomes tipsy or a Blacksmith drives

[1] Trs. G. R. Noyes and A. Kaun.

off the Business Man who tries to turn the new state of affairs to his own profit. But the chief quality is the lyrical exaltation which shows Mayakovsky's finest qualities of work in his conviction that natural powers will now serve man and lay the universe at his feet. It is this which the Locomotive Engineer sings towards the end :

> We are the architects of earths,
> The planets' decorators ;
> We are the wonder-makers.
> The sunbeams we shall tie
> In radiant brooms, and sweep
> The clouds from the sky
> With electricity.
> We shall make honey-sweet the rivers of the world,
> The streets of earth we'll pave with radiant stars.[1]

Then, again like Aristophanes, Mayakovsky ends the whole riotous fantasy in a choral song, a version of the *International*, in which the Unclean proclaim the new birth of mankind and the brotherhood of working men.

In all this fancy and satire Mayakovsky releases his special gifts and keeps up a wonderfully harmonious tone through his bold and adventurous scheme. In the vision of this new world he found something which satisfied his oldest and deepest longings. As one who knew the privations and humiliations of the outcast, he gladly sang the new hopes which he saw before him. And because he was so sincerely engaged in his task, at times he goes beyond his farce and speaks in more solemn tones about the kind of man whom this new world will produce. When *Mystery-Bouffe* was first acted, Mayakovsky took the part of the Man of the Future who appears across the water to the Unclean when they are voyaging to no known goal. This was the human ideal which he had formed in the Revolution, and it shows an unexpected prophetic quality in him. He uses the language of the Gospel to controvert its doctrines and proclaims :

> My paradise is for everyone
> Except for the poor in spirit,

---

[1] Trs. G. R. Noyes and A. Kaun.

and says that his is a new Sermon on the Mount :

> I do not speak to you of Christ's Paradise,
> Where penitents drink tea without sugar.
> I proclaim the true Paradise on earth.

Instead of the old religious outlook he offers his new faith in a mankind which has no divisions of class or nation and finds delight in work. He offers men this new world of plenty and beauty instead of the unsubstantial promises on which they have hitherto been nourished.

At this stage of his career, in the years immediately after 1917, Mayakovsky flung all his gifts into his poetry. He had always been a child of nature, and now he believed that he was nature's ally and agent in bringing her gifts to a liberated world. How much this belief meant to him can be seen from *An Extraordinary Adventure* (1920). He tells of a hot summer in the country when he finds the sun unendurable. He playfully summons it to visit him — and the sun comes. The poet strikes up a friendship with it and finds that they have much in common, and so the poem ends :

> Shine everywhere,
> Shine every day,
> Shine till the world's last station —
> Always to shine — the sun and I
> Make this
> Our proclamation.

The vivid myth has its moments of fanciful absurdity, as when the sun shines " overtime " and smacks the poet affectionately on the back. But there is truth behind it. Mayakovsky really felt that he was inspired by natural powers and to some degree resembled them. He felt so sure of his task and his place in the new society that he could compare himself to the sun and think the comparison not entirely absurd. He believed that his own gifts were an example of what belong to most men when the bondage of an effete system is broken, that what matters most is this new confidence which he had found and thought that others had found too. If he had a gospel, it was that for free men nothing is impossible.

Yet while he was thus indulging his newly found liberty,

Mayakovsky, with a curious contradiction that lay deep in his nature, was not entirely convinced that a poet must follow his own fancies and not make himself immediately useful by advocating urgent social and political causes. He was so much a man of the Revolution that he had to take an active part in it and set his gifts at its disposal. He believed that the right poetry for the new society was of his kind, and he argued, with sincerity if not with cogent logic : " Only the proletariat will create new things, and we, the Futurists, are the only ones to follow in the footsteps of the proletariat. . . . Futurism is the ideology of the proletariat. . . . Futurism is proletarian art." This was his way of saying what he had always believed, that his special kind of creative energy was that of the revolutionary forces. But an inner doubt was at work in him. A poet indeed he must be, but should he not subordinate his gifts to the clamorous needs of the new world ? In *Command to the Army of Art* (1918) he shows how he interprets his task. He vents his old contempt on established writers and summons his Futurists to action :

> The doddering old brigades
> Spin out the old rigmaroles.
> Comrades !
> On to the barricades,
> The barricades of hearts and souls !

He argues that there is still a need for poets because they give life to other men. He is convinced that they have a social task and that their place is in the midst of new developments and their work among the common people :

> On to the streets, Futurists !
> Drummers and poets !

He did not at first notice that this conception of poetry was at variance with his own lyrical spirit, that it demands a different technique and a different outlook from what had hitherto been his. Mayakovsky still believed that he could combine his old gifts with his new social outlook, and for a short period he succeeded in creating a compromise between them.

Mayakovsky soon felt pressure not only from his own sense of social responsibility but from external powers. In 1921 the

Proletcult, which claimed to represent proletarian art, passed a resolution : " As we consider Futurism an ideological trend of the last period of imperialistic bourgeois culture, we proclaim it antagonistic to the proletariat as a class ". Nor could Mayakovsky be quite insensitive to the difficulty of making his kind of poetry effective with the masses. *Mystery-Bouffe* was not a great success either in its first form in 1918 or in its expanded and revised form in 1921 ; and if that failed, what would his other work do ? So at the very time when he was at the height of his creative excitement over the Revolution and its prospects, Mayakovsky began to simplify his art and to bring it more closely into touch with immediate needs. One day in 1918 he was asked to read to the sailors of the Baltic Fleet, honoured as heroes of the Revolution, and he wrote a poem especially for them, *Left March*. In it we can see how far he had begun to move from *Our March*, written a few months before :

> Fall in and prepare to march !
> No time now to talk or to trifle.
> Silence, you orators !
> The word
> Is with you,
> Comrade Rifle !
> We have lived long enough by laws
> Of which Adam and Eve made the draft.
> Stable history's poor old horse !
> Left !
> Left !
> Left !
>
> Hullo, bluejackets
> Up in the tops !
> Or
> Have your battleships in the docks
> Lost the edge that they had before ?
> See,
> Showing the teeth of its crown,
> The British lion rebuffed.
> The Commune will never go down.
> Left !
> Left !
> Left !

Out there
Past fiery peaks advance
To a sunny land unknown.
Past hunger,
Past oceans of pestilence,
Let millions march on.
Though hirelings circle to crush us
And the lava of steel flow swift,
The Entente cannot conquer the Russias.
Left !
Left !
Left !

Does the eagle's eye grow dim
While on old haunts it lingers ?
Make fast
On the throat of the world
Proletarian fingers.
Fling chests out straight.
In the sky let the banners drift.
Who marches there with the right ?
Left !
Left !
Left !

In this poem there is still much of the ecstatic, visionary Mayakovsky. The prospect of great worlds to conquer still inspires him to grandiose images of cosmic forces and unexampled achievements. But his scope is narrower. His revolutionary vision is now almost confined to a special situation, in which Russia is threatened by the Entente, and his feeling for the brotherhood of man has become belligerent and national. Even the play on the word " Left ! ", so characteristic of Mayakovsky's ingenious fancy, has an aggressively partisan air. Mayakovsky treats his duties so seriously that he has begun to control his fanciful outbursts and to accommodate himself to the requirements of special occasions.

The message of *Left March* was enlarged and elaborated in Mayakovsky's next great work, *150,000,000* (1922). This was written when the young Soviets felt themselves cut off by a *cordon sanitaire* from the rest of Europe which financed and encouraged counter-revolutionary armies within their borders.

The Revolution, which had begun by thinking that all men would open their arms to it, found itself assailed with abuse and violence. In *150,000,000* Mayakovsky justifies the Russian system and proclaims its ultimate triumph over its enemies. The title stands for the population of the U.S.S.R., and Mayakovsky identifies himself with a whole people :

> 150,000,000 speak through these
> Lips of mine.

The poem, writen with great force and with much of Mayakovsky's old brilliance, falls into two parts, the first dealing with a general justification of the Soviets, the second with a myth which portrays their future victory over the forces of Capitalism. In the first part Mayakovsky has hardened and clarified his ideas and brought them into harmony with current thought. His old playful blasphemies are replaced by a conscious conformist atheism. He proclaims his new god :

> Call
> Not from an easy
> Bed in the stars,
> A god of iron,
> A god of fires,
> No god who from Mars is,
> Vega or Neptune,
> But God from the masses,
> God who is man.

This new humanity will have all the resources of nature on its side, and Mayakovsky has transformed his admiration of machines and contempt of sentiment into a new romance of mechanised life. With trains for feet, steamers for fins, and aeroplanes for wings, the new age will increase its speed and scope. It will not need roses, for it will have

> Roses of crowds in the petalled squares,

and its love will be the love of men for one another :

> Understand
> That men
> Will be gentle
> Like love
> That swells with light to a star.

So Mayakovsky created the poetry which his time demanded. His contemporaries, released from their old religion and trusting innocently in the promises of science, believed that with a little effort they could realise the dreams of Jules Verne and H. G. Wells. Mayakovsky agreed with them and proclaimed that theirs was a force that nothing could withstand.

The rest of the poem consists of a kind of myth in which the forces of Communism, embodied in the gigantic figure of Ivan, oppose the forces of Capitalism, embodied, rather oddly, in the figure of Woodrow Wilson. The myth bears no relation to reality, and we cannot complain that when Mayakovsky wrote, Wilson was a dying man. Mayakovsky is concerned not with facts but with wild abstract ideas. His work bears some resemblance to the Russian traditional lays in which heroes of prodigious strength and iron determination, like Volga and Mikula, engage with opponents hardly less formidable than themselves. The scene of the struggle is Chicago, a dream-city, where every mechanical device exists, but man is a slave. Mayakovsky leads up to the encounter with his usual inventiveness and vigour. Ivan's appearance in the United States is like an eruption of natural forces. He breaks up into countless small Ivans who engage Wilson in battle and rout him. In this conflict not only are human beings engaged but natural powers, like wind and water, and the creations of man, like telegraph-poles, skyscrapers, bridges, railway-lines, hospitals, tables and chairs. The result of course is that Communism triumphs in the United States. Despite its purely mythical and fantastic air *150,000,000* is based on a dogmatic belief that the Communist system is bound to conquer because it makes a proper use of human nature and natural resources. Mayakovsky indicates the power behind mechanisation with his poetry of an enormous people on the march, and his irresistible Ivan, who is like a volcano or a tidal wave. The poem takes full account of revolutionary doctrine and is in many ways a glorification of it. It has been transformed into poetry and engages Mayakovsky's most characteristic gifts.

150,000,000 is Mayakovsky's last attempt to combine Futurism with political poetry, the last poem in which he gave full rein to his ebullient fancy. After it he wrote a great deal, but not in this way. He became more and more a public figure, a tribune of the Revolution, who through his rhetorical verse did much to convince the proletariat that it lived in a wonderful world and must make every effort to preserve and improve it. To make his message more effective he trimmed and simplified his style and abandoned most of his earlier wildness. The change in his art reflected a change in his time. The first ecstatic years of revolutionary optimism were finished, and the time of organisation and discipline followed. Futurism of Mayakovsky's kind was no longer appreciated, and Mayakovsky himself decided to compose in a different way. But in these first years, between 1912 and 1922, he had done something sufficiently remarkable. He had created a special kind of poetry in which his words were not only poured out in a white heat of excitement but succeeded in reflecting important elements in the contemporary consciousness. More than anyone he broke down the hieratic dignity of Russian poetry and replaced it with a special version of living experience. His technique, which owed so little to anyone else, was highly modern in the exactness and truth which it allowed, and his own instinct for poetry guided him on a way where few others could go but where he himself was perfectly at ease. His was a peculiar creative gift, half lyrical and half satirical. It was well suited to these years of change, and though some may not like it, we cannot deny its originality and its power.

V

BORIS PASTERNAK,
1917-1923

The peculiar direction which Mayakovsky gave to Russian poetry from 1912 to 1922 was part of a greater movement. The collapse of Symbolism had prepared the way for new kinds of poetry, and for a few years different parties competed for the lead. Each little group had its own title and its own programme, and though members and programmes changed with bewildering rapidity, certain main tendencies can be seen which show that Russian poets were keeping in line with their fellows in other European countries and transforming foreign ideas to suit their special national needs. The Revolution of 1917 gave at first a great impetus and encouragement to fresh kinds of poetry. The Futurists were on the victorious side and proclaimed that theirs was the only truly revolutionary poetry, but other groups made similar claims, and for a few years many experiments were made. The new poetry was on the whole a denial of the past. It wished to be contemporary and realistic and revolutionary, but the different groups were not agreed on what were the best means to secure such ends. The Futurists were too violent and too deliberately crude to suit all tastes. The Acmeists, led by Nikolai Gumilev and Anna Akhmatova, stressed the claims of actuality and real experience, but their political opinions were not well suited to the time, and the movement collapsed when Gumilev was shot in 1921 for counter-revolutionary activities, and Anna Akhmatova, after her noble *Anno Domini* (1922), was condemned to silence. A third group, the Imagists, appeared in 1917 and was less political in its views, though it welcomed the Revolution. Deriving some of its ideas by indirect channels from American poets like Amy Lowell and Ezra Pound, it stressed an aspect of technique, dismissed matter and content as " the vermiform appendix of art " and concentrated on the image as the one thing that really counts.

They would have been of little importance if they had not been joined for a time by Sergei Esenin, a peasant of astonishing genius, whose natural eye for imagery drew him to them but whose sensibility and insight were quite beyond anything possessed by his fellows. For a time these, and other schools with not dissimilar aims, competed for the loyalty of young Russian poets. None of them survived for long. The Futurists took more and more to political poetry and abandoned in fact, if not in theory, most of their original tenets ; the Acmeists were repressed as counter-revolutionaries in politics ; the Imagists, except for Esenin, produced no work of lasting value, and Esenin's short and hectic career ended with suicide in 1925 after he had written poetry of an exquisite, wild sweetness in which the image is kept in a subordinate place.

None the less the new movements had made discoveries of some importance. From their different angles the Futurists, the Acmeists and the Imagists had some real contribution to make. While the Futurists stressed the call to a renewed language and a more vivid concern with actual life, the Acmeists stressed the virtues of a polished technique and the need to make vivid effects in a limited compass, and the Imagists aimed at the greater intimacy and charm which can be secured through a bold exploitation of imagery. Each school suffered from exaggerating its claims. The Futurists' love of violence excluded many legitimate effects, the Acmeists were too traditional for a revolutionary age, and the Imagists spoiled their work by turning a means of poetry into its chief end. What was needed was a poet who could pick up the different threads and combine them, correct the excesses of the various creeds and turn the modern movements to meet modern needs without giving too much emphasis to this or that claim of the competing antagonists. The man appeared in Boris Pasternak, who may be said to have seen almost from the start what truth there was in the several theories and what contribution each had really to make to the general problem of poetical composition. In his beginnings he had some association with the Futurists and was a member of a small association called " Centrifuga " which used to meet in

Moscow. He was also a great admirer of Mayakovsky's early poetry. Pasternak's first verses show some traces of Futurist violence and over-emphasis in their abrupt movement and exaggerated effects, but this manner did not last long. When Pasternak was twenty-seven he had found his style and his own approach to poetry, and we can see how the different influences of his training had come together in a peculiar unity.

Pasternak was in full agreement with the new poets in his rejection of the mystical ideals held by the Symbolists. He was concerned not with some supra-mundane state but with the actual world that he knew. He did not however agree with the revolutionary rejection of the poetical past. He came from a family which represented in its highest form that devotion to the arts which cultivated Russians used to maintain with so unusual an accomplishment. His father was a painter of the Impressionist school ; his mother was a brilliant musician. In his boyhood he not only learned what painting is but studied music with Scriabin. His culture spread outside his own country when, after taking a course in philosophy under Hermann Cohen at Marburg, he visited Italy and saw the great monuments of the European past. To an eye trained on painting and an ear trained to music he added a grasp of abstract problems and a natural gift for words which may have gained something from his study of foreign languages. The man who was later to translate Shakespeare and Kleist and poets from Georgia possessed from the start a remarkable vocabulary and a great sense of the worth and power of words. The authors whom he most admired were Shakespeare and Lermontov. On these he trained his taste and learned that poetry must both be true to experience and as expressive as possible. He absorbed much from the past and formed his standards by it, but he was no slave to it and saw that a poet must create his own style and be faithful to his own outlook.

It was the need for a new style that drew Pasternak to the Futurists. It was because Mayakovsky really gave a new worth to words that Pasternak admired him. But this use of words reflected something else which Pasternak admired. On Mayakovsky's death in 1930 Pasternak compared him to Etna. It was this volcanic eruptiveness that he prized, the enormous elemental force which Mayakovsky put into words. Pasternak knew that he himself possessed a similar kind of force, even though it worked in a different way, and his intention was to make the most of this, to make his poetry as powerful as possible. Though his gifts were very unlike Mayakovsky's, and he ceased to admire Mayakovsky's work when it abandoned its first concentrated ecstasy, he cherished an ideal of a poetry which should be extremely expressive without breaking too violently with the traditions of Russian verse. Without going all the way with the Futurists and other advanced poets of his youth, he saw that they had something which older poets lacked, a fiercer approach to life, a greater power of giving an experience in its whole range, a readier and more sincere response to their creative inspiration. In his long struggle with his art he has always kept true to this ideal, though he differs from the Futurists in the means which he uses and the kind of experience which he puts into poetry.

Pasternak's resemblance to the Imagists was more personal than intellectual. He was not of their number and was too good a craftsman to accept their extreme claims. But, like other modern poets, he saw that the image has a special part to play and that it is almost impossible to express complex states of mind without an adventurous and extensive use of it. It is customary to say that his use of images reflects the world of painting in which he grew up, but though Pasternak's visual sensibility is extremely keen, it does much more than mark and record. It carries with it something which is more than visual. Indeed we might say that his musical training has been quite as important as his knowledge of painting, since it has taught him to give a precise sensuous form to otherwise undefined feelings and to realise what strength can be added to words through combinations of sound. What he sees awakes in him so many remarkable trains of thought and sound that his poetry is packed and complex. It deals with many obscure states which might be material for a musician but are beyond the scope of a painter. Everything that he notices is fraught with mystery and meaning for him. He lives in the real world and observes it intently, but his rapt observation uncovers much more than meets the seeing eye. In the inextricable combination of his senses and emotions he both sees and interprets nature, both marks its manifestations and understands what they mean and what relations they suggest beyond the immediate " given ". No doubt the Imagists hoped to do something of this kind through their cult of the image, but they defined its purpose too narrowly. Pasternak, consciously or unconsciously, has picked up their doctrine and shown how it should really be applied.

Pasternak did not burst into poetry in extreme youth. His early verses are not numerous and still show an experimental quality. At moments there are forecasts of his most mature manner, at others mere attempts to write like other men. Then in 1917 he flowered astonishingly and marvellously. His volume *My Sister Life*, which was not published until 1922, was written in the summer of 1917 and shows how perfectly Pasternak had found himself. The flood of inspiration in which he wrote this book continued for the next few years and produced the no less remarkable *Themes and Variations* in 1923. These two volumes are the essential core of his work, the climax of his first endeavours and the inspired product of his young manhood. In them his temperament and his circumstances combined to produce the new kind of poetry which was his to give and which his time needed. His later work contains many beauties, is always truthful and original, but it is sometimes too experimental, too much at war with his circumstances, to have the final harmony of these two books. In them Pasternak has done something which is unique in his time.

An outlook like Pasternak's demands its own technique, and he has found a form which is firm and concentrated and powerful. In an age of metrical experiments he normally uses stanzas of fixed length and regular rhythms. On the printed page his verses look perfectly normal. He also uses rhyme, though he goes far in his use of half-rhymes and assonances. While the formal plan of his verses binds its different elements together and reduces them to order, the unusual character of his contents is marked by his unusual rhymes. By this means Pasternak avoids that looseness of form which suits the surging moods of the Futurists but is unsuitable to a poet who wishes to give to a poem some of the balance and pattern of a painting or of a musical composition. Pasternak makes us feel that even the most complex of his themes has its own harmony and order and that, however surprising what he says may be, it has a controlling design. The strictness of the form adds dignity to the rich and unusual vocabulary which is in turns allusive, conversational and majestic, and does not shrink from elliptical expressions or from neologisms : it even controls the imagery which is always original and sometimes startling. The formality of Pasternak's verse holds the rebellious material together. Without it the complex themes would not be fused into a unity, and the final result would be far less satisfying.

In his instinctive knowledge of what poetry is, Pasternak is determined that his work shall be essentially and purely poetry. No doubt his standards owe much to the great Russian writers like Blok who brought poetry back to itself in the first decade of this century, but he must also owe something to the discriminating devotion to the arts which he learned in his family circle, especially from his father. If his determination to maintain always a level of pure poetry sometimes makes him obscure or even awkward, it also means that he never writes below a certain standard and never wastes his time on irrelevant matter. The close texture of his verse, which at times makes it difficult to grasp all his implications at a first reading, is an essential feature of his art. It helps him to convey his intense, concentrated experience and is a true mirror of his moods. He looks at objects not in isolation but as parts of a wider unity, marks their relations in a complex whole, and stresses the dominant character of a scene as much as the individual elements in it. His work is therefore extremely personal, but not so personal as to be beyond the understanding of other men. He assumes that others will recognise the truth of his vision and come to share it with him. For, in his view, what he gives them is not a scientific, photographic transcript of an impersonal, external reality but something intensely human, since reality and value are given to things by our appreciation of them and by our absorption of them into our consciousness. Man is the centre of the universe, and human consciousness is its uniting principle. Therefore he can say with perfect sincerity :

> Gardens, ponds and palings, the creation
> Foam-flecked with the whiteness of our weeping,
> Are nothing but categories of passion
> That the human heart has had in keeping.

Pasternak is a poet of sensibility in the sense that for him sensibility is both physical and intellectual, the means by which he gets a full and firm grip on reality, and that nothing counts but those moments when he has a vivid apprehension of something that happens both inside and outside himself.

To convey the results of this sensibility and this outlook demands a special technique. Since what the senses give us must be presented in its fullness, it is not right to use conventional means of description which presuppose an artificial arrangement of experience. The poet must convey his sensations exactly as they strike him. So Pasternak often presents a visible scene in a way which at first seems paradoxical but later reveals its essential truth and exactness. For instance he writes of a road so polished in summer by cart-wheels that it reflects the stars by night :

> By the road age-old midnight stands,
> Sprawls on the trackway with its stars ;
> You cannot pass the hedge without
> Trampling upon the universe.

At first sight this looks like an imaginative trope, but it is really a truthful transcript of the poet's sensations. On crossing the road in such conditions he notices the reflected stars and for the moment believes that he is treading on them. That is the experience which inspires him, and that is precisely what he says. So somewhat differently, when he tells of a journey in a train at night, he assumes that, in his seat, he is the fixed centre of reality and that what he sees is a passing phenomenon. Everyone will know what he means and recognise how precisely he records it :

> And, with its third splash, off the bell goes swimming,
> Still making apologies : " Sorry, not here,"

And under the blind the night passes flaming,
And the plain crumbles off from the steps to a star.

The train has just left the station to the usual Russian signal
of a bell rung three times. When the journey begins, the train
seems to be fixed, and the night behind the blind to move,
so that the country slowly disappears between the steps of the
railway-carriage and the distant star which is relatively
stationary. The description is careful and accurate. This is
just what he feels in a train, and to put it differently would be
to falsify it. But just because Pasternak sees it so clearly and
knows exactly what it is, he is able to awake a delighted and
surprised admiration at his exactness and truth.

The same art is applied to sensations other than visual and
to these mental states which begin with sensations of eye or
ear but contain something else in their mental appreciation of
a situation. Pasternak, for instance, writes of a thunderstorm
at the end of summer :

> Summer then to the flag-station
> Said good-bye. That night the thunder
> Doffed its cap and as memento
> Took a hundred blinding snaps.

The sight and the sound of the thunderstorm are inextricably
mingled with the thought that the summer is over, and this
combination comes out in original and consistent imagery.
In Pasternak's poetry visible and mental things are closely
associated, and he hardly troubles to distinguish between
them. So he describes a view through the impression which
it makes on his mind :

> The mind is stifled. The horizon is,
> Like thoughts, the colour of tobacco.

The thing seen and the thought of it are one, and there is no
call to separate them. The ultimate setting is in the poet's
mind : this holds the phenomena together and gives them
their character, but the physical sensations are none the less
acutely felt and recorded. The watching mind observes them
as they really are and sees their significance. Indeed the actual
facts take on a symbolical importance and convey the char-

acter and atmosphere of the poet's state as he observes them. Pasternak's images deepen his meaning not merely because they give a greater exactness, but because they show the relation between a given event and other events not immediately connected, which are none the less of the same kind. They show that no event can be treated in absolute isolation but that any proper appreciation of it must take into account its universal qualities and relations.

This poetry is difficult just because it reflects the poet's sensations so exactly, especially when he advances beyond visual effects to the associations which they awake and with which they are inextricably united. Pasternak has a remarkable gift for giving shape and colour to these inchoate states of the mind in its moments of excited sensibility and uses vivid concrete images for much that poets usually leave undefined. He seizes on some significant trait in what he sees and relates it to something wider by his choice of a significant image. When, for instance, he writes :

> But people in watch-chains are loftily grumbling
> And sting you politely like snakes in the oats,

the primary effect is visual, but the scene, so clearly portrayed, suggests the character and habits of a class of persons who are coldly polite and use good manners to inflict wounds. So, more strikingly, in *Spring* Pasternak moves from the seen to the unseen, from an actual place to its character and meaning for him :

> It's spring. I leave a street where the poplar is astonished,
> Where distance is alarmed, and the house fears it may fall,
> Where air is blue just like the linen bundle
> A discharged patient takes from hospital,
>
> Where dusk is empty like a broken tale,
> Abandoned by a star, without conclusion,
> So that expressionless, unfathomable
> A thousand clamouring eyes are in confusion.

This is a real place with its street, its houses, its poplar, its sky with the colour of a blue bundle. But the visual effect is made more significant by the imaginative and emotional tone which it gets from the imagery. The poet leaves the place because it is somehow frustrated and incomplete. It has the confused pathos of an interrupted story, and this spreads to all who are interested in it and have hopes for its future. We all know how a visual scene may excite emotions in this way and contain in itself a power to move us to grief or pity. Pasternak describes such a state with admirable truth and appropriateness. He does not exaggerate his feelings, but passes with easy skill from one aspect of the situation to another until the short poem gives a complete and faithful picture of what has struck him.

This pictorial method enables Pasternak to deal with undefined and impalpable feelings and to give them a remarkable brilliance of colour and outline. He finds his images in what his eyes and ears have noted. These become his instruments for showing the obscure movements of the human soul. In particular when he tells of some action and wishes to show its full significance, he sometimes uses its actual features symbolically. The symbols exist both in themselves and for what they represent, and a poem written in this way seems to call for understanding at two levels, literal and symbolical. One of his most quoted poems will show how Pasternak faces this technique with all its difficulties :

> Stars raced headlong. Seaward headlands lathered.
> Salt spray blinded. Eyes dried up their tears.
> Darkness filled the bedrooms. Thoughts raced headlong.
> To Sahara Sphinx turned patient ears.
>
> Candles guttered. Blood, it seemed, was frozen
> In the huge Colossus. Lips at play
> Swelled into the blue smile of the desert.
> In that hour of ebb night sank away.
>
> Seas were stirred by breezes from Morocco.
> Simoon blew. Archangel snored in snows.
> Candles guttered. First draft of *The Prophet*
> Dried, and on the Ganges dawn arose.

The last verse explains the whole. *The Prophet* is Pushkin's famous poem and Pasternak's subject is its composition. To

this all the themes are related. In the first place we hear of
the circumstances in which the poem is written. It is begun
at night, and finished at dawn. The dark bedrooms, the
guttering candles, the racing stars, are the accompaniment of
composition. The geographical setting, from Africa to Archangel, from the Ganges to Morocco, places the poem in its
wider, cosmic relations and sets its birth on the stage of the
world. But each of the details serves a second purpose. They
are symbols for the act of composition as it takes place in the
poet. The storm at sea is his tumultuous energy, the freezing
Colossus his state when the work begins, the listening Sphinx
his expectant consciousness on the verge of starting, the
swelling lips his joy that expands into creation, the snoring
city of Archangel his indifference to all around him, and the
dawn his final triumphant achievement. But though we may
treat the poem at two levels, literal and symbolical, they are
fused into a single result. The actual circumstances illuminate
the significance of such an event and become symbols of its
character. The composition of *The Prophet* is a display of
creative energy in which the workings of the poet's inspiration
have the power of natural forces and closely resemble them.

Pasternak uses imagery to give to his poems a high degree
of exactness and individuality. For instance, he often writes
about rain, but he distinguishes between its different aspects.
At one time, on a summer evening, it advances through a
clearing as a surveyor walks with his clerk : at another time
a solid sheet of rain is like charcoal in a drawing : in *Sultry
Rain*

> Dust simply soaked the rain in pills
> Like iron in a gentle powder.

The different parallels show variously the gentle approach of
rain, its black torrential downpour, its disappearance in a
parched landscape. When this art is applied to mental and
emotional states, it gives a new significance and clarity to them.
The unmarked passage of time becomes " the hour is scuttling
like a beetle ". A mood of quiet satisfaction appears as

> In fur-coat and arm-chair purrs the soul
> In the same way, always, on and on.

The sense of time lost is conveyed through a new adaptation of an old theme :

> The year's burnt out in paraffin,
> Like a moth drawn into the lamp.

The hour which threatens us with a feeling that we are insane is

> Blacker than monks, more stifling than clergy.

So the methods of the Imagists are given a new and much more impressive purpose. The image, as Pasternak uses it, is as rare and striking as they could demand, but instead of being given pride of place as the only thing that matters, it concentrates the poem's essence in itself and at the same time serves to make clearer the complex unity with which the poem as a whole deals.

The desire to make his imagery exact sometimes leads Pasternak into curious results. We may even feel that, like Apollinaire, he enjoys startling us by unexpected effects as when he says that a frosty night is " like a blind puppy lapping its milk " or that the dew " runs shivering like a hedgehog ". But if we look closely at these, we see how apt they are in that a frosty night has really something primitively greedy about it and that the shivering of the dew is like the shivering of a hedgehog. The danger of this method is that the desire to make the image extremely precise may give it too great an emphasis and upset the balance of tone. For instance when Pasternak says that scorched rye is like " down on erysipelas ", the comparison is visually correct and even emotionally relevant ; for the scorched rye is in its own way a horrifying sight. But the surprise caused is so great that it tends to distort the impression made by the rest of the poem and to detract from its effect. This is a minor fault, and there are not many instances of it, but it shows the difficulty of using images which are both striking and exact.

Pasternak uses this technique to convey his own vision of reality. He is perfectly at home in a real, physical world, but he sees it in a special way and gives his own interpretation of it. He believes that it has its own powers and forces and that it is for him to understand these and bring them into closer touch with himself. Just as the Futurist Khlebnikov believed that the earth is full of unacknowledged or neglected powers which he identified with the old Slavonic gods, so Pasternak, more realistically and more reasonably, sees in nature real, living powers with whom he can enter into some kind of communion and whose influence he can to some extent fathom. For him trees and flowers, skies and winds, clouds and light, are in their own way alive with a special energy and character of their own. Naturally he speaks of them in the language of human actions and relations, but his conception of nature is not simply of something akin to mankind. He sees that it works differently, and he is content to observe it as it is and to show how it affects him and other men. He can mark natural details as attentively as Tennyson, but he does more than this. He passes from his delighted observation of them to interpreting what they mean, what dramatic parts they play, what effects they create, what powers lie behind these common and apparently innocent phenomena. For him the natural world is a busy active place, full of strange forces and energies, which are often almost unintelligible but none the less exciting or disturbing. He feels that he stands in some relation to them, and tries to show what this means. Few poets have approached nature quite with these beliefs. Pasternak delights in it and feels that it is alive and powerful, but does not make a god of it or expect it to reveal oracular messages.

Pasternak is so at home with nature and treats it with so easy and affectionate a familiarity that we do not always notice how special his vision is and may even assume that his treatment of a natural subject is fundamentally conventional. Such is an obvious judgment on such a poem as this :

> Swung down from the fragrant branches
> That drank of such bliss in the night,
> A rain-drop drunk with the thunder
> Slipped from flower to flower in flight.

> From flower to flower dripping
> It slid over two, and stayed
> On both, a great agate hanging,
> And sparkled, and was afraid.

Wind blowing over the meadowsweet
   May flatten and tease that drop :
But the couple will not be parted
   Or from kissing and drinking stop.

They laugh, and they try to sever,
   Stand up and make a new start,
But the drop will not fall from their pistils,—
   Though you cut them, they will not part.

This is not a poem of great importance, but it shows Pasternak's observation and his treatment of flowers as if they were human beings. A tiny episode in his garden so excites his attention that he reads into it far more than any ordinary observer would. This is his way of looking at natural things. He treats the flowers like this because he feels that in some sense they are alive and that the only way to speak about them is in the language of human and personal relations into which he can enter at least as an observer. Such a poem rises from his individual insight and special understanding of natural things, and is much more than a piece of fanciful embroidery. Pasternak's imaginative curiosity is aroused by the behaviour of the flowers, and he records its effect on him.

    This familiarity with nature passes into a deeper and more significant poetry. How much it can mean to Pasternak may be seen from *Sparrow Hills*. Reduced to its lowest terms this is a variation on the old theme of *carpe diem* : since no pleasure lasts for long, let us enjoy what we can, and especially let us enjoy our youth. This is perhaps the fundamental theme, but the variations are what matter and give a unique quality to the poem. Pasternak tells of a real situation — the poem is in a section called " songs to save her from boredom " — and a real landscape. But in this actual scene he shows how close he is to nature and what it means to him : he starts with a hint of active love and shows how into this doubts break with their disturbing presage that this happiness will not last for ever. Even the pleasures of love may become monotonous, and he looks for an escape which shall be more satisfying and more exciting :

Kisses on the breast, like water from a pitcher !
Not always, not ceaseless spurts the summer's well.
Nor shall we raise up the hurdy-gurdy's clamour
Each night from the dust with feet that stamp and trail.

I have heard of age — those hideous forebodings !
When no wave will lift its hands up to the stars.
If they speak, you doubt it.   No face in the meadows,
No heart in the pools, no god among the firs.

Rouse your soul to frenzy.   Foaming all the day through.
It's the world's midday.   Have you no eyes for it ?
Look how in the heights thoughts seethe into white bubbles
Of fir-cones, woodpeckers, clouds, pine-needles, heat.

Here the rails are ended of the city tram-cars.
Further, pines must do.   Further, trams cannot pass.
Further, it is Sunday.   Plucking down the branches,
Skipping through the clearings, slipping on the grass.

Sifting midday light and Whitsunday and walking
Woods would have us think the world is always so ;
They're so planned with thickets, so inspired with spaces,
Spilling from the clouds on us, like chintz, below.

This is Pasternak's *L'Invitation au Voyage*, but he invites his beloved not to an imaginary paradise but to a real wood in a real summer, and the renewal of life which he seeks is to come not from intellectual or artistic pleasures but from the presence of nature.   The almost pantheistic language of the second verse, with its fear that the years may turn the poet's beliefs into illusions, prepares the way to the enhancement of the senses which is to be found in the woods, to the frenzy and the foaming which he believes to be at his command.   In such an expedition the driving force is the belief that nature provides an invigorating relaxation, not supernatural peace but an enlargement of faculties in young lovers.

In nature, as Pasternak sees it, human beings are a constituent part.   It interpenetrates their being and controls them in such a way that they are in some sense its creatures, swayed by the moods and subject to the influences of their surroundings.   This interrelation raises many questions, and Pasternak sometimes forces us to look in quite a new way at man in his natural setting. For instance in *In the Wood* the scene is again a summer day in a wood, where a couple are asleep while the dusk gradually advances. What holds the poem together is the idea that, as they sleep, nature constructs a kind of natural clock which tells the hours, though the couple are insensible to the passage of time. We might almost say that the fundamental theme of the poem is that time flies for lovers while they do not notice it ; but this flight is vividly expressed through the actual place where the lovers sleep. They, their sleep, and their surroundings are a single unity which Pasternak depicts :

> A lilac heat was heavy on the meadow ;
> High in the wood cathedral's darkness swelled.
> What in the world was left still for their kisses ?
> It was all theirs, soft wax in fingers held.
>
> Such is the dream : — you do not sleep, but only
> Dream that you thirst for sleep, that someone lies
> Asleep, and through his dream beneath his eyelids
> Two black suns sear the lashes of his eyes.
>
> Rays flowed, and with the ebbing flowed the beetles ;
> Upon his cheeks the dragon-flies' gloss stirs.
> The wood was full of careful scintillations,
> As under pincers at the clock-maker's.
>
> It seemed he slumbered to the tick of figures,
> While in harsh amber high above they set
> Their nicely tested clocks up in the ether
> And regulate and shift them to the heat.
>
> They shift them round about, and shake the needles,
> Scatter shadow, and swing and bore a place
> For darkness like a mast erected upward
> In day's decline upon its blue clock-face.
>
> It seems that ancient happiness flits over ;
> It seems, sleep's setting holds the woodland close.
> Those who are happy do not watch clocks ticking,
> But sleep, it seems, is all this couple does.

The poem begins with a suggestion of love satisfied. The lovers rest in a state bordering on sleep, in which the man is vaguely conscious of the woman at his side. Then gradually nature gets to work and builds in the sky its own kind of clock, and this sign of passing time is not marked by the couple who are now asleep. To this extent the poem is concerned with the state that follows the consummation of love, but just as other poets set love against the menace of fleeting time, so Pasternak makes the passing of the hours an element in the whole situation. Nature herself marks the time, though the human beings do not notice what they are losing.

Nature, which displays so many different moods to human beings, needs a different symbol or myth for each of them, and Pasternak, who has no fixed mythology, creates a fresh myth for each new manifestation of natural powers. Nature is alive with presences whose character cannot be fully known but whose actions are observed with keen curiosity. Spirits are abroad, but spirits of no common sort and with few familiar traits. They can be mischievous and arouse annoyance and even dismay. They have some of the malice of Shakespeare's fairies, but they move in a familiar world and are quite recognisable once our attention is drawn to them. Everyone, for instance, knows the disturbed and disturbing air that comes after the end of winter, and nowhere is the change of season more gusty and more trying to the temper than in the Russian thaw. At such a time uneasy spirits seem to walk abroad, and Pasternak tells of one:

> The air is whipped by the frequent rain-drops;
> The ice is mangy and grey. Ahead
> You look for the skyline to awaken
> And start; you wait for the drone to spread.
>
> As always, with overcoat unbuttoned,
> With muffler about his chest undone,
> He pursues before him the unsleeping
> Silly birds and chases them on.
>
> Now he comes to see you, and, dishevelled,
> The dripping candles he tried to snuff,
> Yawns, and remembers that now's the moment
> To take the hyacinths' night-caps off.

Out of his senses, ruffling his hair-mop,
Dark in his thought's confusion, he
Leaves you quite dumfounded with a wicked
Stupid tale that he tells of me.

The chief character is not named ; he is simply " he " and
is known from what he does. He rises out of the uneasy
atmosphere, and his character and actions embody its untidy,
restless, teasing spirit. He starts trouble not only by frightening the birds and making the candles flicker but in human
beings. The poet feels the uneasiness spread to his companion and have the effect of a story told against himself.
The season has in it a disturbing and grating presence, a kind
of Puck, but a Puck who rises out of the time of year and is
known only from his disorderly and malicious pranks.

This sense of natural powers at work in the world may
even take on an almost tragic intensity. The Russian autumn
has been sung by many poets, and Tyutchev more than once
told of its melancholy character. In *Spasskoye* Pasternak does
something of the same kind, but with a more poignant and
more personal note. He takes the moment when the summer
is over and autumn comes with falling leaves, the felling of
trees, rising mists and anticipations of winter. What strikes
him is the sense of decay and death, of lessened vitality and
of painful separation. His imagery contributes greatly to the
emotional effect ; for each image adds something to the
interpretation of the situation and suggests sickness and death.
But behind the imagery and the description there is something
which only Pasternak can convey, a situation in which man is
so entangled in his natural surroundings that they dictate his
moods and make him seem part of themselves :

Unforgettable September is strewn about Spasskoye.
Is to-day not the time to leave the cottage here ?
Beyond the fence Echo has shouted with the herdsman
And in the woods has made the axe's stroke ring clear.

Last night outside the park the chilling marshes shivered.
The moment the sun rose it disappeared again.
The hare-bells will not drink of the rheumatic dew-drops,
On birches dropsy swells a dirty lilac stain.

The wood is melancholy. What it wants is quiet
Under the snows in bear-dens' unawaking sleep ;
And there among the boles inside the blackened fences
Jaws of the columned park, like a long death-list, gape.

The birchwood has not ceased to blot and lose its colour,
To thin its watery shadows and grow sparse and dim.
He is still mumbling, — you're fifteen years old again now,
And now again, my child, what shall we do with them ?

So many of them now that you should give up playing,
They're like birds in bushes, mushrooms along hedges.
Now with them we've begun to curtain our horizon
And with their mist to hide another's distances.

On his death-night the typhus-stricken clown hears tumult,
The gods' Homeric laughter from the gallery.
Now from the road, in Spasskoye, on the timbered cottage
Looks in hallucination the same agony.

The poem is built on a clear pattern. The first three verses
set out the scene in its melancholy and decay. The actors are
the natural features of the landscape — the echo, the marshes,
the harebells, the trees, all of which are ailing and suffering.
This sense of doom reaches its climax in the comparison of
the trees in the park to an obituary column in a newspaper.
In the fourth verse the purpose of this detailed setting emerges
mysteriously and allusively. The undescribed " he " is surely
one of Pasternak's natural powers, the genius of the place at
this season who haunts and dominates the wooded park. It
makes the poet feel as if he were again fifteen years old and
again suffering from some childish melancholy and uncertainty
with the sense that comes at such an age that life has lost its
range and contracted its horizon. This feeling dominates the
present moment and gives to the cottage and its surroundings
a tragic air, as if it were being mocked by inhuman powers,
like the people in the gallery of a theatre, in the hour of its
death. The tense poignancy of the close is enhanced by the
suggestion that the poet has been thrown back into his childhood and feels some old misery, awakened by the chance air
of the season. All this is forced on him by natural powers at

work in Spasskoye. He is their victim, and in their dealings with him they show the callous indifference which the ancient gods showed to men. His keen ears and eyes miss nothing in the scene, and everything which Pasternak gets from them starts something else in his mind, some parallel or illustration or symbol, which drives home with compelling precision his full response to the situation. Nature is the first source of his poetry and calls out his finest powers.

Pasternak's view of nature is central to his work, and his poetry illustrates his belief that a creative force is at work in everything and that elements in the natural scene are as powerful as those in man and closely connected with them. His special interest is in his contact or conflict with such powers. He sees himself and other men as moved by strange energies and influences which are not fully intelligible but can be grasped only through a special insight and represented only through myth or symbol. Even when he writes specifically about himself and his own feelings, his outlook is the same. He still treats of strange, undefined forces which sweep into or rush over him and are outside his control and full comprehension. This outlook, which rises from his acute sensibility, gives a special character to his poems of love. For him love breaks the ordinary rules of life and creates its own world. In *From Superstition* Pasternak shows how love transforms his circumstances and gives a new meaning to everything. For him " a box with a red orange in it " is all the lodging that he now needs : the dappled wall-paper becomes an oak-tree : the entry to this setting is gained by song : when he kisses his beloved, he tastes violets : her dress is like a snowdrop which chirrups a greeting to April. The casual encounter takes on all the charm of the country in spring, and it is not surprising that the poet feels as if his beloved has taken his life down from the shelf and blown the dust off it. Love imposes its laws on reality and makes the lover enjoy a state which is more real than the reality around him. A similar capacity to transform is more elaborately and more forcibly portrayed in *Do not touch* where what looks like a pretty trope takes command of the poem and gives to it an unusual power :

" Don't touch. Fresh paint," the notice said.
  Soul no attention paid,
And memory's in smears that cheeks,
  Legs, hands, lips, eyes have made.

More than for all good luck or bad
  I loved you just because
All in this white and yellow world
  Through you still whiter was ;

And my own gloom, my friend, I swear,
  Will whiter be somehow
Than fever, lampshade, or the white
  Bandage upon a brow.

Here the transforming power of love is displayed in the image of the white light which comes from the beloved and changes the poet's world. And this power, which arises from what might seem to be an unhealthy or abnormal condition, exerts itself especially on the poet's melancholy until it makes even that luminous.

If love is like this, it is a little disturbing. Such an incalculable power is not to be welcomed lightly. It comes from unplumbed depths of nature and may well cause havoc. That is why Pasternak sometimes treats of the disintegrating effects of love and shows how afraid he is of them. In one poem he draws a strong contrast between the ordinary view of love and his own. While other people treat weddings as occasions to get drunk and to shut " life, that is like a pearly dream by Watteau, into a snuff-box ", he finds that it releases primaeval energies in him :

  Chaos again crawls out upon the world
  As in the ages when the fossils lived.

Ordinary people are jealous of him and do not like it when he raises a girl from the earth " like a bacchante from an amphora ". But against this critical opposition his own powers are all the more enhanced. The Andes melt in his kisses : it is like dawn on the steppe where stars fall in dust. The result is that in commonplace surroundings, amid the flat ritual of marriage, a strange, chaotic power is released.

Pasternak sees love as brutal, irrational, and uncontrollable ; it breaks into life and turns everything upside down. It is therefore appropriate that his most effective love-poetry should be the series called *Rupture* which treats love as a morbid condition in which the mind is infected with a kind of disease and the lovers are haunted by a sense of shame and guilt :

> O grief, infected with lies in its roots,
> O sorrow, leprous sorrow !

For a moment Pasternak may accept love's illusions and imagine that he and his beloved can escape, like Actaeon and Atalanta, into the woods, but the mood does not last, and reality soon asserts itself again. At the end the separation comes, quietly, but not without leaving a wound :

> I do not hold you. Spread your charms again.
> Go to others. *Werther* is written now.
> Odours of death into our day-time blow ;
> An open window is an open vein.

Pasternak accepts love and its results because it is a natural process, but he finds in it much that is disturbing and distressing.

Most of this highly personal and lyrical poetry was written by Pasternak at a time when his country was in great turmoil and confusion. *My Sister Life* was composed for the most part in the summer of 1917 between the February Revolution of Kerensky and the October Revolution of Lenin. *Themes and Variations* was written during the no less crowded and eventful period between the triumph of Bolshevism and the end of the Civil War. In these years, when the poetry of Mayakovsky and Khlebnikov was inspired by popular emotions and largely directed to revolutionary ends, Pasternak might seem to have kept himself detached and independent outside the battle. We might think that this time of violent changes made little impression on him : so faithful is he to his personal vision and to such themes as his immediate circumstances suggest to him. But this is to misunderstand him. Pasternak was neither unpolitical nor reactionary. As a boy of fifteen he had shared the revolutionary fervour of 1905.

The Futurists were his friends, whose political aims and ambitions he shared. For him, as for them, the Revolution was a prodigious manifestation of natural forces which had hitherto lain dormant in Russia, and he could hardly fail to see that it answered to his own dynamic conception of life. In his own way his poetry contributes to the revolutionary period and owes much of its inspiration to the spirit of the time. But it is very much in his own way. Pasternak's manner of writing, sensitive, personal and lyrical, is quite different from the broken epics of Khlebnikov or the enthusiastic rhetoric of Mayakovsky. His genius forces him to assimilate his political experiences until they are part of himself and to present them precisely as he feels them. He understood the Revolution through his insight into the powers which stir in nature and in man, and it was this side of it that challenged his creative energies. It belonged to the same order of things as his other subjects, whether nature or love, and he wrote of it in the same way, as of something that touched him deeply in the roots of his being and was yet another sign of strange forces at work in the world.

The result is that Pasternak assimilates his political experiences so closely to his central outlook that he seems for the moment to detract from their importance and to reduce them to mere natural events. Yet this is precisely the importance that he finds in them. They are indeed natural events and therefore full of majesty and mystery. They are a special manifestation of the strange powers that can be observed in physical nature. Pasternak believes that, like other human actions, they rise naturally from the landscape and stand in some close relation to it. Even the Revolution is a natural event in the sense that it rises from the Russian soil no less than from the Russian soul. A hint of this outlook, and an example of how Pasternak treats it, can be seen from *Summer*, written in 1917, in the lull before the storm :

> Athirst for insects, butterflies,
> And stains we long had waited,
> And round us both were memories
> Of heat, mint, honey plaited.

No clocks chimed, but the flail rang clear
From dawn to dusk and planted
Its dreams of stings into the air ;
The weather was enchanted.

Strolled sunset to its heart's content,
Then yielded to cicadas
And stars and trees its government
Of gardens and of larders.

The moon in absence, out of sight,
Not shade but baulks was throwing,
And softly, softly the shy night
From cloud to cloud was flowing.

From dream more than from roof, and more
Forgetful than faint-hearted,
Soft rain was shuffling at the door
And smell of wine-corks spurted.

So smelt the dust. So smelt the grass.
And if we chanced to heed them,
Smell from the gentry's teaching was
Of brotherhood and freedom.

The Councils met in villages ;
Weren't you with those that held them ?
Bright with wood-sorrel hung the days,
And smell of wine-corks filled them.

The first five verses, written in Pasternak's most delicate and sensitive manner, are a preliminary and a preparation for a hint of political events. The penultimate verse touches on the vague talk of the time and suggests that even the landed classes were touched by its ideals, and the last verse explicitly names *zemvstva*, the village-councils which voiced the ambitions and hopes of the common people. For Pasternak these political happenings, so big with promise for the immediate future, are part of the summer scene, of the harmony and beauty that pervade the air. But they are also its climax and its culmination. The brotherhood of men rises from the natural setting and shows its affinity to it.

Pasternak is fully aware of the human side of the Revolution and sees that, though it holds out great promises, it also brings many anxieties and troubles. A hint of what he himself suffered in the first months after the Revolution and what solution he found may be seen in *January 1918* where he greets with relief the coming of a new year with its promise of better times :

> That year ! How often " Out you fall ! "
> The old year's whisper at my window said.
> The new year makes an end of all
> And brings a Dickens Christmas tale instead.
>
> He murmurs ; " Shake yourself. Forget."
> Mercury rises with the sun outside,
> Just as the old year strychnine set
> And fell down in the glass from cyanide.
>
> For by his hand, and by his dawn,
> And by his hair that indolently stirs,
> Outside the window peace is drawn
> From birds and roofs, as from philosophers.
>
> Now here he comes, lies in the light
> That shines from panels and from snow out there.
> He's boisterous and impolite,
> Shouts, calls for drink ; it is too much to bear.
>
> He's off his head. With him he brings
> The hubbub of the yard — what can we do ?
> In all the world no sufferings
> Are such that they will not be cured by snow.

Here, as so often with Pasternak, the actual situation provides the symbols for something more abstract. After the suicidal terrors and deathly chill of the old year, the new year promises light and comfort and, above all, peace. Peace comes alike from nature and from men, both of whom are in their separate ways philosophers and know what it means. None the less the new year is not quite what is expected. It is noisy and vulgar and embarrassing. After the agonies and the sacrifices, after the bold Utopian hopes, reality gives something of a shock. But Pasternak accepts it with philosophic wisdom and cheerfulness and humour. The last two lines proclaim his trust in the future. The snow stands for the purifying forces which are abroad and will in the end produce a cure for present discontents. This poem shows the quality of Pasternak's detachment. He sees the events from his own point of view and is not afraid to say what he feels, but at the same time he appreciates their importance and foretells the good things that lie ahead.

The optimistic note on which this poem ends shows Pasternak's feeling towards his time. True to his trust that such an eruption of natural forces must in the end be right and prevail, he finds in them a source of vitality and energy. What matters for him is this release of nature's powers which bring man closer to itself. Pasternak is not a partisan of particular causes but a poet of the whole movement for liberation and a new life. That is why he is not too hard on his opponents. He feels that they have lost the battle and that they do not deserve too much attention. So he dismisses them ironically or contemptuously. He knows that there is a vast difference between his own exultant confidence and the straitened outlook of his adversaries, and that he has something which they cannot hope to have. What this means can be seen from *May it be*, written in 1919 :

> Dawn shakes the candle, shoots a flame
> To light the wren, and does not miss.
> I search my memories and proclaim
> " May life be always fresh as this ! "
>
> Like a shot dawn rang through the night.
> Bang bang it went. In swooning flight
> The wads of bullets flame and hiss.
> May life be always fresh as this.
>
> The breeze is at the door again.
> At night he shivered, wanted us.
> He froze when daybreak brought up rain.
> May life be always fresh as this.
>
> He is astonishingly queer.
> Why rudely past the gate-man press ?
> Of course he saw " No thoroughfare ".
> May life be always as fresh as this.

> Still with a handkerchief to shake,
> While mistress still, chase all about,
> While yet our darkness does not break,
> While yet the flames have not gone out.

The dawn symbolises the coming of the new order, and it breaks like a rifle-shot. The breeze shows that new movements are active, though their meaning is not fully understood and they do not conform to old proprieties and prohibitions. The poet welcomes the situation and knows that all will be well. In the last verse, the woman whom he addresses stands for the old ruling class which may for the moment continue its sentimental or authoritarian tasks but will before long have to change its ways. The poem is written in gaiety and confidence. What others may find frightening, Pasternak finds inspiring and exciting.

Pasternak's political poetry in the first years of the Revolution is nearly all composed in this special way. He tells how events strike him personally and what part they take in his scheme of things. But the Revolution called for more than this, and it was almost impossible for Pasternak to be deaf to it. Just as in these years Khlebnikov wrote heroic poems about Russian characters who fought for liberty, from the old rebel Stepan Razin to a nameless seamstress of 1917, so others felt the need to display the events of their time with a full sense of their grandeur. Among them Nikolai Tikhonov turned his experience in the Red Army into powerful poems in which he depicted nature as the ally of his cause. In tune with his time he did not shrink from portraying the harder and more brutal side of such a life, though he justified it by the results which it brought. An example will show his manner with its mixture of animistic and realistic themes :

> A fire, a hawser, bullets and an axe
> Like flunkeys greeted us and followed after.
> In every drop a deluge slept,
> Through little stones hills sprang into existence,
> And in the briar trampled underfoot
> Loud was the sound of forests with black arms.
>
> With us untruth partook of food and drink,
> Bells rang their changes in the usual manner,

Coins lost their weight and lost their ringing sound,
And children were not startled by dead bodies.
And in that time we were the first to learn
To use words bitter, beautiful and cruel.

This is revolutionary heroism seen from the inside : it bears
no relation to Pasternak's meditative and essentially detached
poems of the same time. But he wrote something in the same
spirit and showed how well he understood this new, creative,
realistic love of adventure :

We're few, perhaps not more than three,
Flaming, infernal, from the Don,
Beneath a sky racing and gray
Of rain, clouds, soldiers bent upon
Soviets, verses and long talk
Of transport and the artist's work.

Once we were men ; we're epochs now.
Knocked, whirling in a caravan,
Like tundra 'neath the tender's sough,
While pistons, sleepers rattle on.
We'll join our flights, break through, make touch,
Spun round in ravens' eddying rush.

And on ! Later you'll understand.
So at dawn, striking on piled straw,
Instantly hurling all around,
The wind becomes eternal where
Trees in a meeting's stormy din
Talk as a ruined house falls in.

Pasternak's manner is perfectly adapted to this heroic subject.
His revolutionary soldiers are almost natural forces, like
ravens or the wind, and these are no mere similes. Pasternak
really sees his men like this. It shows how close man is to
nature in the Revolution. Even the concise, packed sentences
help to secure a special impression of lives rich in enterprise
and incident. In the short space of three verses Pasternak
reflects something like an epic spirit.

In nature, in love, in stirring political events Pasternak
found the subjects of his mature poetry. In all of them was
something primaeval and forceful which appealed strongly to
him and echoed something in himself. This something was

the spirit in which he composed poetry. He felt himself at home with such subjects because in them he saw powers at work which were closely related to his own powers when the spell of composition was on him. And just as these subjects excite his curiosity and vivid interest, so his own creative spirit is a burning question for him. He more than once writes about it and seems to have more than one view of it. Its aspects strike him differently at different times. He is so modest and truthful that we cannot expect him to produce a grandiose metaphysic of art or even to reveal his whole feelings about it. But his career shows how much it means to him and how he puts it first even when he feels a strong call to serve other ends. Sometimes when he speaks about poetry he seems to assume an ironical or paradoxical air as if he were on the defensive and unwilling to put forward his whole case. But this is the reflection of an extreme honesty which refuses to speak dogmatically about something which means a great deal to him but cannot really be grasped or explained. That is why in *Definition of Poetry* his definition is a series of images which convey many qualities of poetry but do not actually define it :

> It's a whistle's precipitous rise,
> It is icicles broken and ringing,
> It is night when the frost on leaves lies,
> It's a duel of nightingales singing.

Nor is he prepared to make vast claims for the mood in which the poet composes. There is nothing of Blok's *Artist* in what Pasternak says of his work, no timeless ecstasy or vision of Paradise. In one poem he suggests that the images of his poetry come to him by an almost automatic process :

> Images fly aslant in torrents,
> Gather in rhythm from hook and wall
> And road that has blown out the candle.
> I do not stop their measured fall.

He even denies that composition gives him any pleasure and says in *Poetry* :

> You're summer with a third-class ticket,
> A suburb and not a refrain.

It is as stifling as May or a crowded quarter of the town or a fort over which clouds pass. Even the final consummation is not claimed to be at all impressive or wonderful :

> Poetry, when an empty truism,
> Like a zinc bucket, stands below
> The tap, is certain to be spouting.
> The copy-book is open. Flow !

This is Pasternak's modest way of not claiming too much for his art. It is, it seems, a perfectly natural process and he must not pretend that it is more.

Yet it is a natural process and all that this means to Pasternak. Whatever difficulty he may find in explaining his art to others or in justifying its place in society, he is quite confident and explicit about what it means to himself. In one poem he admits that a poet is a peculiar kind of being, but insists that he follows a special destiny and wins special rewards. He looks back on childhood and tells how from the beginning he has known the magical power of words and found his own most vivid experiences through them :

> So they begin. With two years gone
> From nurse to countless tunes they scuttle.
> They chirp and whistle. Then comes on
> The third year, and they start to prattle.
>
> So they begin to see and know.
> In din of started turbines roaring,
> Mother seems not their mother now,
> And you not you, and home is foreign.
>
> What meaning has the menacing
> Beauty beneath the lilac seated,
> If to steal children's not the thing ?
> So first they fear that they are cheated.
>
> So ripen fears. Can he endure
> A star to beat him in successes,
> When he's a Faust, a sorcerer ?
> So first his gipsy life progresses.
>
> So from the fence where home should lie
> In flight above are found to hover
> Seas unexpected as a sigh.
> So first iambics they discover.

So summer nights fall down and pray
" Thy will be done " where oats are sprouting,
And menace with your eyes the day.
So with the sun they start disputing.

So verses start them on their way.

This is Pasternak's apology. It tells how marvellous discoveries reward him for feeling that he is odd and unlike other men. His course follows an inevitable rhythm from the start, and though his early shocks are more violent than those of other men, his compensations are correspondingly great. He has his wonderful dreams, his moments of rapture and exaltation, his conviction that he is at one with nature and shares her strength. By such means Pasternak does more than defend himself against utilitarian or mechanistic notions of poetry : he shows that so far from being an artificial adjunct of society he is a magician who releases nature's powers through his art.

Pasternak responds to the special character of his calling by a special sense of the responsibilities which it puts upon him. He believes, above all, that everything that he writes must be a work of art, complete and independent with its own life, the final vehicle by which experience is selected and organised and transformed into a permanent shape. He also believes that no work of art has any value unless it is true in a rigorous and exacting sense, true not merely to fact but to experience, to all that the poet sees in it and feels about it. This double ideal is perhaps responsible for his complexities and roughnesses, but it is no less responsible for his final success and for his special importance. In a revolutionary age Pasternak has seen beyond the disturbed surface of things to the powers behind it and found there an explanation of what really matters in the world. Through his unerring sense of poetry he has reached to wide issues and shown that the creative calling, with its efforts and its frustrations and its unanticipated triumphs, is, after all, something profoundly natural and closely related to the sources of life.

VI

T. S. ELIOT,
THE WASTE LAND

In 1922 an American living in England, Thomas Stearns
Eliot, then in his thirty-fourth year, published *The Waste
Land*. Eliot was already known to the discerning few by two
slim volumes of verse in which the manner of Jules Laforgue,
tempered by an Elizabethan eloquence, was artfully adapted
to the English language. But *The Waste Land* found a resounding and popular success. It was quoted far and wide :
the younger generation saw in it a mirror of its own aspira-
tions : poets imitated its technique and its temper. To-day
it still holds its place, and in retrospect its publication is seen
to be a landmark in modern English poetry. For with it the
new manner won a place in the hearts of those who love poetry,
and became almost respectable. The First World War had
evoked some good poetry in England, and some of it was
written with a regard for new manners, but it seldom seemed
to speak for more than an initiated few. Eliot made the new
manner acceptable, because in his hands it seemed to be the
right, the only style for the confused issues of the age and for
the disillusion which followed the armistice of 1918. Young
poets who were tired of the trim elegances of the Georgian
poets were satisfied by Eliot. He was an apostle, a pioneer,
a guide to new realms of the spirit. Though Eliot wrote good
poetry before *The Waste Land*, and has written equally good
poetry of a different kind since, this is perhaps his most
characteristic book, and certainly the most influential volume
of verse published in England in the nineteen-twenties. In it
the new manner was presented by a man who spared no pains
to make every word tell, and who subjected everything that
he said to a searching and sensitive criticism.

The Waste Land made a twofold appeal to the men and
women of 1922, in its language and in its matter. Whatever
Eliot's critics might say of him, they had to admit that his

language had a notable purity and brilliance, that he had got rid of the outworn vocabulary of the later Victorians and the Georgians and found a new manner of speech which was at once vivid and contemporary. In his own way he was a remarkable revolutionary in language. Trained on the great masters to be extremely attentive to the value of words and laboriously critical in his selection of them, he created a style which is entirely his own and never fails to be significant and lively. Like all fresh poetical styles, it experiments with sounds, and Eliot, alive to the dangers which English suffers from its deadened vowels and its slurred consonants, makes a special choice of words whose sound is clear and pure. When, for instance, he writes

> A rat crept slowly through the vegetation
> Dragging its slimy belly on the bank,

the dentals of the first line and the labials of the second convey with vivid precision the sinister, silent passage of the rat. We can imagine how the Greek critic, Dionysius of Halicarnassus, would have appreciated the cunning effects of sound in these lines; for he saw that much of the beauty of poetry depends on the juxtaposition of dentals and labials and the contrasts of rough and smooth which it gives. So too Eliot knows the worth of varied and uncorrupted vowels. When he writes

> Supine on the floor of a narrow canoe,

we can almost say what Tennyson said of Milton's

> In th' ascending scale
> Of Heav'n the stars that usher evening rose,

that " this last line is lovely because it is full of vowels, which are all different ". Eliot's first appeal was through his words. He used them as a master uses them, with a full sense of their sound and of its value for a poetical effect.

In the second place, Eliot appealed to the spirit of the time by writing a poetry of frustration and disorder. It is possible to interpret *The Waste Land* in different ways and to apply quotations from it to many kinds of situation. But the spirit which inspires it, the dominating thought which holds it together, the tone and temper of its poetry, are the product of a spirit which is profoundly dissatisfied with existing conditions and, in judging them by high standards, finds them pathetically wanting. Before his poem Eliot prefixes a quotation from Petronius which shows what we are to expect : " For I myself saw with my own eyes the Sibyl hanging in a cage at Cumae, and when the boys said to her : ' Sibyl, what do you want ? ', she used to answer : ' I want to die '." After the exacting claims and the vaulting hopes of the First World War disillusion and scepticism set in. The younger generation, feeling that they had been tricked by the slogans of their elders, developed so sharp a critical sense that they liked to show how far practice fell short of principle and on what humbug and hypocrisy modern civilisation is based. The crusading spirit of the Russian Revolution hardly touched Western Europe, where the belief that old-fashioned standards were no longer adequate produced a sceptical and ironical art. Eliot, in some ways so unlike his contemporaries, was at one with them in his conviction that something was severely wrong with civilisation and that life had lost its old dignity and savour. While writers like D. H. Lawrence advocated an artificial return to primitive virility and brutality as a cure for modern discontents, Eliot, who felt the need quite as strongly, had as yet no cure to offer. He was content to brood over the barrenness of the age and to awake a response in many of those around him. Historically *The Waste Land* reflects the reaction and defeat which followed the high hopes raised by the idealism of Woodrow Wilson. It was clear all too soon that the new world was not likely to be an improvement on the old, and that the war had in many lands and sections of society created irreparable devastation.

The form which Eliot chose for *The Waste Land* was not that of his first verses. He abandoned Laforgue for Ezra Pound, to whom the poem is dedicated with the suggestive words " il miglior fabbro ", which Dante makes Guido Guinizelli use of Arnaut Daniel. For Dante, Arnaut is the great poet of love and romance, and though Eliot can hardly mean this of Pound, he clearly feels for him some of the respect which Dante felt for the obscure and difficult Arnaut. Arnaut was pre-eminently the poet of *trobar clus*, of that allusive, hermetic poetry which was practised in Provence and which combined great technical dexterity with a refusal to write in the sweet, lyrical manner of such poets as Giraut de Borneil, whom Dante expressly puts below Arnaut. In his dedication Eliot shows his affection for the new, harsh, cryptic manner which he finds in Pound, as Dante found it in Arnaut. In the history of modern English and American poetry Pound holds a strange place. He has won many distinguished admirers. Yeats, Edith Sitwell and Eliot alike have held him in high regard and considered him to be one of the most influential spirits of the time. But the common reader seems unable to share this enthusiasm. There is undeniably something repellent in Pound. His claims to vast learning are not justified by his own displays of it ; the personality revealed in his poetry is uncongenial ; the movement of his verses is often cacophonous ; his work has a distasteful air of pretentious smartness, of being altogether too " knowing " ; his political opinions are brutal and angry, and have earned him the unenviable name of traitor. But whatever the merits of Pound's work may be, there is no doubt of his influence. He was one of the first poets writing in English to attempt a poetry in which the feelings and thoughts of urban, cultivated man are expressed in a modern idiom. To justify his practice he has called in examples and precedents from the past, and the emphasis which he gives to Provençal and Chinese poetry shows how far he thinks Victorian ideals have led literature astray and what new directions it can find by purifying its outlook of the standards of the last century. In particular, Pound invented a kind of poetry which on the one hand sought to convey the consciousness of modern man and on the other hand to introduce echoes from the past, often by way of quotations, and so to stress the contrast with the dismal present. This appealed to Eliot, whose first two volumes turn largely on the contrast which he finds between literature and life, between the masterpieces which he has read and the actual conditions which prevail in society. When in *The Waste Land* Eliot set out to write a poem on the impotence and failure of the modern world, he decided that Pound's method was what he needed.

The Waste Land is a difficult poem. For its full understanding it requires knowledge which is not always to be found in the author's professorial notes ; it treats punctuation with an almost Futurist nonchalance ; its subject and main thread are not easy to define ; it uses new and heterogeneous symbols, and it is entirely symbolical. From Pound Eliot has taken the use of quotations from other writers, and there are allusions to, and adaptations of, thirty-five different writers, and passages in six foreign languages, including Sanskrit. From Pound too comes the abrupt method of progression, in which explanatory aids are lacking and what matters is the emotional sequence, the impact which the symbols make on us as they appear. If we wish to detect the intellectual structure behind this, we must make a considerable effort, and there is a chance that our conclusions will be wrong. For it is primarily the emotional sequence that matters. The successive scenes and images, which melt into each other and seem to have no logical connection, dictate what we are to feel and carry us from one stage to the next. If we follow them and respond to them, we find the main experience that the poem has to give. *The Waste Land* does in its own way what Valéry's *La Jeune Parque* does in its, though Eliot's art is even more allusive and evokes more varied responses. Its symbols create states of mind and feeling which are not and cannot be clear, and which would lose their essential character if they were presented more definitely. Even the author's notes may at first be neglected. Many readers have responded to *The Waste Land* without having followed Eliot's advice to read Jessie Weston's *From Ritual to Romance* and without knowing what a Tarot pack of cards is. Such is Eliot's power that his images, gathered from so many sources, have an almost independent existence and make an immediate appeal to many who do not care about their origins or original significance.

None the less, if we extract its framework from *The Waste Land*, we are well rewarded. For an intellectual analysis of it adds to our appreciation of its poetry by giving a background to a purely emotional enjoyment, and the poem is seen to be constructed not dithyrambically in response to a haphazard series of moods but with a real design. This framework comes largely from anthropology. The central idea is that of a waste land, such as we find in legends of the Grail. Its prosperity and fruitfulness are inseparably connected with the physical powers of its king, and it suffers from drought because he is impotent. This condition can be remedied only by some magically appropriate act, usually performed by some other person, who through sexual intercourse breaks the doom of sterility. In the ritual which underlies these legends it seems that the king, commonly called the Fisher King, dies and is either restored to life like the year-gods Adonis and Osiris, or is succeeded by someone who can do what he himself cannot. Eliot has absorbed some elements of this ritual and finds in them his chief symbols. His poem is of a parched land which needs refreshment and a new life. Its sterility is, of course, not physical but spiritual, and its sense of impotence is a dire malady of the soul. This land is much more than post-war Europe or the poet drooping among the Philistines. It is something desiccated which needs refreshment, and it can hardly be defined more closely. Of course it can be related to countries and individuals, but it has no such limited reference. The apparent disarray of the poem and the very varied figures who flit across it are arranged round a central conception and best understood through it. The poem is not Futurist nor, in any derogatory sense, Impressionist. Hard brain-work has gone to its making, and if we wish to explain it intellectually, we are justified in doing so, and well rewarded.

The thirst of the waste land is presented through different settings and different characters. Scene fades into scene and character into character, because ultimately there is only one scene and not more than three characters. The setting and its persons exist in some mental and imaginative condition which does not belong to ordinary space or time and is identifiable only through its essential nature. Thus the first scene comes from Ezekiel, but it soon turns into a huge modern city There is a fundamental connection between

> A heap of broken images, where the sun beats,
> And the dead tree gives no shelter, the cricket no relief,
> And the dry stone no sound of water,

and

> Unreal city
> Under the brown fog of a winter dawn.

This passes by abrupt changes into a woman's boudoir, where the wind whistles under the door, the deserted, autumnal Thames, the canal behind the gas-house, a typist's squalid lodging, and then reverts to its first form, when the waterless land receives great prominence, and themes from the beginning are repeated and amplified :

> Here is no water but only rock,
> Rock and no water and the sandy road,
> The road winding above among the mountains
> Which are mountains of rock without water.

These different scenes have more than a similarity : they have an identity. They are all aspects of the same barrenness and frustration, and it is with this that the poem is primarily concerned. In different moods the poet displays this fundamental situation, sometimes with irony, sometimes with dramatic excitement, sometimes with tragic consternation and hysterical dismay. This variety of moods adds greatly to the poem's relevance and truth. For most men when faced with a complex, recurring phenomenon like this will see it differently at different times, and there is no single or final view of it.

The characters, like the scenes, melt into each other. Behind their different appearances are the main figures of the Grail ritual, the Fisher King who embodies the sterility of the land, the Deliverer whose task is to break the curse, and the Woman with whom he breaks it. In *The Waste Land* the central figure of the Fisher King does not assert himself, but he is none the less present and may be assumed to be the speaker whenever the first person singular is used. He is the impotent observer, the type of man who knows what is happening and how closely his own fate is connected with it, but is powerless to do anything to change the situation. It is characteristic of him that in this time of crisis he just sits and fishes. He makes his clearest appearance towards the end :

> I sat upon the shore
> Fishing, with the arid plain behind me
> Shall I at least set my lands in order ?

From this we can trace him back   He appears in the scene of autumnal desolation :

> While I was fishing in the dull canal
> On a winter evening round behind the gas-house,
> Musing upon the king my brother's wreck
> And on the king my father's death before him.

Through the poem he keeps up this helpless role.   In the first section he sees the crowd of dead flowing over London Bridge, marvels at their number and sees among them one who is an image of himself.   In the third section he takes on the significant part of Tiresias, who is not only a prophet :

> I Tiresias, old man with wrinkled dugs
> Perceived the scene, and foretold the rest,

but combines the attributes of man and woman and, as such, shows the special nature of his understanding, which is more than that of ordinary men or ordinary women.   In the fifth section the Fisher King is back at his old pastime of fishing. Nothing has happened to him, and he is incapable of any decisive action.   He is the passive consciousness which combines a wide understanding and knowledge with a singular ineffectiveness in doing anything that matters.   His crisis is the crisis of the modern soul as Eliot diagnoses it.   His life, which is also the life of his people, is terribly impoverished and weakened, and he needs some tremendous act to restore him and them.

This restoration is the task of the Deliverer, who in the Grail legends is usually a knight like Gawain or Percival, but to whom Eliot gives new and unexpected shapes.   His figures of the Deliverer embody the different activities and ideas by which man seeks in vain to give a greater richness to life. A forecast of his character is given by the Clairvoyante when she gives a warning against death by water.   He appears in the second section, first as a demobilised soldier, who has been dubiously faithful to his wife since she no longer attracts or pleases him.   Seen through her eyes and the eyes of her woman friend he represents some deep domestic discontent and failure, and is a typical victim of a system which has lost the sanctity of marriage without finding anything to take its place, and which shows the nervous uneasiness of the years after the war. In the third section the Deliverer appears in another form, as

> Mr. Eugenides, the Smyrna merchant
> Unshaven, with a pocket full of currants
> C.i.f. London : documents at sight,

and at once passes into a more familiar and more suburban figure :

> He, the young man carbuncular, arrives,
> A small house-agent's clerk with one bold stare,
> One of the low on whom assurance sits
> As a silk hat on a Bradford millionaire.

He makes perfunctory love to a typist and is satisfied with her mechanical response. In these appearances of the Deliverer Eliot conveys two important interests of common life, in money-making and in love-making, and shows how empty and unsatisfying both are. An age which puts its trust in activities like these for its redemption is not likely to be satisfied.

There is, however, another side to the Deliverer which excites other feelings. To the Fisher King, who needs him, he presents a more attractive shape as Ferdinand, Prince of Naples, from Shakespeare's *Tempest*. He is youth obsessed by a sense of a great loss and haunted by a terrible feeling of deprivation. The Clairvoyante in the first part gives a hint of his feelings when she says :

> (Those are pearls that were his eyes. Look !)

and shows how this insistent regret haunts him. Then in the third part his grief for his father's death hampers his activity and makes him almost one with the Fisher King in his impotent idleness. But his haunting dreams prevail, and he becomes the symbol for the dreaming homesickness of youth, the longing for something unlike ordinary life, or the memory of magical moments which are painfully at variance with ordinary habits :

> " This music crept by me upon the waters "
> And along the Strand, up Queen Victoria Street,
> O city, city, I can sometimes hear
> Beside a public bar in Lower Thames Street

> The pleasant whining of a mandoline
> And a clamour and a chatter from within
> Where fishermen lounge at noon : where the walls
> Of Magnus Martyr hold
> Inexplicable splendour of Ionian white and gold.

In this form the Deliverer is quite different from the Merchant or the Bank Clerk. He has his moments of imagination, of aesthetic delight. But he is still incapable of a truly restoring effort, because he is cut off from life and lives among dreams and desires. The spiritual life of the time will not be renewed through haunted spirits of his kind.

The Deliverer fails. The Clairvoyante has said, " Fear death by water ", and in the fourth section death by water comes. The Merchant and Ferdinand are combined in the single character of Phlebas the Phoenician, who has the money-making interests of the one and the romantic youth of the other. The short section is composed with much point and care to emphasise its important part in the poem and has its own kind of pathos :

> Phlebas the Phoenician, a fortnight dead,
> Forgot the cry of gulls, and the deep sea swell
> And the profit and loss.
> A current under sea
> Picked his bones in whispers. As he rose and fell
> He passed the stages of his age and youth
> Entering the whirlpool.
> Gentile or Jew
> O you who turn the wheel and look to windward,
> Consider Phlebas, who was once handsome and tall as you.

In the image of a young man drowned at sea Eliot presents his climax of the soul lost through routine and unimaginative desires. Phlebas has his finer side when he listens to the gulls and the sea, but his directing principle is " profit and loss ", and this is his ruin. Nor is it without significance that he meets " death by water ". The waste land needs water, but not in this way. It needs real refreshment, not activities which devour those who take part in them. In Phlebas' death Eliot shows the failure of false efforts at redemption. Neither money nor debased love nor nostalgic regrets enhance life.

The cures are useless, and in the next section it is clear that the Deliverer has failed and that with his death the situation is worse :

> He who was living is now dead,
> We who were living are now dying
> With a little patience.

The waste land is still waste, and nothing has happened to redeem it.

Finally, there are the women, or rather there is the one woman, who takes different shapes according to the needs of the poem and the status of the Deliverer. In the first section there is a hint of what she might be, the object of an almost ideal love, the creature that one imagines in listening to Wagner's *Tristan und Isolde*, but who somehow eludes her lover because he is too shy to speak to her :

> " You gave me hyacinths first a year ago ;
> They called me the hyacinth girl."
> — Yet when we came back, late, from the Hyacinth garden,
> Your arms full, and your hair wet, I could not
> Speak, and my eyes failed, I was neither
> Living nor dead, and I knew nothing
> Looking into the heart of light, the silence.

Against this ideal Eliot sets the facts as he sees them in his different types of womanhood. In the second section his woman is a Cleopatra or Dido, who lives in magnificence among jewels and perfumes and passes imperceptibly into a neurotic modern woman who hears presentiments of evil in noises under the door and tries to drown her anxieties in useless activities and wonders what she can ever do. Then she becomes a woman of the working classes whose husband is back from the war and who is so caught up in her trivial occupations that she is quite out of touch with him and has lost any meaning for her life. From this she sinks to the typist who satisfies the carnal desires of the bank-clerk and gets little pleasure from it :

> She turns and looks a moment in the glass,
> Hardly aware of her departed lover ;
> Her brain allows one half-formed thought to pass :
> " Well now that's done : and I'm glad it's over."

Then the tone deepens. Against a picture of Elizabeth and Leicester on the Thames Eliot sets his " Song of the Thames-daughters ", each of which has a poignant, almost tragic quality in its suggestion of corruption, failure and guilt. The first turns a theme from Dante's account of La Pia into a squalid modern story of lost innocence :

> " Trams and dusty trees.
> Highbury bore me. Richmond and Kew
> Undid me. By Richmond I raised my knees
> Supine on the floor of a narrow canoe."

The second is hardly less callous in its lack of remorse, and shows how the woman is impervious to the emotional reactions of the man :

> " My feet are at Moorgate, and my heart
> Under my feet. After the event
> He wept. He promised ' a new start '.
> I made no comment. What should I resent ? "

The third is grimmer and more searching. It shows the sense of defeat which accompanies such love-making, a new kind of humility which accepts the loss of virtue as part of the debased human lot :

> " On Margate sands.
> I can connect
> Nothing with nothing.
> The broken fingernails of dirty hands.
> My people humble people who expect
> Nothing."

These different women are aspects of the one Woman who should help the Deliverer to break the curse of impotence in the waste land. But their acts with him are always somehow failures, hysterical or frustrated or perfunctory or guilt-ridden. Such love-making cannot bring a spiritual revival. Over it hangs the menace of frustration and misery, and we may well expect that something more than this is needed to bring back life.

The waste land needs water. In childhood or the past this refreshment is familiar, and the opening lines touch on the contrast between the old times when

> Summer surprised us, coming over the Starnbergersee
> With a shower of rain

and the present with its insistent question :

> What are the roots that clutch, what branches grow
> Out of this stony rubbish ?

The desire for water runs through the poem, and there are many hints of water which mocks those who need it and fail to see how near it is to them. In the first section it is not without significance that the dead cross the Thames in their meaningless procession :

> A crowd flowed over London Bridge, so many
> I had not thought death had undone so many.

In the third section the Thames, degraded and empty, calls up not the pleasant days of summer but desolation and gloom. The regal grandeur of Elizabeth and Leicester on the river falls into the sad songs of the Thames-daughters, and places on the river-bank are the scenes of their degradation. The recurring theme of water suggests that the revival which the world needs is near and possible but is somehow missed or put to the wrong purpose or undertaken in the wrong spirit. Just as the Deliverer and the Woman fail in their task, so the water, which should flow and revive the waste land, plays a different part and drowns Phlebas.

After these efforts and failures, we can hardly expect any fine consummation, nor does any come. In the last section Eliot returns to the theme of his start and tells of the dry land which has become harsher and more full of mockery :

> There is not even silence in the mountains
> But dry sterile thunder without rain,
> There is not even solitude in the mountains
> But red sullen faces sneer and snarl
> From doors of mudcracked houses.

As the air grows drier and more cruel, illusions breed, and the thirst for water is mocked by the song of the hermit-thrush, whose

> Drip drop drip drop drop drop drop

ironically gives the sound of falling water but brings no consolation to the parched land and its people. In the general desolation the scheme of the Grail legend takes a new form. In its old form the Deliverer has his last fight, his great struggle with evil and his ordeal through courage, in the Chapel Perilous. This is the risk he must take to prove his valour and to set the seal on his quest. But in the waste land he is dead, and the Chapel Perilous has become a ruin :

> In this decayed hole among the mountains
> In the faint moonlight, the grass is singing
> Over the tumbled graves, about the chapel,
> There is the empty chapel, only the wind's home.
> It has no windows, and the door swings,
> Dry bones can harm no one.

Modern life offers no final and decisive struggle, no hard ordeal, no test of real worth. The Deliverer is dead, and his task has lost its meaning, since there is no demand for it. Life is revived neither by finance nor by sex nor by adventure. It has no fierce struggle with evil, but continues as before, unredeemed and barren.

None the less there is a presage of storm. The " dry sterile thunder " is not without its hints of something to come, and in due course it sounds. In its thrice repeated rumble *Da* there speaks a message from the *Upanishads* which is *Datta, Dayadhvam, Damyata* — give, sympathise, control. If this is obeyed, if men show more generosity, more sympathy, more self-control, the waste land may still be redeemed. Nor do the words fall on entirely deaf or unresponsive ears. Yet they fail to be effective, because those who hear them are ordinary men and women occupied in themselves and their own affairs, hardened by habit to caution and afraid of taking risks. The thunder's demands strike against fatal and final obstacles in men's hearts. It tells them to give, but they feel that they have already given as much as they dare in the past and are not prepared to give so much again :

> The awful daring of a moment's surrender
> Which an age of prudence can never retract.

Then they are told to sympathise, but each lives in himself as in a locked prison and cannot break out from the private peculiar world of his own soul. This imprisonment is not absolute :

> Only at nightfall, aethereal rumours
> Revive for a moment a broken Coriolanus,

but it is too strong for the prisoners to escape. Finally, they are called to control, but this too they cannot do completely. They would rather obey others and receive orders :

> The sea was calm, your heart would have responded
> Gaily, when invited, beating obedient
> To controlling hands.

So the message fails, and the poem ends with the Fisher King sitting on the shore and asking when new life will come to him. The various efforts have ended in defeat and failure, and all goes on as before.

If such are the main elements in the symbolism of *The Waste Land*, they may help to explain its development. Its main lines correspond to them and mark different stages in the scheme of impotence and the unsuccessful attempts to cure it. The poem is composed in five parts or movements, each of which has a definite character. The first is called " The Burial of the Dead " and sets out the position at the start. Anthropologically it is the season when the year-god has died and the Fisher King is barren, and poetically it shows a futility which amounts to spiritual death. In such a situation forecasts are inevitably made, and Eliot uses the device of a clairvoyante with a pack of cards to foretell the future and utter warnings. Her advice is needed, since the situation is indeed grave. In the spectacle of crowded urban life Eliot sees the triumph of death, and his image of dead men crossing London Bridge shows the extent of this terrible flatness and staleness :

> Sighs, short and infrequent, were exhaled,
> And each man fixed his eyes before his feet.
> Flowed up the hill and down King William Street,
> To where Saint Mary Woolnoth kept the hours
> With a dead sound on the final stroke of nine.

The sound of the clock reflects the deadness in the human beings, and it is not surprising that the poet or his chief character becomes almost hysterical in addressing a friend who is dead and in whom he sees a reflection of himself. This is the situation as the poet diagnoses it, and from it he advances to the various cures attempted for it.

The second section is called " A Game of Chess " and owes something to Middleton's *Women beware Women*. Its central feature is that it stresses the urgency of the situation and suggests the need for something to be done at once. It falls into two halves. The first conveys the agony of the human soul in its uncertainty and lack of purpose, its pretensions and its fears, and the second half transposes this spirit to a lower order of society, to show how common and widely spread it is. The figure of the game of chess indicates how men and women pursue futile occupations in the face of doom and are so engrossed in them that they fail to see what awaits them. So here the woman of society and the woman of the people are entirely occupied, each with her own kind of life, muddled and pointless and purposeless. But just as the rich woman hears voices which frighten her and hint that her life is a sham, or, as the interrupting voice says :

> I think we are in rats' alley
> Where the dead men lost their bones,

so the poor woman's chatter is broken at intervals by a menace of hurrying time so insistent that it is printed in capital letters :

HURRY UP, PLEASE, IT'S TIME.

The closing of the public-house with the haste and hurry that it causes is the symbol for some much more significant change when the round of petty activities will be suddenly ended, and there is a special irony in the closing words :

Goonight Bill. Goonight Lou. Goonight May. Goonight.
Ta ta. Goonight. Goonight.
Good night, ladies, good night, sweet ladies, good night, good night.

Eliot deftly marks first the scene and then what he feels about it. The first two lines realistically conjure up closing-time, but the third line, being what Ophelia says in her madness, hints that deep in the characters lies something bordering on insanity.

The third section is called " The Fire Sermon " after a work attributed to the Buddha which describes the lusts of the flesh and their corrupting effect on the human soul. The fire is that of the lusts which consume men, and they are the subject of the section. As it proceeds it shows more and more how violent and deadening these are. The episode of the bank-clerk and the typist is followed by the darker songs of the Thames-daughters, and then comes the abrupt, powerful conclusion :

> To Carthage then I came
>
> Burning burning burning burning
> O Lord Thou pluckest me out
> O Lord Thou pluckest
>
> burning.

The first line comes from St. Augustine, who in his *Confessions* describes his own entry into a life of sexual licence by a violent metaphor which is also almost a pun : " veni Karthaginem, et circumstrepebat me undique sartago flagitiosorum amorum". Carthage is a " sartago ", a " cauldron of unholy loves ". The decline in morality which the section marks leads to this conclusion and shows what end awaits such trust in the worth of sexual desire. Eliot follows it up at once with a theme from a work attributed to the Buddha which sets out his central doctrines of purification and redemption. The soul is consumed by its lusts, but there is still a hope that it may be saved, — a hope but no assurance, and the broken sentences, which Eliot cunningly contrives, leave us in doubt about what happens. The last word, isolated in its fearful menace, suggests that the fire goes on.

After the short fourth section of " Death by Water " which tells of the end of the Deliverer and the failure of his efforts, the fifth section is called " What the Thunder said ". Its tone is less ironical and less realistic than that of the earlier sections and it carries on at the level of grave seriousness with which the third section closes. Eliot is no longer concerned with prospects and menaces but with fears realised and with a terrible disintegration which has begun in the soul. Not only

is it the victim of illusions and false hopes : it has in itself a
fearful disorder which is like the disorder in the starving
European countries in the years after the war. It has mad
mirages of hunger and thirst, which are even more powerful
in the spirit than in the body The solid cities of the earth are
no longer solid :

> What is the city over the mountains
> Cracks and reforms and bursts in the violet air
> Falling towers
> Jerusalem Athens Alexandria
> Vienna London
> Unreal.

The whole order of nature seems to be breaking, and strange
sounds and sights testify to the general decomposition :

> A woman drew her long black hair out tight
> And fiddled whisper music on those strings
> And bats with baby faces in the violet light
> Whistled, and beat their wings
> And crawled head downward down a blackened wall
> And upside down in air were towers
> Tolling reminiscent bells, that kept the hours
> And voices singing out of empty cisterns and exhausted wells.

Against this hysteria and disorder come the failure at the
Chapel Perilous and the voice of the Thunder. They show
how great the need for recovery is, but also how extremely
difficult it is to get it. Things have gone so far that the
demands of the Thunder can hardly be met when they come.
The Waste Land then is concerned with the sickness and
inadequacy of the human soul. So far from following a
psychological or purely emotional sequence it moves according to a plan which first sets out a situation in its many
implications and then shows how there is no cure for it. It
does this in a strictly poetical way. The true character of the
situation is presented through the poetry, and is thus much
richer than any analysis of it may suggest. Eliot's subject is
so complex that his presentation demands time before we can
grasp his implications at their true value. But so far from
letting his thoughts run wild, he arranges them with consider-

able care and has his own devices for holding the poem together. Not only do his central characters represent principles
or outlooks which persist through the different scenes, but
certain themes supply a similar need. For instance, Eliot at
intervals uses the theme of the nightingale with an insistence
which shows that it means much to him. In the second
section his rich woman's room is decorated with scenes, and
one receives special attention.

> Above the antique mantel was displayed
> As though a window gave upon the sylvan scene
> The change of Philomel, by the barbarous king
> So rudely forced ; yet there the nightingale
> Filled all the desert with inviolable voice
> And still she cried, and still the world pursues,
> " Jug Jug " to dirty ears.

Then in the third section, with its insistence on the squalour
of love, the mention of Mrs. Porter and her lover—types of
commonplace self-indulgence — is succeeded by another
reference to the nightingale :

> Twit twit twit twit
> Jug jug jug jug jug jug
> So rudely forc'd
> Tereu.

On each occasion the nightingale is brought into relation with
a woman who is deluded or dissatisfied or vulgar, and on
each occasion a sudden, almost tragic note breaks the atmosphere. It is impossible not to connect this contrast with
Eliot's earlier poem, *Sweeney among the Nightingales*, where a
scene of coarse debauch is contrasted with the beauty of
nightingales singing :

> The host with someone indistinct
> Converses at the door apart,
> The nightingales are singing near
> The Convent of the Sacred Heart,
>
> And sang within the bloody wood
> When Agamemnon cried aloud,
> And let their liquid siftings fall
> To stain the stiff dishonoured shroud.

There the music of the nightingales, immortalised and sanctified by great poetry, presents a sharp contrast to the life which takes place beside them. In *The Waste Land* Eliot must intend a similar contrast. The nightingale of Greek legend is the type of beauty which is foully done to death and yet survives through the gift of song, and in Eliot's new mythology the contrast is between the superficial, almost frivolous nature of sexual love and the serious tragic character which the old story gives to Philomela. In introducing the nightingale Eliot shows by a hint of real depths how shallow his characters are.

The art of contrast used so subtly here is used on a larger and more impressive scale elsewhere. Eliot indeed seems to feel that the true significance of his situations is best seen when they are set against something else. For instance, in the first section between his account of the waste land in its barrenness and his echoes from *Tristan* with their hints of unsatisfied longings, he puts some lines which seem to contrast with both :

> Only
> There is shadow under this red rock,
> (Come in under the shadow of this red rock),
> And I will show you something different from either
> Your shadow at morning striding behind you
> Or your shadow at evening rising to meet you ;
> I will show you fear in a handful of dust.

The red rock is a symbol different both from the waste land and from the hyacinth girl. Its function here is to hint that even in the waste land there is some hope of salvation in fear and self-abasement. On one side of it is the general sense of futility, on the other the regret for something lost. Through such fear a man may perhaps see his way to redemption.

Another powerful contrast comes in the third section. Before the distressing, poignant songs of the three Thames-daughters Eliot sets two verses, lyrical in their lilt and sprightliness, which tell of Elizabeth and Leicester on the Thames. The occasion was one when they almost came to being married and the two verses give a charming sketch of love conducted in a high style between great persons. The hints of an old London and of invigorating waters give a special grace to the second verse :

> Elizabeth and Leicester
> Beating oars
> The stern was formed
> A gilded shell
> Red and gold
> The brisk swell
> Rippled both shores
> Southwest wind
> Carried down stream
> The peal of bells
> White towers
>> Weialala leia
>> Wallala leialala.

The love of Elizabeth and Leicester is conducted in a high style, and the setting reflects it. Its place in the poem is clear. It provides a contrast to what follows, but only a contrast of style and manners. The famous couple are no more satisfied by love than are Eliot's more squalid modern lovers. The gay meaningless refrain, with its sound of rippling water, both reflects their empty hearts and mocks their pretences.

The life set out so mercilessly in *The Waste Land* is not merely feeble and deficient : it is assailed by strange anxieties and fears. The innocent longing for what is lost, which is displayed especially by the Deliverer in his incarnation as Ferdinand, Prince of Naples, turns almost imperceptibly into illusions which are ironical and even sinister. In " A Game of Chess " the society woman is haunted by such fears. There is a dramatic conflict between her eager, nervous questions and the cold answers which reality makes to them. At first her questions remain unanswered : then the central character of the poem answers in a forbidding and menacing way :

" What is that noise ? "
>> The wind under the door.
" What is that noise now ? What is the wind doing ? "
> Nothing again nothing.

She gets more and more nervous and almost loses control of herself, and the answer comes relentless and insistent that she is caught in the mechanical routine of life and will do in the future what she has done in the past :

> " What shall I do now ? What shall I do ? "
> " I shall rush out as I am, and walk the street
> With my hair down, so. What shall we do to-morrow ?
> What shall we ever do ? "
>   The hot water at ten.
> And if it rains, a closed car at four.
> And we shall play a game of chess,
> Pressing lidless eyes and waiting for a knock upon the door.

The answers that come to her strike cold on the imagination and convey a hint of the doom that waits for her beyond her purposeless activities.

Again, in the last section, before the Thunder speaks, Eliot introduces remarkable symbols to show the kind of illusion from which the modern world suffers. Thirst and hunger create mirages, and one is of a special poignancy :

> Who is the third who walks always beside you ?
> When I count, there are only you and I together
> But when I look ahead up the white road
> There is always another one walking beside you
> Gliding, wrapt in a brown mantle, hooded
> I do not know whether a man or a woman
> — But who is that on the other side of you ?

This strange effect is made from two elements. First, the poet recalls the Disciples who on the road to Emmaus met the risen Christ, but secondly he recalls how some Antarctic explorers " at the extremity of their strength, had the constant delusion that there was *one more member* than could actually be counted ". The two elements are fused into a single experience in which the figure seen by the Disciples becomes an illusion of exhausted men and the sense of Christ's presence a mockery. The imagery fits wonderfully into some aspects of the troubled conscience. Many men and women have ceased to believe in Christ but have not quite rid themselves from some consciousness of Him. His presence in a way haunts them, without seeming real or truly important. In the collapse of their confidence and in their sense of inadequacy this presence becomes more insistent but has no more meaning. If they could believe in Him, their lives might perhaps be redeemed, but as the Clairvoyante has said,

> I do not find
> The Hanged Man.

In the anthropological scheme Christ Himself should become the Hanged Man, the Scapegoat in Frazer's sense, who takes the sins of others on himself and suffers for them, but in the waste land there is no such redemption, and the figure of Christ is no more than a haunting phantom.

In *The Waste Land* Eliot judges the actual world by high standards which he conveys not only by explicit contrasts like that of Elizabeth and Leicester with the Thames-daughters but by a special use or adaptation of quotations from other authors. This technique has an ancient precedent. The Greeks sometimes used what they called παραδιόρθωσις, which is the adaptation of one poet's line by another poet for a different use. This sometimes has an ironical effect as when Solon's line

> τίκτει γὰρ κόρος ὕβριν, ὅτ' ἂν πολὺς ὄλβος ἔπηται,
> Pride begets surfeit when it has great wealth,

is altered by Theognis to

> τίκτει γὰρ κόρος ὕβριν, ὅτ ἂν κακῷ ὄλβος ἔπηται.
> Pride begets surfeit when the base have wealth.

While Solon was concerned with the corrupting effects of wealth as such, Theognis, a resentful reactionary, was concerned with its effects when it belongs to the basely born. In this way Greek poets paid a tribute to their predecessors and brought familiar maxims up to date. Eliot learned this device from Pound, who uses it to display his distaste for the present by contrasting it implicitly with the nobler past. In his earlier poetry Eliot had created a special art by which actual life is compared with the world of great literature and found sadly wanting. In *The Waste Land* his comparison is more embracing and goes beyond literature to a wide vision of human values. To make his comments clear he takes up this device and makes considerable use of it.

Eliot adapts quotations from other poets to show the gap between the spiritual level at which man should live and the actual level at which he does live. They provide a contrast between the ideal and the actual and throw into a single phrase a complex emotion in which respect for high standards and consciousness of their absence are fused into a single ironical result. For instance, Day had written in his *Parliament of Bees* :

> A noise of horns and hunting which shall bring
> Actaeon to Diana in the spring.

This is charming and graceful, with all the confidence of a great classical tradition behind it. Eliot needs something to convey the quite different character of ordinary lovers, and he alters Day's lines to

> The sound of horns and motors which shall bring
> Sweeney to Mrs. Porter in the spring.

The characteristically modern sound of motor-horns replaces the old music of hunting-horns, and Actaeon and Diana give place to two typical figures of Eliot's world. Sweeney comes from Eliot's earlier poetry where he represents some violent, coarse and disagreeable type, " apeneck " and " broad-bottomed, pink from nape to base ". Mrs. Porter has a different origin. She comes, as Eliot says, from an Australian song, though he does not add that this was the song which the Australian soldiers sang when they landed on Gallipoli in 1915, and that Mrs. Porter, who seems to have kept a bawdy-house in Cairo, was a legendary figure with them. Eliot goes on to quote the song in an inevitably bowdlerised form and shows how fit a companion Mrs. Porter is for Sweeney. The process of adaptation is complete, and judgment is passed by the old on the new.

When he does not alter his quotations in this way but keeps them intact, Eliot secures a somewhat different kind of effect. He still relates the present situation to some high example from the past, and still makes the gap obvious between the two; for the quotation, placed as it were in inverted commas, is too emphatically a quotation to ring quite naturally and suggests that the present is trying to live up to something beyond its reach. But the emphasis is perhaps less on the discord between ideal and real, between past and present, than on the real seriousness of the present crisis. The quotation dignifies something that might otherwise be too depressing and even too trivial. Eliot's use of this device can be seen from the last words of the poem which are a *cento* of lines from other works. It is perhaps not entirely successful — the crisis seems to need something more original and more authentic than this, but it illustrates this branch of Eliot's technique :

> London Bridge is falling down falling down falling down
> *Poi s' ascose nel foco che gli affina*
> *Quando fiam uti chelidon* — O swallow swallow
> *Le prince d'Aquitaine à la tour abolie*
> These fragments I have shored against my ruins
> Why then Ile fit you. Hieronymo's mad againe.
> Datta. Dayadhvam. Damyata.
>   Shantih. Shantih shantih.

Before this the Fisher King has gone back to his fishing and thinks of putting his lands in order. Now the poet, speaking for the general consciousness, sums up the emotional state to which his poem has led him. An English nursery rhyme conveys his sense of a collapsing world. Like Dante's Arnaut Daniel in Purgatory, he goes back into the refining fire. Like the poet of the *Pervigilium Veneris* he asks when like the swallow he will be able to sing again. Like the nightingale in Swinburne's *Itylus* he laments his misery. Like the speaker in Gérard de Nerval's sonnet *El Desdichado* he feels himself disinherited, and like a character in Kyd's *Spanish Tragedy* he tries to create some shelter for himself in the general ruin, while in his ears there rings the summons from the *Upanishads* with its promise of unreckonable peace. The quotations piled up in this way relate the living situation to various situations as poets have seen them and bring the present crisis into touch with the past.

In *The Waste Land* Eliot makes a full use of the modern

technique of poetry as Pound evolved it. It tries to secure two ends, to be always poetry and to be realistic and contemporary. The two ends are not always easily harmonised, and we may think that sometimes Eliot's realism interferes with his poetry. This is perhaps not quite justified. For Eliot really does create a peculiar kind of poetry even when it is a studied effect of common speech. The woman of the working classes in the second section speaks in her colloquial vernacular, and though the result is extremely conversational it has its own kind of dramatic power. The dull, trite words ring so true that they achieve the effect of drama, and their succinct, practical air has its own attraction. There is an undeniable power in such drab phrases as

> If you don't like it you can get on with it, I said,
> Others can pick and choose if you can't,

or

> But if Albert makes off, it won't be for lack of telling.
> You ought to be ashamed, I said, to look so antique.

It is true that the whole of this passage creates an effect of being written in dialect, and it is hard to judge dialect as poetry when it is not spontaneous. But Eliot seems to have foreseen this difficulty and to have concentrated on a human situation which is interesting for its own sake and gains much from his discriminating presentation.

The great variety of tone in *The Waste Land* is largely due to Eliot's realism. Though he is capable of lyrical effects, as in the verses on Elizabeth and Leicester, and of a grand, imaginative manner, as in the mirages of the last section, he tries other effects which bear much less resemblance to familiar kinds of poetry and are often consciously conversational. When he does this, Eliot avoids Pound's mistake of thinking that the correct representation of current speech in itself makes poetry. Eliot is enough of a dramatist to make something even of what might at first sight seem pallid and lifeless words. For instance, his hysterical woman in the second part speaks in the language of her kind, but her words have a strong reserve of emotion and show her neurotic condition, as when she says :

" My nerves are bad to-night. Yes, bad. Stay with me.
Speak to me. Why do you never speak. Speak
" What are you thinking of ? What thinking ? What ?
I never know what you are thinking. Think."

So too the reminiscences of childhood with which the poem
begins have a complete simplicity, almost a baldness of
statement :

And when we were children, staying at the arch-duke's,
My cousin's, he took me out on a sled,
And I was frightened. He said, Marie,
Marie, hold on tight. And down we went.

But the baldness is suitable, because it conveys the situation
as it really is and has its own kind of poetry in the simple
interest of a small but not unimportant occasion. There is a
considerable element of drama in *The Waste Land*, and it
accounts for the variety of style. Eliot is not in the least
concerned to create a single, harmonious language, as a poet
of the nineteenth century might have done, but varies his style
with his subject, with the result that his poem has its own kind
of richness by presenting its themes from different angles and
in different voices.

The special success of *The Waste Land* is that its style suits
its subject as Eliot sees and feels it. The decomposition of
civilisation, the poverty-stricken nature of the modern consciousness, its moments of fear and of hysteria, its lack of
conviction and of direction, fit easily into this abrupt, allusive
manner. In his later work, especially in *Four Quartets*, Eliot
had adopted a different manner, less abrupt and less allusive,
simply because his subject is different and would hardly fit
into the manner of *The Waste Land*. Nor would this manner
be suitable if Eliot did not keep his own feelings in the background. It is possible because his presentation is so largely
dramatic, because each scene tells its own story and creates
its own kind of effect without requiring any personal comment
from the poet. Indeed this dramatic kind of art is Eliot's way
of making his poem contemporary. Words which, coming
from himself in his own person, might seem inappropriate, are
perfectly appropriate when given to his characters. He takes

us through a series of states of mind, differing greatly from each other, and to each he gives its special manner. What unites the style and gives it a unity is its purity and force. It is, even in unexpected ways and through unusual means, poetry.

But of course *The Waste Land* has a greater unity than this. The plan which so skilfully holds it together, rises from Eliot's own anxieties and emotional experience. He is able to give his feelings greater force by attributing them to his characters, but they are in the first place his own, the reflection of a powerful crisis in himself. Of his extreme seriousness there can be no doubt. Eliot wrote *The Waste Land* in a great distress of spirit over the state of the world. What particularly troubles him is the emptiness and futility of much modern life. In his earlier poems something of the same kind can be seen, but there it is largely a question of personal distaste. His dislikes are not founded on any strong principles, but in *The Waste Land* his disgust has grown into a deeper and more human anguish. He often hides the strength of his feelings under an ironical exterior, but no one can read *The Waste Land* without seeing that this irony is simply the cloak which a civilised man puts on to hide emotions whose real force would be too much for him if he were to give free expression to it. It is a kind of control, and it gives a special reserve of strength to his words. It is in its own way modern and contemporary ; for this is the way in which civilised men often speak about matters which concern them deeply.

The Waste Land is almost a poem of despair. It holds out little prospect of regeneration or revival, and the final obstacles to the new life demanded by the Thunder are in men themselves. At the same time it asserts certain values and accepts these as valid in its implicit criticism of the modern world. Not only does it suggest that great literature provides standards by which behaviour can be judged, but through its use of words from the Buddha and St. Augustine and the *Upanishads* it claims validity for something like a religious outlook. Whatever Eliot's religious opinions may have been when he wrote it, he could not dispense with religion altogether, but uses it to support his views on some matters of fundamental importance. In fact the poem displays a great uneasiness over the disparity between spiritual values and actual conduct and suggests that despite the mood of defeated acceptance in which it ends, the poet is not content to accept things as they are but wishes that some cure could be found for them and assumes that it can be found, if at all, in religion. But though *The Waste Land* provides this wisp of hope, it is of little importance to it. Its greatness and the strength of its appeal are due to its penetrating vision of contemporary life. It conveys with a peculiarly personal power the discord between high standards and brutal facts, between the desire to make life more abundant and the obstacles in our souls and bodies which prevent this from happening. It is a poetical diagnosis of a grave psychological malady, an attempt to show from various angles the inability of most men and women to realise a full life of the spirit. Through the power of its words it shows what this malady means and in how many ways it frustrates and corrupts.

In *The Waste Land* Eliot uses an advanced modern technique for purposes unlike those of Apollinaire or Mayakovsky or Pasternak. While they needed new and electrical means of expression because they felt themselves brimming over with creative energy and believed that other means were inadequate to their sense of life, Eliot has no such ebullience. His creative spirit moves slowly and carefully and is inspired more by anguish than by joy, more by depression than by confidence. Whereas they draw strength from the life around them and increase their range through their enjoyment of human contacts, Eliot seems to be a lonely, distrustful, and at times supercilious soul. It is hardly surprising that revolutionary critics have seen in him the last voice of a civilisation which knows that it is doomed and struggles without hope to regain a splendour which is lost for ever. Eliot is indeed a poet of modern failure and distress, but his work is so personal and special that, despite his popularity and influence, he seems to speak hardly for an age or a country or a class but for his own peculiar self. The defects which he finds in common life have an unusual significance because of his unusual sensibility to any imperfect kind of behaviour. In his heart he conceals a stubborn moralist who is more intent on uncovering faults than on recognising virtues. Indeed his prepossessions with morality are more American than European, the product of New England and its Puritan tradition. The strange thing is that this has given Eliot a peculiar insight into human life and a deep concern with it. He is a poet largely because he is so eager and critical a moralist. Most of his emotions seem to rise from this particular approach to life, and though this gives to his work a character quite unlike the creative and vigorous spirit which informs Apollinaire and Pasternak and suggests that his human sympathies are narrower than theirs, it is essential to his art and largely responsible for its integrity and intensity. He has spared no effort to be entirely honest and to give to his own range of experience a most accomplished art of words.

VII

FEDERICO GARCÍA LORCA,
ROMANCERO GITANO

Though Spain lies outside the main orbit of European developments and tends to proceed on its own way, it has a remarkable gift for absorbing foreign influences and transforming them to suit its national characteristics and traditions. The great revival of imaginative literature which came with the generation of 1898 certainly owed much to France through the medium of the Nicaraguan poet Rubén Darío, but the movement which he inaugurated and inspired and which found its chief exponents in Miguel de Unamuno and Antonio Machado was emphatically Spanish in its grand manner, its intellectual discipline and reserve, its religious and philosophical basis. So dominating was it that it ruled the Spanish scene until after the First World War, and Spain felt no need for Futurism or such other creeds as were astir in France and Russia in 1910. But if the younger poets were to do more than imitate their seniors, they had to find new means of expression, and they did so by developing some tendencies which were already noticeable in their elders but had not yet been exploited to the full. Juan Ramón Jiménez had done much to write a poetry pure from political and doctrinal prepossessions : Antonio Machado had made his metres respond with sensitive delicacy to the movements of his powerful personality. It was for the younger poets to create a poetry which should be more vigorous than that of Jiménez and more musical than that of Machado. They could do this only if they shed some of the austerity favoured by the older generation. They must be more outspoken, more intimate, more responsive to impressions, more exact in their account of fleeting moments and complex states of mind. The new movements, which emerged about 1920, were attempts to do something of this kind. Owing much to French example they were also typically Spanish in their background and their outlook.

Despite differences of detail the new poets agreed on some essential matters. They wished to combine a new vivid imagery with contemporary themes and a vivid awareness of modern life. Unlike their predecessors they were not much interested in metaphysical or religious or political questions. Like other Modernists, they wished to be poets of the present day, but their work took a special direction because the Spanish situation was unlike the French or the English or the Russian. Spain had had no war and as yet no revolution. Its intellectual forces were not gathered into a few great cities but scattered over a country which, more than any other, keeps its old regional characteristics and loyalties. The young poets were not revolutionaries inspired by political ideals and passions but artists who wished to make poetry more vivid and more intimate. They were not even metaphysicians ; they were primarily interested in their art and in ways of bringing it up to date. Like other poets of their time, they started with a clear notion of poetry derived from their own experience of it, and they wished to be true to this without reference to extraneous considerations. But because they were artists and eager to create something really new, they were in revolt against the manners and the standards of their elders. The revival of Spanish letters had been so impressive and so successful that to younger men it seemed an exacting tyranny. It had its own rules, its own sense of decorum, its own conception of the poet as the grave prophet who speaks from his solitude on urgent matters of life and death. This was not what the younger men asked from poetry. They were distrustful of such rules and such a discipline. They embarked upon poetry as upon a great adventure, not knowing what would happen but certain for the moment that something would and that they knew what to do. Their poetry was a gamble with circumstances in which, as Gerardo Diego said,

La ruleta celeste
— blanco, verde, rosa, azul —

> gira lenta, lentamente,
> y yo lanzo mi bola imaginaria.[1]

Uninstructed inspiration is a dangerous guide, and this approach raised many new problems. But for the moment the creative principle was given full powers and allowed to find its own way.

The conviction that poetry was this and nothing else inevitably meant that the younger writers could not accept certain standards which their elders regarded as essential. Above all, they did not believe that poetry demands a proud intellectual reserve. They felt that it rises from elemental powers in man and that the closer to nature it is, the better for it. In particular they were fascinated by the more primitive elements in the Spanish character. Of all the Spanish provinces Andalusia is perhaps the least European. It was the last Spanish territory to be delivered from the Moors, and it still bears traces of Moorish blood in its inhabitants whose customs and traditions are often more oriental than Latin. Just as the lush landscape, with its great rivers and abundant orange-groves, stands in marked contrast to the bleak mountains and waterless plains of Castile, so its human inhabitants preserve a special character which has never been absorbed into a common Spanish pattern. The men of '98 looked askance at the Andalusian spirit. Eminent writers like Unamuno, Azorín, and Valle-Inclán stood for a Northern and European ideal and felt that Andalusia with its primitive passions and its lack of education was what the Spanish people ought to suppress if it was to take its proper place in Europe. Their own work reflects an austerer, drier air in which bloodshed and barbarism are kept at bay. None the less Andalusia, with its rich, pulsating life, was the birthplace of poets. In the older generation Antonio Machado and Juan Ramón Jiménez were Andalusians who forsook their local traditions for central Spain and acclimatised themselves to its noble and exacting traditions. But the

---

[1] The celestial roulette
— White, green, pink, blue —
Turns slow, slowly,
And I throw my imaginary ball.

younger generation saw that Andalusia was a real home of poetry with a people given to song and dance and to many graceful rites and ceremonies. It was time for Andalusia to take its place in Spanish poetry, and with Federico García Lorca, who was born at Fuentevaqueros in the Granada valley in 1899, it found its poet. With him the emphasis of Spanish poetry shifted from the refinements of a cultivated and intellectual minority and found new sources of strength in a primitive, unlettered people.

Lorca was from the beginning a pure artist, not only a poet and a dramatist but a draughtsman who drew charming and original sketches, and a musician of whom de Falla said that, if he had chosen, he would have been as good a musician as he was a poet. Those who knew him agree that his personality turned everything about him into poetry. His remarkable vitality and creative imagination imposed themselves on others and created the atmosphere in which they lived. With him the landscape and the human beings in it took on an enchanted air and seemed different from what they had been before. His art was no mere department of his life ; it filled and inspired everything that he did. His sensibility was so vivid that he was able to reveal to others much that they would otherwise not have noticed, to find undiscovered characteristics in trivial things, and to cast over all his irresistible gift of melody. He had no message to give : he followed his instincts and wrote about anything that excited his insight or his fancy. All this made him the poet for which his generation was looking. Though speculations meant nothing to him and he always denied that he had any theory of art, his practice realised many hopes and justified many beliefs. His poetry was really poetry and nothing else ; his imagery was of an enthralling brilliance and originality ; his vision was actual and contemporary in that it centred round his Andalusian homeland and on the varied life which he found in it.

Lorca began by possessing two separate gifts. He was in the first place a lyrical poet who possessed a special gift for song, and in the second place a dramatist with a real love and understanding of the stage. From the start he wrote plays and he wrote songs, and the two seemed to represent quite different aspects of his genius. His songs have a peculiarly diaphanous and evanescent quality. His sensitiveness enabled him to catch those fleeting moments to which coarser temperaments are blind, and his skill translated these into airy melodious verse, in which all that exists is the impression of a single moment. Lorca, intent on conveying the pure essence of poetry, gives only the central thrill. When his sensibility found unexpected relations between things and was able to illuminate what others had only half noticed, with deft brevity he touched on the vital relation, the point of identity or resemblance between one impression and another and produced the image which secured this. What counts is the choice of an image, or of a scene which does the work of an image in suggesting wider associations of thought. Lorca uses his sensibility to evoke something beyond the event which provides his material. These poems are not in any limited sense descriptive, nor are they abstract. They move through varied and vivid stages, through exact and loving observation, to the evocation of an experience in its imaginative unity. Lorca seems to possess by nature the new way of transforming inchoate states of consciousness into concrete pictures. His mind was stored with memories and what his eyes or ears noted passed into his poetry. He could well say of himself :

> Se ha llenado de luces,
> mi corazón de seda,
> de campanas perdidas,
> de lirios y de abejas.[1]

He was indeed filled with such impressions of sight and sound, and his immediate impulse was to translate them into song.

At the same time Lorca was a dramatist, interested in the play of human character and especially in its more violent and more instinctive actions. He looked for drama not among men and women of his own class and breeding, but in those who were nearer to the soil and the struggle for life and whose passions turned naturally into high dramatic action. He had

---

[1] My heart of silk
Is full of light,
Of lost bells,
Of lilies and bees.

no lack of subjects in the Andalusian world which was his home and the source of his inspiration, and for a time he wrote plays with as much ease as he wrote songs. But the two activities could not be kept permanently apart, and before long Lorca began to give greater strength and solidity to his songs by introducing a small dramatic element into them. The unhappy look on the faces of two lizards inspires him to fancy that in a scene of general gaiety they are unhappy because they have lost their little leaden wedding ring. He sees four pigeons shot while in flight through the air and in a miraculously short space tells the drama and conveys its misery. He sees a woman gathering olives in the wind and refusing the invitations of horsemen to go with them to Cordoba or Seville or Granada, and he imagines that the wind is her lover and has his arm round her waist. In a few lines, with full lyrical art, Lorca creates these moments of dramatic fancy, and in them lies the germ of his most mature and most original achievement.

This art soon found its special field and limits. In *Poema del Canto Hondo* (1927) Lorca gave the poetry of Gipsy life. In the Andalusian Gipsies he admired an elemental energy and a closeness to earth while other poets of his time looked to politics or physical nature or the disturbed consciousness of urban man. He responded to the simple passions and uncomplicated emotions of these country folk. His Gipsies keep all the essential qualities of the uncorrupted southern Spaniard and have in addition a full existence of their own. In songs akin to the Gipsies' own and less formal than the traditional songs of Spain he catches the poetry of this society. Each poem has its own little drama, usually violent, always set in some striking setting as if it arose naturally from the Andalusian countryside. He was the first European poet to use modern methods of imagery and suggestion to create a poetry of simple people, and these songs show how well he could do it. Every detail tells. Every touch is not only perfectly conceived imaginatively but is entirely true to the human subject. Though Lorca throws himself into the lives of his Gipsies and sees everything through their eyes, at the same time he keeps his own delicate, special touch in the speed with which he shows just what a situation or a sensation means, what imaginative significance it has, what its decisive impression on him is. Lorca absorbed some of the discoveries of modernism so easily that he seems to have been born into them. His art shows no traces either of effort or of conscious modernity. In him the modernistic ways of looking at experience seem to be perfectly natural not only in himself but in the characters whom he presents.

Lorca's interest in this grim and primitive Gipsy life led him to publish in 1928 *Romancero Gitano* (*Gipsy Ballads*), and to win with it a success unparalleled for poetry in his time. It was his masterpiece. Even he, who was usually diffident and dilatory about publication, felt no hesitation about this book. He knew that it was all that he could make it and that he could neither improve it nor add to it. In it he leaves the restricted scope of song for a form closer to narrative. His dramatic instinct needed something wider than song could give him, and he found it in the Spanish *romance*, the ballad which dates back to the fourteenth century and has been perfected by many great poets both known and unknown. It has none of the slackness and immaturity of the English ballad : it has a regular line based on a fixed number of syllables, and a whole poem is held together by a single assonance which runs through it instead of rhyme. The traditional *romances* have a wonderful economy and concentration, and Lorca could follow their manner without surrendering any of his own special effects. He might even claim that in applying this ancient form to a modern sensibility he had a precedent in Luis de Góngora who in the seventeenth century used the *romance* to blend popular themes with the advanced manner of his epoch. Lorca could not have made a better choice. He wished to create a poetry of living people and to present them through his own special vision and technique. The *romance*, whose themes vary from heroic stories to love-poems, provided him with just what he needed. As the title suggests, Lorca's characters are still Gipsies. He could not lightly forsake this people in whom he found so much to win his affection and awaken his inspiration. The word *gitano* or " gipsy " often occurs, even for the moon or maidens in a biblical story. But the Gipsy colour is diluted. We hear no more of *siguiriya* or *soleá* or *petenera*. The Gipsies have become simple, passionate Spaniards as Lorca found them in Andalusia, and the *Romancero* is the poetry of his own people.

In the *Romancero* Lorca carried to perfection that harmony of primitive and cultivated elements which can be seen in his earlier poetry. Though his subjects are drawn from a small part of life and his characters act on elementary motives, he never fails to set the imprint of his own sensibility on them. There is no artificial simplicity in these ballads. There is no moment which is not pure poetry or in which Lorca does not give an experience in its exciting fullness. The poems are not, even at a first reading, easy. Yet they have won a great popular success and are loved and quoted by many almost illiterate Spaniards. The reason is not only that they reflect some dominant qualities in the Spanish soul but that Lorca's sensibility is so fine and so sincere that simple men, whose minds are not touched by science or its substitutes, can see directly what he means and recognise its affinity to their own experience. Arturo Barea tells of a member of the Republican militia who heard Lorca's description of the Civil Guard :

> Los caballos negros son.
> Las herraduras son negras.
> Sobre las capas relucen
> manchas de tinta y de cera.
> Tienen, por eso no lloran,
> de plomo las calaveras,[1]

and, taking in the lines at once with all their implications, said : " He makes you see and smell the Civil Guard ". Lorca's art is such that he can present something just as he himself feels it and at the same time make this intelligible to men very unlike himself. It is a great triumph of art, but it is more than that. Lorca could do it because he understood his

[1] The horses are black.
The horse-shoes are black.
On the police-caps glisten
Stains of ink and of wax.
Their skulls are of lead,
So they do not weep.

Gipsies with a full imaginative insight and entered into their ways of thought and feeling. He found in their instinctive outlook much in common with his own sensibility, and from this common basis he wrote poems which are not only brilliant and exciting and far-ranging, but firmly founded in human nature.

Lorca presents his complex material with all the fullness that it would have if it were a first impression which has not been clouded by time or thinned by intellectual analysis. He uses his modern technique to convey sensations in their essence without reference to artificial categories of thought. When, for instance, he writes :

> Y un horizonte de perros
> ladra muy lejos del río,[1]

this is the scene exactly as it would strike the senses. The rationalised way of describing it might be that dogs bark on the horizon far from the river. But that is not exact or correct. For no horizon is visible : there is simply a sound of barking in the distance. So it is right to say that a horizon of dogs barks, as if the only horizon that matters were not visible but audible. Lorca's accounts of what is seen or heard have this immediacy and truth. Sometimes he appeals to the ear, as when the starch of a petticoat sounds " like a piece of silk torn by knives " ; sometimes to the eye, as when the fighting Antoñito makes " leaps like a slippery dolphin " ; sometimes to undifferentiated sensations of touch and sound, as when Thamar says her brother's kisses are " wasps and light breezes in a double swarm of flutes ". The effects may be accumulated into a complex result, as in a description of dawn :

> La higuera frota su viento
> con la lija de sus ramas,
> y el monte, gato garduño,
> eriza sus pitas agrias.[2]

---

[1] And a horizon of dogs
Barks far away from the river.

[2] The fig-tree rubs its wind
With the sand-paper of its branches,
And the mountain, thieving cat,
Bristles its sour agaves.

We might paraphrase this by saying that the sound of the fig-tree stirring is like the rubbing of sand-paper and that the mountain bristling with agaves is like a cat bristling when it is out to steal. But Lorca puts his meaning more directly and more faithfully. For him the fig-tree is, so far as his sensation of it is concerned, really rubbed with sand-paper and the mountain really bristles. That is how the situation actually strikes him. The result is far more vivid than if the complex experience had been analysed and arranged to suit ordinary habits of thought. Lorca's sensuous handling of events appeals to much more than the eye. It conveys shades and associations beyond the power of plain statement and despite its apparent strangeness strikes home with immediate and telling effect. For instance in *Preciosa y el Aire* (*Preciosa and the Wind*) a girl is pursued by a lustful wind which says to her :

> Abre en mis dedos antiguos
> la rosa azul de tu vientre,[1]

and the image of the " azure rose " conveys both the wind's desire for the girl and the virginal coldness of her resistance. In *Thamár y Amnón* (*Thamar and Amnon*) the blistering Eastern heat appears in the picture of the wounded earth :

> La tierra se ofrece llena
> de heridas cicatrizadas,
> o estremecida de agudos
> cauterios de luces blancas.[2]

The heat is cruel and devastating and prepares the way for ugly actions to come. No less sinister is the spilt blood in *Reyerta* (*Brawl*) :

> Sangre resbalada gime
> muda canción de serpiente.[3]

---

[1] Open in my ancient fingers
The azure rose of your belly.

[2] Earth presents itself full
Of scarred wounds,
Or shaken by piercing
Cauteries of white lights.

[3] The spilt blood groans
A mute song of a serpent.

The blood, which is said to sing a silent song like a serpent's, has not only an ugly trail but calls with a menace of vengeance. The visual image passes into something more suggestive and more horrifying. The complex emotional and imaginative experience which is the stuff of poetry is brought directly home to us by this art which singles out the significant detail and presents it with all its claims on the imagination.

Lorca's interest in painting enabled him to make a special contribution to this kind of effect. He felt keenly the significance of colours, and in some poems he makes them set the tone of the whole story. For instance, in *Romance sonámbulo* (*Sleepwalker Ballad*) he strikes in his opening lines a note of green :

> Verde que te quiero verde.
> Verde viento. Verdes ramas.[1]

From this he moves to the sleep-walking girl with her green flesh and green hair. The themes are repeated at intervals through the poem until a green light seems to dominate it. The colour suggests an unreal, ghostly atmosphere and is well suited to the sleep-walker as she sways over the face of a cistern and looks like a lunar icicle held above the water. In *Muerte de Antoñito el Camborio* (*Death of Antoñito the Camborio*), a story of blood and death, the dominating colour is red. It appears in different shades, in Antoñito's voice " of male carnation ", in his crimson tie, in his raisin-coloured shoes, in the three spurts of his blood before he dies. In *Romance de la Guardia civil española* (*Ballad of the Spanish Civil Guard*) the colour is black. It appears at the start with black horses, horse-shoes, and ink stains, goes on through the black night and the black dust thrown up by the battle between the Guards and the Gipsies, and ends with the Guards disappearing into the night. The black tone of the poem makes more than a visual impression ; it shows the stupid malice of the Guards. Their night-attack on the Gipsies is typical of their characters, and they fit appropriately into this imagery of darkness.

The subjects to which this art is applied are primitive men

[1] Green, how I love you, green.
A green wind. Green branches.

and women who are moved by violent and unrestrained passions and live in close proximity to blood and death. Lorca's Gipsies are almost outcasts from society. They have little place in its organised activities and are often in conflict with the law as it is embodied in the Civil Guard. The Civil Guard are Lorca's symbols of oppression and tyranny, of that bleak, unreasonable power which interferes with the natural pleasures of man and seeks only to inhibit or destroy. In *Reyerta* they appear at the scene of bloodshed and listen respectfully to the unfeeling decision of the judge :

> — Señores guardias civiles,
> aquí pasó lo de siempre.[1]

In *Romance sonámbulo* they pursue the mortally wounded smuggler into his refuge and beat drunkenly on the door so that, though he is hiding, he does not feel safe :

> La noche se puso íntima
> como una pequeña plaza.
> Guardias civiles borrachos
> en la puerta golpeaban.[2]

In *Prendimiento de Antoñito el Camborio* (*Arrest of Antoñito the Camborio*) they arrest Antoñito as he walks to Seville and take him to prison. In the ballad named after them they burst on the Gipsies' revelries and stop them with acts of hideous violence. As they ride through the night they dream of bloodshed :

> Pasan, si quieren pasar,
> y ocultan en la cabeza
> una vaga astronomía
> de pistolas inconcretas.[3]

---

[1] Gentlemen of the Civil Guard,
This is what always happens.

[2] The night became intimate
Like a little square.
Drunken Civil Guards
Were beating on the door.

[3] They pass if they wish to pass,
And conceal in their heads
A vague astronomy
Of pistols without shape.

They are creatures of brutal reality who invade the dream-city of the Gipsies as they hold a festival in fancy dresses and half-imagine that they are the Virgin, St. Joseph, and the three sultans of Persia. The Guards end the revels and the dreams, and ride away into the " tunnel of darkness ", leaving nothing behind but the play of the sand and the moon. The ballads in which the Civil Guard appears become myths of the struggle between passionate, imaginative, simple life and the cruel, unnatural forces of senseless authority which attack it.

The life which the Gipsies lead against this background is built of simple elements and especially of religion, love and death. Each has its own character and its own appeal. In religion the saints are figures of local sanctity who have been long acclimatised to the ways of a southern, superstitious people. In Granada is St. Michael whose character reflects the luxurious city which he protects. He is covered with lace, and his beautiful thighs show through his bell-shaped clothes. He stands in the alcove of a tower, his petticoats stiff with sequins, while old men and old women come to worship him, and a poor old bishop conducts Mass. The picture is scrupulously correct and conveys a side of Catholicism which has grown up in a country where religion is largely the concern of women. St. Michael is a popular manifestation of the spirit of the Counter-Reformation as it has prevailed since the sixteenth century in Latin countries. The saints attract some of the vague sensual longings which are deep in the Spanish temperament, and the Church has found this a useful outlet and conducive to virtue. As he stands in his girlish elegance, St. Michael presents a marked contrast to the busy life which goes on outside, especially to the caravans of mules that come over the mountains and to the common people who chew sunflower-seeds as they go to worship him.

St. Raphael, of Cordoba, is conceived in a different spirit. He stands on a great classical tower and suggests the Spanish Renaissance. In his splendid detachment he represents one side of the proud ancient city : the other side is represented by all the hubbub of the town and by the river which washes remains of Roman statues and mirrors the coaches that pass along its banks. The contrast is thus made between the two aspects of Cordoba :

> Blanda Córdoba de juncos,
> Córdoba de arquitectura.·

Just as the unmoving saint in the tower stands for the second, so the first is represented by a fish which is equally unmoved as it stays in the water and takes no notice of the attempts made by children to lure it. The contrast is worked out with much charm and point between the noisy town of real life and the celestial town on high, between unmoving fish and un-moving saint, and this conveys the paradox of such a city as Cordoba, where buildings from the great age of Spain rise up in all the uproar and activity of Spanish life to the accompani-ment of the silent water. The effect is largely visual, an impression of the city as it might strike a sensitive visitor. But the visual impression stands for something else, for the harmony and union between the celestial detachment in the saint and the life around him. The two Cordobas are distinct and yet one :

> Córdoba quebrada en chorros.
> Celeste Córdoba enjuta.[2]

The simple Gipsy mind accepts the contrasts without question and sees in Cordoba a single place, full of life and wonder and watched over by its special saint.

In Seville the saint is St. Gabriel, and the ballad about him tells how he comes as a smart, handsome young man to reveal to a Gipsy girl that she will bear a son. It is the story of an annunciation conceived in a spirit like that of Murillo, with the difference that Lorca is simpler and closer to the unsophisti-cated Gipsy spirit. There is a delightful tenderness in his presentation of the episode. The saint is seen with the clear, sensual vision of primitive folk :

> Un bello niño de junco
> anchos hombros, fino talle,

---

[1] Gentle Cordoba of reeds,
Cordoba of architecture.

[2] Cordoba broken in streams.
Heavenly, dry Cordoba.

piel de nocturna manzana,
boca triste y ojos grandes.[1]

He wears patent-leather shoes, and as he comes through the
air there is a sound of celestial lutes. There is no palm-tree
to equal him, no emperor or morning-star. In a charming
interchange, Anunciación, whose child is to be the head of
" a hundred dynasties ", greets the angel with joy and tells
him that she feels the young life stirring in her :

— ¡Ay, San Gabriel que reluces !
¡Gabrielillo de mi vida !
En el fondo de mis pechos
Ya nace la leche tibia.[2]

Lorca's Anunciación is just a Gipsy girl, and his bold conception of her as a kind of Virgin Mary reflects the ease with
which a primitive people gives to its heroes and heroines the
qualities of its gods. The son she is to bear is to be unlike
other children in that he will have three wounds and a mole
on his chest, and his destiny is power and splendour. The
simple Gipsy imagination likes to dream of such hopes as this
and sees nothing strange in the part played by the Archangel.
It transforms an old legend into its own myth and dreams that
one of its own daughters can have so special a destiny. The
Christian religion comes so naturally to it that it can play
with it and invent from it new chapters of mythology.

The peculiar character of the Gipsy faith as Lorca sees it
comes out even more remarkably in his historical ballad
Martirio de Santa Olalla (*Martyrdom of Saint Eulalia*). The
story is ancient, and long before Lorca took it up Prudentius
sang of it in decorous Latin and a French poet of the ninth
century wrote a hymn to " Sancta Eulalia ". Lorca's poem
has its relations with the past and treats history as the Gipsies

---

[1] A beautiful, lissom boy,
Broad shoulders, slim waist,
Skin of an apple at night,
Sad mouth and large eyes.

[2] Oh shining Saint Gabriel!
Dear Saint Gabriel of my life!
In the depths of my breasts
Warm milk is already stirring.

see it with their feeling that it is still present and real. He dwells almost brutally on the circumstances of the martyrdom and shows how well he understands the taste for torture and blood which informs so much of Spanish religion. The Roman consul receives on a platter the severed breasts of the martyr; her hands are cut off and writhe on the ground; blood covers her shoulders like hair. And this brutality is interwoven with a sexual emotion of fascinated horror. As the maiden is tortured,

> Su sexo tiembla enredado
> como un pájaro en las zarzas.[1]

The persecutors are presented with a strong sense of their reality, almost as if they were members of the Civil Guard. The centurions clash in their silver armour; their horses rear and gallop while the bold soldiers of Rome dice or sleep. The end is in the simplest spirit of traditional religion. Eulalia's body hangs on a tree, blackened by death, above the white snow. Then the skies flare, and Eulalia turns white as Angels cry, " Holy, Holy, Holy ! " The story of the martyrdom gives another aspect of Spanish religion. In his poems on the saints of the great cities Lorca shows the gay side of what the Gipsies believe; in the martyrdom he strikes a more cruel note. But the two sides are equally true and relevant. In both there is a strong undercurrent of sensuality. The Gipsies turn to their faith for instances of the violent passions which belong to their own lives and which they accept as inevitable to the human lot. In its elements of suffering and reward, of brutal passions and insensate power, the *Martyrdom of Saint Eulalia* conforms to an ancient and popular tradition.

In a religion of this kind even those whose task it is to promote it have their extremely human sides and must not be expected to conform to exacting standards of behaviour. In particular its monasteries and nunneries have developed lives which are not only strange to a Northern outlook but sometimes repellent even to Spaniards. Institutions of this kind have existed for so long and been so cut off from common

---

[1] Her sex trembles in disarray,
Like a bird in the briars.

ties that they develop abnormalities which are more or less accepted by those who are familiar with them. In nunneries the inmates combine a life of prayer and self-denial with little customs like embroidery or the making of sweets, and it is not difficult to imagine that these reflect their repressed desires and longing to partake of more ordinary human activities. Lorca takes up this subject in *La Monja Gitana* (*The Gipsy Nun*) which shows a nun in her closeness to nature and is much more realistic than his ballads about saints. In her nunnery, with its whitewash and flowers, she embroiders carnations on cream-coloured cloth, while the lights flutter in the chandelier and in the kitchen other nuns make sweets called " the five wounds of Christ ". Her work is interrupted by the distant sight of two horsemen galloping, and she is deeply disturbed :

> Un rumor último y sordo
> le despega la camisa,
> y, al mirar nubes y montes
> en las yertas lejanías,
> se quiebra su corazón
> de azúcar y yerbaluisa.[1]

Momentary fancies sweep into her mind : then she turns her eyes away and goes on with her embroidery. This picture of a nun who is suddenly assailed by lusts of the flesh might be taken to show that Lorca disapproved of the whole system of nunneries with their denial of the body and the hypocrisy which it breeds. But Lorca is no moralist. He enjoys the dramatic situation, feels its charm and human appeal, and presents it as a touching and attractive episode.

If religion provides the brighter side of Gipsy life, love provides some of its more sombre tones. When he deals with it, Lorca still keeps his detachment and his objectivity, though he does not shrink from depicting its harsher and more brutal manifestations. *La Casada infiel* (*The Faithless Wife*) is a

---

[1] A last muffled sound
Ruffles her garment ;
She looks at the clouds and hills
In the motionless distances,
And her heart is bursting
With sugar and rosemary.

masterpiece which deserves its great popularity. As Arturo Barea has shown, it contains all the elements of a typical Spaniard's attitude to women and turns on " the point of honour " that, since the woman is not a virgin, the man feels himself cheated and pays her for her compliance as if she were a prostitute. Into this frame Lorca weaves his story, and stresses its tense excitement and rampant sexuality. The setting is an obscure corner of the town, and it is growing dark. Beyond the blackberry-bushes, the reeds and the haw-thorns, the man makes a hollow in the earth, takes off his tie and his belt, while the woman takes off her four bodices. The physical sensations are conveyed with unshrinking candour. In the opening stages the man says :

> En las últimas esquinas
> toqué sus pechos dormidos,
> y se me abrieron de pronto
> como ramos de jacintos,[1]

and later he praises the woman's shining skin, and adds :

> Sus muslos se me escapaban
> como peces sorprendidos,
> la mitad llenos de lumbre,
> la mitad llenos de frío.[2]

His sense of honour prevents him from telling what she said to him, and he pays her off with a sewing-basket of straw-coloured satin. But his male pride has been offended, and he refuses to fall in love with her. The whole poem is true to Spanish manhood. It catches the mood of an exciting adventure and sets it out with dramatic realism and truth.

A counterpart to this modern scene can be found in *Thamár y Amnón* where realism is replaced by a powerful

---

[1] In the remotest corners
I touched her sleeping breasts
And suddenly they opened to me
Like stalks of hyacinth.

[2] Her thighs fled from me,
Like frightened fish,
Half full of fire,
Half full of cold.

erotic fancy.   The biblical story of Amnon's incestuous love
for his sister becomes the story of a brutal, uncontrollable
passion, as a Gipsy imagination might see it.   The atmosphere
is of a stifling, moonlit night in a parched season.   In such an
air all control is thrown aside and sexual passions rise in their
naked violence.   Lorca conveys this both directly and in-
directly.   He shows the youthful figure of Amnon :

> Llenas las ingles de espuma
> y oscilaciones la barba,[1]

and the fancies which fill his mind as he lies on his bed :

> Toda la alcoba sufría
> con sus ojos llenos de alas.[2]

When Thamar begs him to leave her in peace, he answers in
words of oracular insistence :

> Thamár, en tus pechos altos
> hay dos peces que me llaman,
> y en las yemas de tus dedos
> rumor de rosa encerrada.[3]

Lorca's imagery falls easily to this task, but it plays a more
subtle part in the choice of details for their relevance to the
unconscious psychology of sex.   The heat itself is physically
excited :

> Por encima de los techos
> nervios de metal sonaban,[4]

and there is something ugly and brutal in the general silence :

> En el musgo de los troncos
> la cobra tendida canta.[5]

---

[1] His loins full of foam
And his beard of vibrations.

[2] The whole alcove suffered
With his eyes full of wings.

[3] Thamar, in your high breasts
Two fishes are calling to me,
And in the tips of your fingers
Is a murmur of sealed rose.

[4] Above the roofs
Nerves of metal were sounding.

[5] In the moss of tree-stems
The stretched cobra sings.

The setting prepares the way for Amnon's rape of his sister, when he grabs her by the hair and claws her dress. The poem is a remarkable example of Lorca's ability to weave fact and fancy, plain statement and vivid sensation. The biblical story takes on a new fierceness and horror through his genius which gives to it all the erotic concentration that it would have for a Gipsy.

The theme of passion is close to the theme of death. The lives of Lorca's Gipsies, passed in passion and violence, are liable to end in tragedy. Particularly when their honour is assailed, they feel that they must make atonement with blood. This spirit gives a special point to the two ballads about Antoñito the Camborio. The first tells of his arrest by the Civil Guard on his way to Seville. He has an excellent style and appearance, as he moves slowly and gracefully, with his blue ringlets shining between his eyes, and shows his careless gaiety as he goes :

> A la mitad del camino
> cortó limones redondos,
> y los fué tirando al agua
> hasta que la puso de oro.[1]

But this brave figure shows no fight when the Civil Guards arrest him and take him off to prison. This is a grave dereliction of honour and shows that Antoñito is untrue to his breeding. The second ballad tells how he makes amends by a heroic death. In his last fight against his four cousins he shows all the courage that can be asked of him. His courage is beyond praise, but the odds are against him, and he knows that he is dying :

> Ya mi talle se ha quebrado
> como caña de maíz.[2]

His death is tragic because he is a splendid creature, " worthy of an empress " and " living coin that will never be repeated ".

---

[1] Half-way along the road
He cut round lemons,
And threw them into the water
Until he turned it to gold.

[2] My waist has snapped already
Like a stalk of maize.

His death is his finest moment, and after it there is silence :

> Voces de muerte cesaron
> cerca del Guadalquivir.[1]

His heroism sets the seal on his life and atones for its failures.

Lorca's ballads do more than present scenes of Gipsy life through a sensibility which marks their picturesque and dramatic elements. They present events as Gipsies themselves see them, and for this reason many of the poems have a strange quality of mystery, as if their episodes were not really intelligible. Lorca is so faithful to the Gipsies' own outlook that he presents the vague and almost nameless powers which govern their lives behind the façade of their religion. When Preciosa is chased by a wind, the wind may be St. Christopher, but his lustful habits are those of Pan. In *Romance de la Pena negra* (*Ballad of the Black Sorrow*) more sinister powers are at work. A fearful dread assails a girl while she is busy with her household tasks, and drives her out to seek comfort in human society. It is quite irrational and throws her into frenzied misery :

> ¡ Qué pena ! Me estoy poniendo
> de azabache carne y ropa.
> ¡ Ay, mis camisas de hilo !
> ¡ Ay, mis muslos de amapola ! [2]

There is no cure but air and quiet. This sudden fear is typical of Gipsy life, and the poet comments on it :

> ¡ Oh pena de los gitanos !
> Pena limpia y siempre sola.[3]

In *Romance de la Luna, Luna* (*Ballad of the Moon, the Moon*) the moon is a baleful power which kills a child for making fun of it. We are not told how this happens, though the presage

---

[1] Voices of death were silent
Near the Guadalquivir.

[2] What sorrow ! My dress and my flesh
Are becoming black as jet.
Oh my garments of linen,
Oh my thighs of poppy !

[3] O sorrow of the Gipsies,
Sorrow pure and always alone.

of it is clear enough, and the moon is seen carrying the child
off through the sky :

> Cómo canta la zumaya,
> ¡ ay, cómo canta en el árbol !
> Por el cielo va la luna
> con un niño de la mano.[1]

For the Gipsies this needs no explanation, and Lorca presents
it through their eyes.

The same mysterious uncertainty fills the wonderful
Romance sonámbulo. A sleep-walking girl lingers over a balustrade and dreams of the sea. The silence is broken by a
wounded smuggler who has the police after him. He knows
that he is dying, and he wishes to die in comfort in a proper
bed with sheets, but his host cannot help him :

> Pero yo ya no soy yo,
> ni mi casa es ya mi casa.[2]

There is no explanation of this refusal, and no account of the
circumstances which prompt it. Then both men climb up to
the balustrade where the sleep-walker sways over a cistern
while the Civil Guards beat on the door. We assume that
before he dies the smuggler wishes to see the girl, who in the
past has loved him :

> ¡ Cúantas veces te esperó !
> ¡ Cúantas veces te esperara,
> cara fresca, negro pelo,
> en esta verde baranda ![3]

But this love is not stressed, and the smuggler's motives are
not mentioned. The action, which is intensely vivid and

---

[1] How the barn-owl sings
How it sings up in the tree !
The moon goes up in the sky
With a child in its hand.

[2] But I am no longer I,
And my house is no longer my house.

[3] How often she waited for you,
How often she would wait for you ;
Cool face, black hair
On this green balustrade.

exciting, has some of the qualities of a dream ; so clear are its outlines and so inexplicable its motives. But such actions do not need to be explained. What count are the atmosphere and the sense of mystery. The girl becomes a kind of unattainable goal, a love which cannot be satisfied, and which the smuggler will never know before he dies.

How deeply some of Lorca's themes are founded in Spanish tradition can be seen from *El Emplazado* (*The Cited*). In history King Ferdinand IV was known as " the cited " because he died from no explicable cause exactly thirty days after he had put two brothers wrongly to death, and was believed to have been cited before God for it. The impression which his death made on the public mind was confirmed, says the historian Mariana, when in the next two years Pope Clement V and Philippe le Bel, King of France, both died on the date cited for them by Jacques Moloy, the Grand Master of the Templars, whose execution they had arranged. The notion of *el emplazado* has played its part in Spanish history, and Lorca takes it up. With his usual economy he does not say what crime has been committed or who cites the guilty man : he dwells almost entirely on the actual citing and the anticipation of death in which the man spends his last days. The curse is laid on him on the 25th of June, and on the 25th of August he is laid in his shroud. This is the situation as Lorca gives it, and into it he infuses a strange, powerful poetry of a man who knows that his end is near. The setting is realistic and painfully impressive. There is a cold savagery in the curse which his enemies have put on him :

> Pinta una cruz en la puerta
> y pon tu nombre debajo,
> porque cicutas y ortigas
> nacerán en tu costado,
> y agujas de cal mojada
> te morderán los zapatos.[1]

---

[1] Paint a cross on the door
And put your name under it ;
For hemlock and nettle
Will grow in your side,
And needles of wet lime
Will bite into your shoes.

The poem gives the haunted, hunted state of a doomed man who cannot sleep while he waits for the end which he cannot escape. It needs no more explanation and no more details than it has. Magic is at work, and Lorca shows what it does.

Though the eighteen poems of the *Romancero Gitano* vary greatly in subject and considerably in spirit, they are not merely alike in their style and outlook but are held together by certain recurring themes which stress points of significance for Lorca's conception of his Gipsies. For instance, he often speaks of razors and knives and swords. In *Reyerta* they strike a dominant note at the start :

> En la mitad del barranco
> las navajas de Albacete,
> bellas de sangre contraria,
> relucen como los peces.[1]

Antoñito falls to the " four daggers " of his kinsmen. When he is taken off so unheroically to prison, it is a sign that he has fallen short of traditional standards, and that manners are not what they once were :

> Están los viejos cuchillos
> tiritando bajo el polvo.[2]

Since the Gipsies take so easily to knives when their passions are aroused, it is right that their fiercer actions should sometimes be symbolised through the imagery of knives. So the starch of the woman's petticoat in *La Casada infiel* sounds like " silk rent by ten knives " : so the Wind-man pursues Preciosa " with his flaming sword " : so Thamar screams at her brother's assault of her,

> Qué espesuras de puñales
> y túnicas desgarradas.[3]

---

[1] In the middle of the gully
Razors of Albacete,
Lovely with combatant blood,
Glitter like fishes.

[2] The old knives are shivering
Underneath the dust.

[3] What thicknesses of daggers
And of tunics ripped.

These weapons strike a note of cruelty and violence, whether literal or symbolical, and show the fierce spirit in which the Gipsies conduct their lives.

Another favourite theme is horses and horsemen. They are of course a familiar element in the Spanish scene, and they often complete the landscape with a touch of life. But their appeal is stronger than that of mere decoration. The Gipsy nun sees the horsemen in the distance and is troubled by obscure desires. The man who makes love to the faithless wife rides away on his mare without bridle or stirrups. The scene for the martyrdom of St. Eulalia is set by a horse galloping and rearing. The dying smuggler's life has been passed in ships on the sea and with horses on the mountain. When the child mocks the moon, a horseman gallops over the plain. Such a life is passed among horses. They are an integral part of it, and for this reason they easily take a symbolical significance. The horse suggests physical strength and health, vigorous activity and grace and speed. That is why St. Gabriel tells Anunciación that her eyes are like " a horseman's landscape ", and why the arrest of Antoñito is twice associated with the imagery of horses, first when he sets out for Seville in fine style, and the wind reflects his spirit :

> Y una corta brisa, ecuestre,
> salta los montes de plomo,[1]

and later, when he is arrested and the still sky shines above him,

> Como la grupa de un potro,[2]

as if it mocked his humiliation and despised him for not living up to his proper standards. In horses and horsemen Lorca stresses the noble side of the Gipsies, their physical strength and beauty.

The strange world of the *Romancero* has its moments when it seems strange and remote, as if it were governed by its own inscrutable laws, and this element Lorca stresses through his frequent use of the moon and of imagery drawn from it. The

[1] And a sharp breeze, like a horse
Leaps over the mountains of lead.
[2] Like the croup of a foal.

moon brings frenzy and seems to account for some of the strange actions which take place. In the ballad named after it it dominates everything :

> En el aire conmovido
> mueve la luna sus brazos
> y enseña, lúbrica y pura,
> sus senos de duro estaño.[1]

Preciosa's tambourine is like a moon, and the comparison is not merely of shape but of character. In *Romance sonámbulo* the moon is called " gipsy ", no doubt because its ways are as uncertain as those of the Gipsies : the balustrades seem to be made of moonlight, and the moon holds a girl above the water as if it were an icicle. In *San Miguel* the moon is full of voices and fading shapes. In the ballad of the Civil Guard the moon seems to take part in the Gipsies' revelry :

> La media luna soñaba
> un éxtasis de cigüeña.[2]

In *Thamár y Amnón* the moon is one of the chief characters, as it shines over the parched land, and Amnon looks at it and sees the breasts of his sister. It is a power of deceit and illusion : it draws men's dreams to itself and breeds folly and infatuation.

The poems have a deeper unity than this. Though Lorca tells his stories for their own sake with an almost dramatic impartiality, he creates his own self-consistent world of the imagination. He reduces human life to a few essential elements, to the unrationalised emotions and desires of simple men and women. The humanity which Lorca portrays has a natural directness and candour. The characters, sketched in a few deft strokes, stand in their own strength with all their primitive forces at work, like Preciosa playing her tambourine or the man who courts the faithless wife and is confident that he has acted " like a true gipsy ", or Anunciación, " well

[1] In the troubled air
The moon moves her arms
And shows, lustful and pure,
Her breasts of hard tin.

[2] The half-moon dreamed
An ecstasy of a stork.

favoured, badly dressed ", or the incomparable Antoñito with his scarlet tie, his blued hair, and his magnificent profile. These characters are not facets of the poet's inner life or symbols of his thought ; they are figures of drama who engage our interest by their personalities and their destinies. Even when Lorca shifts his point of vision from the present to history or legend, his characters are equally alive, and his Eulalia and his Thamar are fit companions for Preciosa in their passionate simplicity and their undeserved sufferings. Lorca's dramatic and plastic genius created a homogeneous world in which some simple and essential kinds of human life are vividly presented in his dramatic persons. He makes his own little universe which so imposes itself on us that we accept its laws without question.

The *Romancero* is much more than dramatic : it is almost pure poetry. To every phase of his Gipsy lives Lorca gives the abundant riches of his sympathy and sensibility, and weaves his visual fancies in the frame of their dreams and deaths. His unexpected juxtapositions of images, the brilliance of his details and of his symbols, his complete avoidance of anything trite or false or exaggerated, all help to secure an astonishing level of imaginative achievement. He sees not only the physical setting of his characters but its meaning for the imagination. When he first mentions the Gipsies, he not only shows what they look like but more subtly what they are :

> Por el olivar venían,
> bronce y sueño, los gitanos.
> Las cabezas levantadas
> y los ojos entornados.[1]

The words hold good for nearly all his characters in their pride and their passion, their physical strength and their dominating dreams. When Preciosa walks on " an amphibious path of crystals and laurels " and plays on her " parchment moon ", the figure means more than that she plays a tambourine : it suggests the illusion in which she is sunk, her midway position

---

[1] Through the olive-wood came,
Bronze and dream, the Gipsies,
With their heads uplifted
And their eyes half-closed.

between reality and trance. Even the dead have a similar kind of interest, like the man killed in a brawl :

> Su cuerpo lleno de lirios
> y una granada en las sienes,[1]

or the blood of the dead lover :

> Tranquila de flor cortada
> y amarga de muslo joven.[2]

The poetry which Lorca finds in his Gipsies bears no relation to romantic and picturesque conventions. It is not their clothes that interest him, but the fundamental humanity which displays itself in many ways and calls for his imaginative interpretation.

These characters move in a brilliant natural setting. It has its towns like Cordoba, Seville and Granada, but it is for the most part in the country. There is a hint of the sea in the distance, and in the background are the mountains with their traffic of coaches and horsemen :

> El barco sobre la mar
> y el caballo en la montaña.[3]

The different aspects of the physical scene correspond with the moods and actions of the human characters and seem almost to determine their course. The man who takes out the faithless wife does it on a dark night when the only light is that of the fireflies, and the darkness corresponds to his mood of grim sensuality. The girl who is frightened by the " black sorrow " feels something sinister in the movement of the leaves and needs the free, open air to recover herself. When St. Gabriel leaves Anunciación after his joyous message to her and returns to the sky,

> Las estrellas de la noche
> se volvieron siemprevivas.[4]

---

[1] His body full of lilies
And a pomegranate in his temples.
[2] Tranquil with cut flowers
And bitter with young thigh.
[3] The ship on the sea
And the horse on the mountain.
[4] The stars of the night
Became immortelles.

The stars share the exalted joy which his mission has brought
and the ordered universe of which it is a part. The calm night
which witnesses the incarceration of Antoñito reflects the un-
eventful, unheroic character of his surrender, while his death
takes place in nobler circumstances at night :

> Cuando las estrellas clavan
> rejones al agua gris,[1]

when the stars are almost sinister and baleful. A similar note
of mysterious terror appears when a man dies of love :

> La noche llama temblando
> al cristal de los balcones,
> perseguida por los mil
> perros que no la conocen.[2]

The blistering heat of high summer enters into Amnon and
makes his lust as violent as itself. Even the water in the wells
reflects his state :

> Linfa de pozo oprimida
> brota silencio en las jarras.[3]

Lorca's characters are true children of nature. They live close
to it and its moods are their own.

The lives of Lorca's Gipsies have a strangely immemorial
quality which transcends their local and temporal limitations
and makes them typical of the unchanging elements in Spanish
life. When at their November festival they dress themselves
up and take different parts, the Judge, who comes with the
Civil Guard, says :

> Han muerto cuatro romanos
> y cinco cartagineses,[4]

---

[1] When the stars nail
Spears on the gray water.

[2] The night calls trembling
To the crystal of the balconies,
Pursued by the thousand
Dogs who do not know her.

[3] Oppressed water of the well
Gushes silence in the jars.

[4] Four Romans have died
And five Carthaginians.

and refers to the fantastic costumes worn by different confraternities who take the name of Jews or Romans or Carthaginians or Phoenicians and often end their celebrations in blows. To the Gipsies these disguises are quite real. They feel for the moment that they really are Romans or Carthaginians, and their belief is based on some ancient memory of a past when the two races contended for the dominion of Spain. The Roman past is buried, but it is still there, at least at Cordoba :

> Donde las ondas alisan
> Romano torso desnudo,[1]

and at Merida where the martyrdom of St. Eulalia is connected with vague memories of Roman soldiers, and broken statues testify to Roman rule and are believed still to have power as they lie under the earth :

> Noche de torsos yacentes
> y estrellas de nariz rota
> aguarda grietas del alba
> para derrumbarse toda.[2]

These remains of the Roman world have a more than historical or local interest. They show how ancient the Gipsy life is and how deep its roots are in the Spanish earth.

The *Romancero* is a book of astonishing brilliance, of unfailing poetry, in which a modern technique is adapted to traditional means and primitive subjects. In it Lorca has absorbed the most important lessons of modernism and avoided it excesses. His tone is marvellously sustained. We never cease to feel that we are seeing things as the Gipsies see them or would see them if they had the power to make their feelings definite. By a remarkable stroke of insight Lorca uses his modern manner for a primitive outlook, and the fit is perfect. His sense of mystery, of irrational actions, of magical powers in the universe, of the way in which passion dominates

[1] Where the waters wash
A naked Roman torso.

[2] Night of resting torsos
And stars of broken nostrils
Waits for the fissures of dawn
To crumble away completely.

the mind and imposes illusions on it, is not only true to his Gipsies but perfectly adapted to his impressionistic method. People so unsophisticated as these see things in this vivid, unrelated way and do not wait to arrange their thoughts in logical categories. The ease of Lorca's purely poetical appeal owes much to his subject. Through it he can take great risks of expression but be sure that they will succeed, because after all his Gipsies are human beings whose approach to life has the instinctive immediacy which is also that of a poet. Nor is it fair to complain that in taking such a subject Lorca shirks the urgent issues of his time. His Gipsies are the humble people of Southern Spain and differ in few essentials from true Spaniards of the same district and class. These were the people whom Lorca knew, and he was right to make them his subject because he felt for them that special affection which awoke his curiosity and his imagination and set his powers to work. The result is a book which has a special place in our time because it shows not only that the outlook of a highly civilised poet is in many ways that of the simplest men and women, but that the new devices which have been invented to express a modern sensibility are not restricted to urban and sophisticated subjects but may be applied with great success to the dark passions and obscure fancies of an almost primitive consciousness.

VIII

RAFAEL ALBERTI,
SOBRE LOS ÁNGELES

At the same time that Lorca was writing his *Romancero*, his friend, Rafael Alberti, wrote *Sobre los Ángeles*, which for originality, sustained and concentrated power, and masterly handling of a modern technique is worthy of comparison with Lorca's book. Published in 1929, *Sobre los Ángeles* is the work of a young man who was born in 1902 and proved in early manhood his ability in more than one kind of poetry. At first sight Alberti presents certain obvious points of similarity to Lorca. He too was an Andalusian who studied the ways and songs of his own country ; he too had a gift for painting and trained his eye through it ; he too began by writing songs, not indeed so delicate or diaphanous as Lorca's but composed with a sure insight into the use of traditional measures for a modern sensibility. But these similarities are much less than the differences, mainly of temperament, which distinguish the two men. Alberti was from the start more intellectual than Lorca. Even his charming songs about the sea and sailors, with which he made his name in 1924, lack Lorca's effortless flight and suggest a background of intenser thought. And with the years this element asserted itself and became more emphatic. While Lorca was content to live on his sensibility and to lose himself in the lives of other men, Alberti found his subjects more and more in himself, in his own struggles and contradictions and problems. With his keen intellect he watched and analysed his emotions, tried to find what they meant, and adapted his technique to his discoveries. He lacked Lorca's instinctive joy and instinctive melancholy : his gifts were more varied and more conflicting. He wrote with apparent ease, and his production in his twenties was abundant and well sustained, but his complex, self-analytical character was soon to create for him difficulties such as Lorca never knew.

Alberti's chief problem in these first years seems to have been to find an art which should express the whole of himself. The conflicting elements in his character refused to cohere into a single form. In his first songs he presented with much charm and fancy his lyrical feeling for the sea, and his success was immediate and deserved. But this was only one part of him. Though the form of the song appealed to the craftsman in him and raised problems of technique which were much to his taste, he had other things to say which could not be held in so small a compass and demanded a different form. He answered this by writing in the grander measures of Spanish poetry as the poets of the sixteenth and seventeenth centuries had used them. In odes, sonnets, madrigals, *terza rima* and *romances* he tried to combine a formal elegance with a modern temper and sensibility and to impose a special kind of external order on his conflicting and often turbulent emotions. His accomplishment is astonishing. At one time he writes a poem in honour of Góngora which has much of Góngora's own elaborate richness ; at another time he writes a madrigal on a tram-ticket which is more than a *tour de force* and shows how the old form can be adjusted to entirely new purposes. But such experiments were not entirely satisfactory. No doubt Alberti saw that this traditional formality was ultimately hostile to some things that he had to say, that it restricted his scope and gave the wrong intonation to his emotions. So, always adventurous, he tried something much more modern and in poems like *A Miss X* and *Platko* used free verse and an almost jaunty manner to create a realistic, ironical, astringent poetry of actual life. Although Alberti succeeded remarkably in each kind of poetry that he attempted, and we cannot but admire his dexterity and sincerity, it is clear that his creative gifts had not reached a final means of expression and that a division of his powers between quite different kinds of poetry was really a confession of his inability to find the ultimate single form which he needed. At this stage Alberti illustrates a risk inherent in the modern conception of poetry. Just because it concentrates on its essential task and regards matters of technique as secondary and subordinate to this, it may leave a poet in a quandary about what means to use, especially when his gifts are unusually assorted and he sees no obvious means to give shape to his experience.

The answer to these questions came with *Sobre los Ángeles*. Into it Alberti put the whole of himself and found a medium entirely appropriate to what he had to say. It is his masterpiece, as the *Romancero* is Lorca's. It reflects both his powerful intellect and his no less powerful emotions : it makes the most both of his lyrical and his contemplative gifts : it shows his ability to use a variety of forms without any hint of strain in them and without any discord between them : it is both intensely imaginative and intimately realistic. Indeed so well does it unite Alberti's gifts that after it his later books seem something of a disappointment. He has indeed written much excellent poetry since the publication of *Sobre los Ángeles*, but no book with quite its finality and completeness. Alberti seems to be an experimenter who is always trying to do something new and is so good an artist that he usually succeeds in creating real poetry. But his own restless and disturbed spirit, no less than the catastrophes which ruined his country and sent him into exile in Argentina, has prevented his later work from having the balance and sustained harmony of *Sobre los Ángeles*. He is still quite a young man, and it is perfectly possible that he may yet produce another masterpiece. But for the present it is his most complete and satisfying work. And it is more than that. In a general picture of European poetry in this century *Sobre los Ángeles* has a special place through the intensity of vision with which it presents the crisis of an imaginative spirit and through the extraordinary degree of precision with which it portrays dark movements and situations in the soul.

Sobre los Ángeles is concerned with a terrible crisis in which Alberti finds that for no explicable reason he has lost his trust in himself and his hold on existence, that things which have hitherto meant much to him and guided and sustained him have suddenly left him, that he has been robbed not merely of his dreams and visions but of everything which gives savour and significance to life, and he does not know what to think or what to do. Other men have gone through crises not entirely dissimilar. The mood which Coleridge sets out so poignantly in *Dejection*, the torturing doubts which Tolstoy felt after the publication of *Anna Karenina*, the collapse of confidence and zest of which Mill speaks in his *Autobiography*, are a few among many examples of the dangers which threaten a man who gives all his powers to his work only to find that he has lost something of inestimable value. Alberti's crisis has something in common with all of these. He too finds suddenly that his self-confidence has gone, that he has no taste for what used to delight him, that he sees no direction in which to move, that he is the prey of strange emotions and dark doubts. But in other ways his position is different. While Tolstoy and Mill encountered these obstacles in ripe middle age after busy lives, Alberti was still in his twenties. And partly because he is still a young man, he resists his crisis and fights against it with a violence and a vigour which show that his state is not really like that which Coleridge expresses so poignantly :

> A grief without a pang, void, dark, and drear,
> A stifled, drowsy, unimpassion'd grief,
> Which finds no natural outlet, no relief,
> In word, or sigh, or tear.

Though Alberti feels empty and useless, he continues to hope for better things and to assert his will against his circumstances. He has indeed found that the spirit in which he has hitherto composed poetry has unaccountably left him. He has assumed that he will always be carried along by it, that he will continue to enjoy his wonder and delight in the mystery of the universe, that no problem faces him more serious than to make the most of his golden opportunities. Suddenly he finds himself flat and sour, robbed of the most important thing that he knew. He has not indeed lost the power to create but he has lost the conditions in which he has hitherto exercised it. It is not surprising that in the first poem of *Sobre los Ángeles* Alberti laments his loss of a Paradise which he has known and loved, his home and his inspiration. No one can answer his questions or tell him how to regain it. He can only look for it and hope to find it :

> Ya en el fin de la Tierra,
> sobre el último filo,
> resbalando los ojos,

muerta en mí la esperanza,
ese pórtico verde
busco en las negras simas.[1]

It is the agony of this loss which inspires Alberti's book. What is for him a terrible personal disaster becomes the poetry of all such disasters in whatever forms they come to others, and so nobly does he tell of it that his voice is not only that of an individual who has lost a most precious possession but of a generation which fears that it has lost its way in the world.

Though *Sobre los Ángeles* is a collection of short poems, each of which is complete in itself, these are arranged in a sequence which gives shape to the whole book. It falls into three parts, each with its dominating character and range of subjects. The first part tells of the actual crisis immediately after it has happened, of the sense of emptiness and meaninglessness which it brings, and of the different ways in which the poet realises this and regrets what he has lost. He cannot at first quite assess the full extent of his loss, but he knows how futile he feels and what fierce forces of disillusion and despair are at work in him. He feels dispossessed of his home and himself, a man robbed of his proper personality, a body which is only a body and nothing else, the ready prey of forces now violent, now deceitful, now furious. In this section Alberti gives the poetry of a soul which has lost its bearings and is unable to withstand the new and fearful powers which assail it. In the second section this sense of emptiness grows into something more anxious and more troubled, a conflict of light and darkness, and darkness triumphs. Alberti's spirit is now a battlefield for ugly and angry passions of anger, envy, vengeance and avarice. His desolate condition has made him painfully conscious of primitive passions which lurk in his being and come to the fore when his system of life is broken.

[1] Now at the end of the earth,
Over the last line,
My eyes wandering,

Hope dead in me,
That green gateway
I seek in the black gulfs.

He is not entirely empty after all. Some things survive in him, but they are powers of destruction and death, enemies of the living soul. In this state he feels like a sleep-walker whose actions and words are mechanical and meaningless and who is haunted by menacing noises and phantoms from the dark. He has still his cherished memories of his earlier happiness, but they serve only to make his present condition more bitter and more distressing. In the third section Alberti slowly and laboriously picks up the broken pieces of himself and sees what remains after the catastrophe and what lessons he has learned from it. He recognises that his paradise, his confident youth, is lost for ever, but from the present there is after all something to be gained, in unexpected corners of experience, even in ugliness and suffering. His task is to make the most of this, and he closes, if not with any lively hope, at least with a determination to take what reality has to offer. The end of *Sobre los Ángeles* is not a despairing confession of defeat like that of *The Waste Land*, though the experience through which the poet has passed is no less disturbing and destructive.

The subject of *Sobre los Ángeles* is well fitted for a modern treatment. A devastating experience of this kind, with its apprehension of disaster and chaos, finds a faithful reflection in the movements of free verse and the sharp concise language of an impressionistic style. So powerful are the emotions at work that every subject, however commonplace it may seem at first sight, is turned into poetry through the poet's agonised vision of it. Moreover, Alberti is concerned entirely with something that happens in himself, with what he thinks and feels in this crisis. The external world and its events hardly count in comparison with his inescapable private troubles. This is an extremely intimate, self-examining, self-revealing poetry. Alberti turns the full strength of his intellectual passion to understanding his state and to giving an exact account of it as it strikes him in its bleakness and its horror. In this condition his intellect becomes much more than an interested observer : it is a witness deeply engaged and disturbed by what it sees. And this is beyond the bounds of the rational. Elementary subconscious and half-conscious forces are at work : they cannot be explained ; they can only be noticed and set down as the poet sees and feels them. In this specially interior poetry, with its unfamiliar moods and violent impressions of disorder and disaster in the soul, a highly modern technique does its work well. It is able to respond to the different movements of the subject and to catch its different aspects as they really strike the poet. Indeed a more regular and more conventional manner might almost destroy the subject by omitting those confused and fleeting elements which are most important to it. In its own way *Sobre los Ángeles* justifies a modern method as *The Waste Land* does, and shows that when the spirit is stirred by violent and disrupting emotions, the poet's art must give a true impression of the chaos that follows.

Alberti is so accomplished a craftsman of verse and so well trained in its different forms that he has no difficulty in finding the right measures for his different moods. His first section is on the whole composed in short lines : in the second section the lines become longer, and in the third they develop the wide sweep which Apollinaire gives to some of his poems about war. This variation is clearly deliberate. In the first section Alberti's exhaustion and emptiness forbid extended rhythms because they would be inappropriate to his mood, but as he faces the new issues of the second and third sections, and his imagination begins to work more adventurously, the lines respond to his efforts and carry a greater weight of words. And as the lines become longer, so do the sentences. In his shorter lines Alberti often uses a highly impressionistic method of putting down the vital words without forming them into grammatical units, as in

> Sin ojos, sin voz, sin sombra.
> Ya, sin sombra.
> Invisible para el mundo,
> para nadie.[1]

---

[1] Without eyes, without voice, without shadow,
Now, without shadow,
Invisible to the world,
To everyone.

or

Y tú, mar,
y tú, fuego,
y tú,
acelerado aire de mi sueño.[1]

This method shows that to the poet in his broken state every word is an effort, that explanations are easier for him than statements and that he can do no more than point to what he means in the shortest possible way. But, as he collects his strength and determination and tries to master his circumstances, his sentences become longer with his lines, and he keeps his rhythms taut and strong through the structure of the words in them, as in

Pero por fin llegó el día, la hora de las palas y los cubos.
No esperaba la luz que se vinieran abajo los minutos,
porque distraía en el mar la nostalgia de los ahogados,[2]

and

Porque hay siempre ún ultimo posterior a la caída de los páramos,
al advenimiento del frío en los sueños que se descuidan,
a los derrumbos de la muerte sobre el esqueleto de la nada.[3]

Each line, and each clause, stands in its own strength, with its own muscular control and discipline. The change from the short spasmodic lines of the first poems reflects the change in the poet's spirit. He has passed beyond his agonised dismay to some control of his situation and himself.

Alberti's technique has finer subtleties than in his use of short and long lines. He had, after all, practised with great skill the traditional Spanish art of song and used it for new purposes, and there are occasions in *Sobre los Ángeles* when he makes use of this experience and gives even to his disordered emotions a certain ordered elegance, as if he were trying to subdue his crisis by giving it a shape. He does not do this

[1] And you, sea,
And you, fire,
And you,
Hastened wind of my dream.

[2] Yet at the end came the day, the hour of shovels and pails.
The light did not expect the fall of the minutes,
Because it was distracting in the sea the desire of the drowned for the earth.

[3] Because there is always an end, even after the fall of the bare, bleak plateau,
After the advent of cold in dreams that forget their purpose,
After the impacts of death on the skeleton of nothing.

(J. M. Cohen)

for his annihilating agonies, but at times, when some memory or hope comes to him, he allows it to fall into a more regular form. For instance in *Invitación al aire* (*Invitation to the Air*) he expresses a strong desire to escape from his gloom to a freer state, and the dominating symbol in his mind is the air with its suggestions of space and cleanliness and freedom. So he writes almost a formal song with a refrain :

Te invito, sombra, al aire.
Sombra de veinte siglos,
a la verdad del aire,
del aire, aire, aire.

Sombra que nunca sales
de tu cueva y al mundo
no devolviste el silbo
que al nacer te dió el aire,
el aire, aire, aire.

Sombra sin luz, minera
por las profundidades
de veinte tumbas, veinte
siglos huecos sin aire.
sin aire, aire, aire.

¡ Sombra, a los picos, sombra,
de la verdad del aire,
del aire, aire, aire ! [1]

For the moment Alberti's emotions have coalesced into a single mood, and he thinks less of his chaos than of some hope to

[1] I invite you, shadow, to the air,
Shadow of twenty centuries,
To the truth of the air,
Of the air, the air, the air.

Shadow, you who never come forth
From your cellar, and to the world
Have not given back the whistle
That the air gave you at birth,
The air, the air, the air.

Shadow without light, miner
In the depths
Of twenty graves, twenty
Empty centuries without air,
Without air, air, air.

Shadow, at the picks, shadow
Of the truth of the air,
The air, the air, the air.

redeem it, and for this purpose the regular form is admirably suited with its equal movements suggestive of a quieter condition, and its repetitions which show how a single idea dominates his mind.

Against such occasional examples of a regular form we may set the poems in which Alberti trusts to his ear to secure a free, full movement for his themes. In some we can perhaps still detect faint traces of the old song-form, but it has been changed into something more irregular, and its music is sharper and less melodious. This hint of a lost or abandoned form suits Alberti's sense of having been robbed of something most vital and important. The movement of the verse is now broken and incomplete, as if it missed something. So for instance in *El ángel ángel* (*The Angel Angel*) Alberti speaks of the vast difference between his lost world and what he now feels. His poem has hints of a regular movement, but even in its short space this is broken, and the contrast between order and failure is marked in the mixture of regular and irregular rhythms :

> Y el mar fué y le dió un nombre
> y un apellido el viento
> y las nubes un cuerpo
> y un alma el fuego.
>
> La tierra, nada.
>
> Ese reino movible,
> colgado de las águilas,
> no la conoce.
>
> Nunca escribió su sombra
> la figura de un hombre.[1]

The poem begins almost with a melody but soon slows its

[1] And the sea was, and gave it a name,
And the wind a surname,
And the clouds a body,
And the flame a soul.
The earth nothing.
That moving kingdom,
Hanging from the eagles,
Knows it not.
Never did its shadow write
The figure of a man.

pace and breaks it to suit the change in the poet's mind as he turns from what might be to what is, from the ideal to the real.

The art of free verse attempts many more adventurous results than this, especially in the third section where it moves in nervous sympathy with the demands which Alberti's packed emotions make of it. It has much to do, since Alberti says much in a little space, and the rhythm must allow each image to make its effect and each sentence to come triumphantly to its close. How skilful his technique is can be seen from *El mal minuto* (*The Bad Minute*). In this poem Alberti comes nearer than anywhere to describing the actual crisis which is presupposed by the book, but now he sees it in retrospect, though not without horror, and is able to sum up its significance for him :

> Cuando para mí eran los trigos viviendas de astros y de dioses
> y la escarcha los lloros helados de una gacela,
> alguien me enyesó el pecho y la sombra,
> traicionándome.
>
> Ese minuto fué el de las balas perdidas,
> el del secuestro, por el mar, de los hombres que quisieron
>   ser pájaros,
> el del telegrama a deshora y el hallazgo de sangre,
> el de la muerte del agua que siempre miró al cielo.[1]

The rhythm follows the movement of the poet's feelings. In the first verse, so long as he thinks of his childhood, his words have a noble flow ; then, as he remembers how he lost this vision, the rhythm becomes sharper, and the fourth line conveys his catastrophe in a single tremendous word. In the second verse he gives the nature of his shock, and the rise and fall of the rhythm corresponds with his passage from anger and indignation to acceptance of defeat.

[1] When the wheat for me was a dwelling place of stars and gods
And the frost the frozen tears of a gazelle,
Someone plastered my breast and my shadow,
Betraying me.

That was the minute when the stray shots were fired,
When the sea kidnapped the men who wanted to be birds,
Of the untimely telegram and the discovery of blood
And of the death of the water that always gazed at the sky.

(J. M. Cohen)

If the versification of *Sobre los Ángeles* shows Alberti's mastery of a modern technique, the same can be said of his imagery. Since he deals almost exclusively with psychological states, he uses imagery all the time. Indeed he hardly ever uses plain descriptive statement, but plunges into imagery without introduction or explanation. In this he may be compared with Eliot, who does not explain what his images mean, but trusts that they will force themselves on us, and make us see their significance. Again, just as Eliot gives a certain order and homogeneity to his images through his use of the Grail legend and its figures but diversifies this with images from quite different and disparate sources, so Alberti gives a dominating pattern to his book by the imagery of angels but diversifies this by a great variety of images which have no essential or obvious connection with angels. But his angels give a greater consistency and coherence to his book than Eliot's anthropological figures give to *The Waste Land*. For they have a more immediate appeal and gain through the simplicity of their outlines and characters. We pick up their meaning at once, and since they are seldom far away, they give a shape and direction to the whole book. Alberti has found a mythology which is full of imaginative possibilities and calls for no erudition to understand it. *Sobre los Ángeles* is a single book and not a collection of separate pieces, largely because the dominating imagery has this unity.

In his use of angels Alberti suggests comparisons with other poets and especially with Rilke, who in his *Duino Elegies* gives angels a predominant part and supplements their symbolism with symbols drawn from quite different quarters. But the difference between Rilke and Alberti lies in the significance which they give to their angels. For Rilke the angel is the absolute of inspiration, the symbol of the uninhibited activity which he sought to secure and express. Alberti's angels are powers of the spirit in all its range, not in themselves good or bad, pleasant or unpleasant. They are not even habits of thought or emotions, but simply powers which any man may recognise in himself, forces of the spirit or flesh which give meaning to what he feels or does. He may welcome them or resist them, but they exist, and their strength is not to be denied. Even their origin is obscure. They have been connected with the angels depicted in primitive Catalan art, but they have no specifically Christian qualities, and their activities are not such as we associate with angels good or bad. But we can see why Alberti uses them. They are symbols of powers outside the control of man but connected with the secret springs of his nature. Just as he regards his crisis as a spiritual event which involves fundamental issues in the value of life and the stricken state of man, so he introduces angels because they embody his sense of powers not himself which come from unknown regions and determine the course of his life and personality. They are both alien and extremely intimate, and he is fully entitled to make use of them because the violent nature of his crisis raises questions so fundamental and so searching that his work has inevitably something like a religious character.

Alberti's angels are best understood if we set them against the background of crisis and collapse which he presents in his first poem through the image of a lost Paradise. He has suffered a fearful deprivation and longs to recover what he can. Above all he has lost his taste for life and his sense of the significance both of great and little things. He sets out the themes of his loss and his search :

> —Ángel muerto, despierta.
> ¿Dónde estás ? Ilumina
> con tu rayo el retorno.
>
> Silencio. Más silencio.
> Inmóviles los pulsos
> del sinfín de la noche.
>
> ¡ Paráiso perdido !
> Perdido por buscarte,
> Yo, sin luz para siempre.[1]

---

[1] Dead angel, awaken.
Where are you ? Shed light
With your ray on the way back.

Silence. Silence still.
Unmoved the pulses
Of night's endlessness.

Lost Paradise !
Lost for seeking you,
I, without light for ever.

Expelled from his Paradise, Alberti finds himself the plaything
and victim of unfamiliar forces which he calls angels, and
feels that somehow these forces are of the same kind as those
which he used to know before his collapse. In the first part
his angels belong largely to his lost world. They are what he
tries to find again, the unknown angel on whom he calls for
help, the good angel whom he once knew and who inspired his
being, the angel of numbers who stands for an ideal of order
and clarity, the unlucky angel who eludes his summons. But
these lost angels are soon replaced by others who are insistent
and present and less desirable. He feels that fierce forces are
at war in himself, and they are bellicose angels ; he believes
that he has been tricked, and puts the blame on a lying angel ;
his world has been burned and shrivelled, and it is the work
of the " angel of coal " ; he feels that he is decaying or being
burned to ashes, and his angels are rusty or ashen ; he ascribes
his fierce passions to an angel of fury. These new passions
grow stronger, and with the process the angels become more
formidable. They assail him with red-hot coals ; they are
cruel, angry, vengeful, stupid, greedy. Such are the forces
at work in himself, and though they have no celestial splendour,
they are terrible and powerful and unearthly, and he knows
that they are no less closely related to the sources of life than
the gentle angels whom he has lost. In the third stage
Alberti's angels lose some of this grimness and are connected
with certain familiar activities. There are angels of the sand,
of the wine-shops, of the college, of the ruins. Just as certain
emotions have their own inexorable force, so have certain
places and activities. These are the means by which Alberti
begins to regain a small particle of his lost confidence and to
strengthen his determination to live. Then at the end there
emerges from the ruins a faint hope with the " faithful "
angels and the " surviving " angel, the powers which remain
after the crisis is over and show the way to the future.

The actions of these strange angels and their various parts
in Alberti's life are conveyed through a wealth of wonderfully
significant imagery. Alberti's images have not merely a strikingly visual appeal : they carry with them a great force of
suggestion in the fewest possible words. Like Lorca, he does

not always make his images strictly coherent with one another, but tries to make them as truthful as possible to the strange conflicts which he feels. His own decayed condition appears in the juxtaposition of images of decay and neglect :

> Por los desvanes de los sueños rotos.
> Telarañas. Polillas. Polvo.[1]

When furious hatreds sweep into him,

> Son puertas de sangre,
> milenios de odios,
> lluvias de rencores, mares.[2]

His greed has a terrifyingly ruthless and merciless quality :

> Los ojos,
> luces de acetileno,
> húmedas, áureas galerías,
> El corazón,
> explosiones de piedras, júbilos, dinamita.[3]

The cosmic character of his catastrophe demands imagery as vast and as violent as itself :

> Es cuando golfos y bahías de sangre,
> coagulados de astros difuntos y vengativos,
> inundan los sueños.[4]

These calcined, ruined relics are set against memories of a better time, and Alberti gives the contrast to his images of destruction through images of sweetness and exaltation, as

[1] In the garrets of broken dreams.
Cobwebs. Moths. Dust.

[2] They are gates of blood,
Myriads of hatreds.
Showers of rancours, seas.

[3] His eyes,
Acetylene flares,
Damp, golden corridors.
His heart
Explosions of stones, outbursts of glee, dynamite.
(J. M. Cohen)

[4] There are times when gulfs and bays of blood,
Clotted from dead and vengeful stars,
Flood my dreams.

when he knew the " good angel " and shared its flight :

> Atrás, montes y mares,
> nubes, picos y alas,
> los ocasos, las albas,[1]

or recalls the lost joys and confidence of childhood :

> Cuando el viento soñaba melenas que peinar
> y claveles el fuego que encender y mejillas
> y el agua unos labios parados donde beber,[2]

or hopes that perhaps after all order may be restored and life resume its regular course :

> Cuidades deshabitadas
> se pueblan, de pronto. Trenes
> descarrilados, unidos
> marchan.[3]

The effect is always immediate and irresistible. Alberti seizes the central point in a situation and drives its significance home.

Alberti's use of imagery changes somewhat as his book proceeds. In the first stages, when he speaks of the chaotic character of his crisis, its chief quality is its terrible clarity, but as he moves to the complex issues which he discovers in regaining his hold on life, his imagery too becomes more complex. A single image or a single arrangement of images is not enough, and he develops a technique by which he moves rapidly from one image to another or qualifies one by something different. The result is that he loses some of his immediacy of effect, but he gains by showing how rich in possibilities these situations are. For instance, he speaks of

[1] Behind, mountains and seas,
Clouds, peaks and wings,
Sunsets and dawns.

[2] When the wind dreamed of tresses to comb,
And the flame of carnations and cheeks to set ablaze,
And the water of lips ready for drinking.

[3] Cities uninhabited
Are suddenly peopled. Trains
Derailed come together
And go.

the essential unhappiness of existence and suggests that man
is doomed to it from before his birth :

> Bambolea el viento un vientre de gritos anteriores al mundo,
> a la sorpresa de la luz en los ojos de los recién nacidos,
> al descenso de la vía láctea a las gargantas terrestres.[1]

He imagines that cries of sorrow exist before life, and sees
them as swayed by the wind in a belly, which shows their
irrational and spasmodic nature. Then, when life begins, the
light in the eyes of children is shocked, and the sorrow to which
men are fated comes into them, as it were down the Milky
Way. It is as if this doom were destined in the nature of the
universe, and Alberti's details stress its universal character.
Again, when he speaks of the way in which men forget the
tragic and confused nature of life, he says :

> Se olvidan hombres de brea y fango
> que sus buques y sus trenos,
> a vista de pájaro,
> son ya en medio del mundo una mancha de aceite,
> limitada de cruces de todas partes.[2]

The images follow one another quickly and change their
character rapidly that we may see at once the complex character of Alberti's thought. Each element in it is presented
with great force through its own image, but this has nothing
to do with the image that presents the next element. What
matters is the series of effects which cohere through the movement of thought which provokes them.

Though *Sobre los Ángeles* tells of a single crisis in the soul
and though the different poems in it are closely welded into
a single design, there is a great richness in its poetry. Alberti
exploits a long scale of experiences and emotions between his
longing for his lost Paradise and the gloom and agony which

---

[1] The wind swayed a belly of cries earlier than the world,
To the surprise of the light in the eyes of the newly born,
To the descent of the Milky Way to earthly throats.

[2] Men of pitch and mud forget
That their boats and trains,
To a bird's eye,
Are a stain of oil in the middle of the world,
Bounded by crosses on every side.

he suffers in having lost it. His poetry moves between these extremes, and since his crisis passes through many stages, his poetry varies greatly from poem to poem and introduces many tones and phases. The bounds of his subject can be seen from *El ángel de los números* (*The Angel of Numbers*) which marks the contrast between his former trust in an absolute, mathematical order and the disorder which he now sees, and its poetry stresses the two extremes of his experience. He begins by sketching the lost order through the image of an angel watching over a school and the display of mathematical problems on blackboards :

> Vírgenes con escuadras
> y compases, velando
> las celestes pizarras.
>
> Y el ángel de los números,
> pensativo, volando
> del 1 al 2, del 2
> al 3, del 3 al 4.[1]

The apparently simple situation shows what ease and security the universe once had for Alberti. It seemed to be governed by intelligible laws which it was pleasant and not laborious to master. But this situation has changed :

> Tizas frías y esponjas
> rayaban y borraban
> la luz de los espacios.
>
> Ni sol, luna, ni estrellas,
> ni el repentino verde
> del rayo y el relámpago,
> ni el aire. Sólo nieblas.
>
> Vírgenes sin escuadras,
> sin compases, llorando.

---

[1] Maidens with squares
And compasses, watching over
The celestial blackboards.

And the angel of numbers,
Pensive, flying
From 1 to 2, from 2
To 3, from 3 to 4.

> Y en las muertas pizarras,
> el ángel de los números,
> sin vida, amortajado
> sobre el 1 y el 2,
> sobre el 3, sobre el 4 . . .[1]

The neat imagery of numbers conveys the transition from a delightful and reasoned order to unreason, obscurity and disaster. The highly individual picture suggests with imaginative precision the character of the poet's crisis.

The world which Alberti has lost has still a reality for him in recollection and desire. It was a harmonious and inspiring condition in which his forces were freely at work without doubt or question. What must have been a time when his trust in life was sure and his creative powers still instinctively certain of themselves becomes an example of something vaster and more exciting, whose loss is an unaccountable catastrophe. Alberti's longings for it are much stronger than the vague desires for the " hyacinth garden " which haunt Eliot, and though they have something in common with the yearning for the lost vision of childhood as Vaughan and Wordsworth and Rilke knew it, they are wider and more poignant. Alberti's lost Paradise certainly has its connection with his childhood, but that is only a part of it. It is something which all men know to some degree, and creative artists know better than others, when their powers are fully at work. For Alberti this lost world is a place where his vision is clear and his faculties

---

[1] Cold chalks and sponges
Crossed out and erased
The light of the spaces.

Nor sun, moon, nor stars,
Nor the sudden green
Of the sunbeam and the lightning
Nor the air. Only clouds.

Maidens without squares,
Without compasses, weeping.

And on the dead blackboards,
The angel of numbers,
Without life, shrouded,
Over the 1 and the 2,
Over the 3, over the 4.

work easily and with assurance. He speaks of it in a way which leaves no doubt :

> Dentro del pecho se abren
> corredores anchos, largos,
> que sorben todas las mares.
>
> Vidrieras,
> que alumbran todas las calles.
>
> Miradores,
> que acercan todas las torres.[1]

He knows that its most precious gift is not quiet or security, but the unimpeded activity of his finest powers, and that it offers not the blank austerity of the moon or snow but something positive and human. He seeks not the ideal of Rilke's angel but an actual life in which his heart and soul play their full parts and gain strength from celestial forces. That is why the angel whom he seeks has a special task, not to conquer death but to make life flow more freely :

> Sin arañar los aires,
> sin herir hojas ni mover cristales.
>
> Aquel que a sus cabellos
> ató el silencio.
>
> Para, sin lastimarme,
> cavar una ribera be luz dulce en mi pecho
> y hacerme el alma navegable.[2]

The lost world gave radiance and strength, and these are what Alberti seeks to regain.

[1] Within his breast there open
Corridors long and wide
That suck up all the seas.

Windows of shops
That light up all the streets.

Observatories
That bring near all the towers.
(J. M. Cohen)

[2] Without scratching winds,
Without wounding leaves or moving crystals.

He, who to his hair
Bound silence.

Without hurting me, to hollow
A river of sweet light in my breast
And make my soul navigable.

In the third section the lost Paradise shows its lineaments more clearly and is presented with something else than the violent emotions of loss. As he gets further from it and begins to know that he will never completely recover it, Alberti sees more clearly and in more detail what it once meant to him. It is indeed the world not only of his childhood but of his youth and first manhood, of the time when his delight in existence was broken by no sceptical doubts but sustained by an unending sense of the miracle of existence. In *Tres recuerdos del cielo* (*Three Memories of Heaven*) he gives three memories of this lost state. In the first he stresses its wonderful silence which is " anterior to the harp and the rain and words " ; in the second he speaks of the epoch when his first dreams and first words come ; and in the third of the visions which filled the sky and had their own independent existence. These poems are dedicated to the memory of Gustavo Bécquer and each is preceded by a quotation from him. Since these quotations refer to poetical inspiration, it is clear that Alberti is treating of a double theme or rather of a single theme from two aspects. His childhood and his inspiration are the same : the second has prolonged into manhood what the first gave him at the beginning. The comparison with Wordsworth is inevitable but incomplete ; for Wordsworth does not say that his inspiration is a prolongation of the visions of childhood. He may indeed live partly on these memories, but his mature life is determined by something else to different ends. For Alberti, childhood and the first creative years are parts of a single process and inspired by the same forces. It is as if his growth had been entirely single and unimpeded until his twenty-fifth year and he had carried into his first manhood all the rounded unity of childhood. His words show what this means. In silence and words and visions he gives the three component parts of his creative life. The first is the ease with which he feels himself at work, ready to absorb and to understand ; the second are his means of expression which come to him from nothing, and the third the results of his creation — figures which are more real and more self-sufficient than anything in the familiar world.

Yet, as he looks more closely into the nature of this vanished experience, Alberti becomes more convinced that it was all a state of dream. Though he deeply regrets the loss of this dream-world, it is still a dream-world. That is why it was so vivid and so full of wonderful surprises, so satisfying and so radiant, but at the same time so remote from common fact and common ways of thought. In *Los ángeles colegiales* (*The Angels of College*) he dwells on the wonderful ignorance and incomprehension of schoolboys :

> Ninguno comprendiamos nada :
> ni por qué nuestros dedos eran de tinta china
> y la tarde cerraba compases para al alba abrir libros.
> Sólo sabiamos que una recta, si quiere, puede ser curva o quebrada
> y que las estrellas errantes son niños que ignoran la aritmética.[1]

The gift which children have of transforming familiar objects through their imagination into something else is also very much what the poet has, and it is this gift which Alberti once possessed and feels that he has lost. His crisis bears some resemblance to that of Rimbaud when almost by an act of will he made phenomena seem to be different from what they were and then suddenly ceased to believe in this gift and flung it angrily aside. The crisis which Alberti suffered is that of the creative artist who lives in his own self-sufficient world and then finds to his horror that it is not real. Slowly the truth forces itself on him until he completely changes his outlook and his work. Such a process is inevitably painful, and it is not surprising that in its earlier stages it brings a mood close to despair.

Sobre los Ángeles is much concerned with the shock of this change. At first Alberti does not see clearly what it means but knows what it costs. He can hardly believe that he is still himself. He wears his old clothes but does not know who he is. He feels empty and meaningless :

> Quedó mi cuerpo vacío,
> negro saco, a la ventana.[2]

---

[1] None of us understood anything :
neither why our fingers were of painted porcelain,
and the evening closed compasses to open books to dawn.
We knew only that a straight, if it wishes, can be curved or broken,
and that the wandering stars are children who know no arithmetic.

[2] My empty body remained,
A black sack, at the window.

Not merely has he lost his intellectual life, but even his senses seem hardly to work, and he tells how each one of them fails him and refuses to answer the calls made on it. Above all, his art of words, upon which he has lived and thrived, is now hollow and mocks him and has passed somehow beyond his control :

> Ya sabéis que mi boca es un pozo de nombres,
> de números y letras difuntos.
> Que los ecos se hastían sin mis palabras
> y lo que jamás dije desprecia y odia al viento.[1]

It is not surprising that in this condition he sees himself as the victim of some fallen angel who reigns in darkness and desolation and burns up his spirit :

> Me estás quemando vivo.
> Vuela ya de mí, oscuro
> Luzbel de las canteras sin auroras,
> de los pozos sin agua,
> de las simas sin sueño,
> ya carbón del espíritu,
> sol, luna.[2]

Alberti creates a special poetry of this empty, ruined state, but unlike some other poets of similar collapses he does not allow his poetry to share in this deadness. Great and impressive though Coleridges's *Dejection* is, it somehow fails to give the last pleasures of poetry because it reflects what is ultimately an uncreative mood, but Alberti succeeds in making his poetry thrilling because, great though his collapse is, he fights against it and resents passionately what it costs him. His poetry is full of fire and force because he feels so acutely what his fall means.

[1] Now you know that my mouth is a well of names,
Of numbers and dead letters,
That the echoes are cloyed without my words,
That all that I ever say despises and hates the wind.

[2] You are burning me alive.
Fly from me now, dark
Lucifer of the pits without dawns,
Of the wells without water,
Of the caverns without dream,
Now, coal of the spirit,
Sun, moon.

Into this empty state new forces enter, and Alberti's old harmony is replaced by terrible discords of primitive passions. At first he is almost too broken to receive them, but the first sign of their presence is a rancour against life which has brought him to this pass :

> ¿ Quién sacude en mi almohada
> reinados de yel y sangre,
> cielos de azufre,
> mares de vinagre ? [1]

Slowly he becomes conscious that he has no control over himself and is a battlefield for contending forces. He figures himself as a tower between battling winds, which break up the cities of the earth and hurl against him people who are somehow both familiar and unfamiliar, as if he had once known them but knows them no more :

> Remolinos de ciudades
> bajan los desfiladeros.
> Cuidades del viento sur,
> que me vieron.
>
> Por las neveras, rodando,
> pueblos.
> Pueblos que yo desconozco,
> ciudades del viento norte,
> que no me vieron. [2]

In this conflict he remains, unmoved and empty, in the middle, but the situation is ready for new forces to enter, and they soon do. First anger appears, almost imperceptibly. The

[1] Who shakes into my pillow
Kingdoms of gall and blood,
Skies of sulphur,
Seas of vinegar ?

[2] Whirlwinds of cities
Come down the defiles.
Cities of the south wind,
Who saw me.

On the ice, rolling
Peoples.
Peoples whom I know not,
Cities of the north wind,
Who saw me not.

poet seems to remember something, without knowing really what it is, and to be angry about it. This state has no clear meaning : he cannot interpret the silence which it brings, but he feels something ugly at work in his blood. Then comes envy :

> Un cielo, verde de envidia,
> rebosa mi boca y canta,
> Yo, un cielo . . .[1]

He feels that this is something false, and he fights against it, that it is killing his soul and breaking his confidence, and that he must bar it out. Next comes the " stupid angel ", the symbol of the deadness which is beginning to dominate him. It is afraid of its powers, and he wonders if it can really be a power of the spirit and not merely of the earth. Then, something more frightening comes. Darker passions are loosed in him, and he is swept by violent desires of destruction and greed. He feels that he is dead and yet at the same time this fierce greed is active in him, so that he is almost a criminal carried away by insane ambitions of wealth :

> Ese hombre está muerto
> y no lo sabe.
> Quiere asaltar la banca,
> robar nubes, estrellas, cometas de oro,
> comprar lo más difícil :
> el cielo.
> Y ese hombre está muerto.[2]

By a natural process the loss of his confidence makes Alberti an easy prey to primitive passions, but even now he keeps some kind of independence from them, fights them as well as he can, and maintains his human dignity against their assaults.

[1] A sky, green with envy,
Overflows my mouth and sings.
I, a sky . . .

[2] This man is dead
And does not know it.
He wishes to break a bank,
To steal clouds, stars, golden comets,
To buy what is most difficult,
The sky.
And this man is dead.

His powerful intellect is not deceived by them, and so great is
his sense of what he has lost that he refuses to give in completely to the disorder which threatens him. His poetry is that
of the struggle of a powerful mind and a strong will against
forces which would be too powerful for most men to resist.

As he passes through his ordeal, Alberti gradually finds
a new outlook on what has happened to him and sees that it is
neither so sudden nor so meaningless as he thought at first.
In *Muerte y juicio* (*Death and Judgment*) he gives his mature,
more considered account of it.   There is no doubt that something in him has died, and he sees this death as the result of
a judgment passed in heaven upon him. What has died is his
youth, which has been shrivelled to ashes and lies at his feet.
This fate is the fate of all human beings, and is predestined
for them before birth. Life is a double process : it both burns
and chills, and it combines laughter and lamentation. Both
sides of it are equally fated.   From excess of heat or excess of
cold it loses its first rapture, and it does this because at first
the soul lives in a world of its own which is not the real world
and cannot be adjusted to it   Into this secluded fastness reality
breaks and works destruction :

> Perdido entre ecuaciones, triángulos, fórmulas y precipitados azules,
> entre el suceso de la sangre, los escombros y las coronas caídas,
> cuando los cazadores de oro y el asalto a la banca,
> en el rubor tardío de las azoteas
> voces de ángeles te anunciaron la botadura y pérdida de tu alma.
> Niño.[1]

From this the young man tries to escape, to sink himself " in
the depth of the tides ", but this only emphasises and increases
his solitude   It is no real escape and no real answer to his
troubles. The result is that he loses his innocence and believes neither in Venus nor in dreams of celestial splendour.
He cannot escape from his destiny, and must yield to it. In

---

[1] Lost among equations, triangles, formulas and precipitated blues,
Among the outcome of the blood, the rubbish and the fallen crowns,
When the seekers for gold and the assault on the bank,
In the evening blush of the roofs
Voices of angels announced to you the looting and loss of your soul.
Child.

this way Alberti sets out the adjustment and the compromise which man has to make with reality. He may try to escape, but he will fail, and his attempt will cost him more than he can well pay. The claims of truth are inexorable, and however great the price may be, it has to be paid. This is the judgment passed by the skies on mankind, and there is no appeal against it.

With the death of the young soul the impulse of instinctive song also dies, but such is the spirit of man that it tries to regain some other way of song and to find new subjects in its new understanding of the world. It cannot hope to recover its old confidence or to see the universe in a splendid, single harmony, but from the broken pieces and the discords it can none the less extract something and find a new reason for work. In *Invitación al arpa* (*Invitation to the Harp*) Alberti shows his struggle towards this different outlook. The reality which he now faces may indeed be fragmentary and forbidding, a country of cobwebs, where things collapse without hope, but it is still real and mysterious and calls for his efforts. It has its own pathos and sorrow, and more than that, just because he has lost so much and knows what such a loss means, there is much for him to think about and to engage his feelings. As a poet, he can still live among echoes and memories and see that they belong to the tragic constitution of the world :

> Siempre, siempre más lejos.
> Adonde las maderas guardan ecos y sombras de pasos,
> adonde las polillas desvelan el silencio de las corbatas,
> adonde todo un siglo es un arpa en abandono.[1]

The whole present century has the appeal of an abandoned harp, of music broken in the middle, and this is what the poet must seek and appreciate and make musical again. Just as in his youth Alberti found his inspiration in a feeling of completeness and harmony, so now he tries to find it through his realisation of imperfection and failure, and just as before his poetry was naturally and necessarily happy, so now it can hope

---

[1] Always, always further.
  Where the woods keep echoes and shadows of steps,
  Where the moths keep awake the silence of cravats,
  Where a whole century is an abandoned harp.

only to dwell on the pathetic aspects of life, its incompleteness and its confusion.

From this Alberti advances to what is in effect a tragic vision of life, and sets it forth with great power in *Castigos* (*Punishments*). Fierce dreams assail him, and the night tastes of sulphur. He realises that he has lived in great ignorance and not understood what things actually are :

> Yo no sabía que las puertas cambiaban de sitio,
> que las almas podían ruborizarse de sus cuerpos,
> ni que al final de un túnel la luz traía la muerte.[1]

It is useless to call for the help of the dead, who are like bodies drifting in the sea with disfigured faces. His thoughts must turn to the sterner aspects of being, to the ruined worlds and the men without homes and the silent centuries. He must recognise that bodies are not what he once thought them to be, and that " the lament of a child deforms the constellations". The universe is full of faults, and corrupts and wrecks those who live in it :

> Cielos enmohecidos nos oxidan las frentes desiertas,
> donde cada minuto sepulta su cadáver sin nombre.[2]

There is always something beyond what we now have, beyond even death, and this sense of an endless process, no matter how disastrous and painful, is what concerns the poet and the man. Decay and death meant nothing in the lost Paradise : now they dominate the whole pattern of existence and give such meaning as it has to it. They must be recognised and respected. To make such an admission costs a man a good deal, especially when, like Alberti, he has lived with quite different beliefs. It is therefore not surprising that he is almost appalled by having to recast his vision of life and believes that in doing so he obeys vengeful powers who work in darkness. This is the poetry of a man still at war with himself and still acutely conscious of terrible issues at stake, but he faces them

---

[1] I did not know that the doors changed their places,
  That souls could blush at their bodies,
  Nor that at the end of a tunnel light brought death.

[2] Mildewed skies oxidise our deserted foreheads,
  Where every minute buries its nameless corpse.

with grim courage and rejects all anodynes. His deepest emotions are called out by the pathos of the human state, and he makes a supreme effort to see what it is and what it means.

This tragic vision has its positive side and inspires its own kind of creative spirit. That is why Alberti speaks of " angels of the ruins ", of the powers which give significance even to what seems to have been irretrievably spoiled or wasted. By curbing his hopes and reducing his horizon, by never expecting too much, Alberti finds the new limits in which he can work and the way in which he can do it. He accepts, almost with joy, these restrictions :

> Y nadie espera ya la llegada del expreso,
> la visita oficial de la luz a los mares necesitados,
> la resurrección de las voces en los eeos que se calcinan.[1]

Nor indeed have his angels entirely forsaken him. In new forms and in new places he seeks them, even though he calls them dead. In *Los ángeles muertos* (*The Dead Angels*) he sets out his present search for the powers of the spirit which hide in unsuspected and humble places, for " a broken ring or a trampled star ". Such angels he has seen and touched, and he continues to look for them :

> Buscad, buscadlos :
> debajo de la gota de cera que sepulta la palabra de un libro
> o la firma de uno de esos rincones de cartas
> que trae rodando el polvo.[2]

He has abandoned his old belief that life is passed in some splendid celestial region and recognises that he must find its secrets in quite different places. The most insignificant thing may be full of mystery and appeal. Just as Wordsworth was content after losing his glory and his dream with " the meanest flower that blows ", so Alberti is content with the meanest

---

[1] And now no one expects the arrival of the express,
The light's official visit to the impoverished seas,
The voices' resurrection in the echoes that burn to ash.

(J. M. Cohen)

[2] Seek, seek them :
Beneath the spot of wax that buries the word in a book
Or the signature on one of those corners of letters
That the dust trails around.

(J. M. Cohen)

things, provided that they yield some unexpected charm, some call to his humanity and sympathy and wonder. His angels are no longer creatures of light or darkness, of heavenly strength or diabolical destructiveness; they are the quieter impulses of the human spirit which have none the less their own peculiar grace. They give meaning to much that is otherwise meaningless, and they make sense of life despite its fragmentary, unsatisfying character.

Then in the last two poems of his book Alberti tells what remains to him after his doubts and his decisions. Something is certainly still there for the seeking, worthy of attainment and able to give him confidence in life. In his search certain powers have remained with him and sustained him, his " faithful angels ". They are the cause of his journey. They have taught him to accept the tragic vision of existence and to see that the highest hopes may end in ugliness or squalor. But they have done more than this. They have also taught him that all these imperfections and failures are as real and important as things perfect and complete and have their own splendour. This is his message :

Pero yo os digo :
una rosa es más rosa habitada por las orugas
que sobre la nieve marchita de esta luna de quince años.

Mirad esto también, antes que demos sepultura al viaje :
cuando una sombra se entrecoge las uñas en las visagras de las
    puertas
o el pie helado de un ángel sufre el insomnio fijo de una piedra,
mi alma sin saberlo se perfecciona.[1]

The failures of life are indispensable to it because through them the soul of man finds its way to perfection. Just as his imagery of angels and of an expulsion from Paradise gives a

---

[1] But I tell you :
A rose is the more a rose when the caterpillars dwell on it
Than over the faded snow of this moon of fifteen years.

Look at this too, before we give burial to the journey,
When a shadow intercepts its nails in the fringes of the doors
Or an angel's frozen foot suffers the fixed insomnia of a stone,
My soul, without knowing it, perfects itself.

religious character to Alberti's poetry, so his conclusion is in its own way religious. The central fact which emerges from his devastating ordeal is not for the world but for his own soul. His catastrophe is private and personal. In his new interests, his warmer sympathies, his greater courage and patience and endurance, his expectation of nothing too much, and his determination to make the most of what he finds, Alberti comes to his conclusion. So in his last poem, *El ángel superviviente* (*The Surviving Angel*) he gives his welcome to the prospect of disaster, to " the dispersion of life and the slow assassination ", and finds something friendly in the fall of the sky. In this cold world phantoms die, and though all his angels will lose their life, yet one, wounded and with clipped wings, survives, — the angel of life itself which still guides and sustains him.

Sobre los Ángeles is in the first place a poet's confession of a tremendous crisis in his life. What Alberti records with such power and insight is by no means unique to him. The struggle and the agony which he has to face in his transition from the dreams of youth to a rigorous grasp of reality is known to other poets. We have seen how it determined the tragic career of José Asunción Silva and turned him from a visionary symbolist into a fierce critic of romantic illusions. Like him, Alberti implicitly criticises any acceptance of another world as the right field for a poet's work. Something of the same kind was known to more than one of the romantic poets. Sooner or later, they were forced into a hard choice between pursuing their dreams to the end and abandoning them for something closer to common experience. Wordsworth solved the problem by concentrating his attention on physical nature and finding in it enough to guide his later work. Shelley tried to turn his dreams into action, and, though in his last years he had begun to see that he might fail and was assailed by moments of dark melancholy, he died before he had to make his final decision. Other poets have been less fortunate, especially those who tried to live their dreams to the last and refused to accommodate them to the world of ordinary men. For Edgar Allan Poe and for Gérard de Nerval the other world was always the real world, and actual phenomena a source of trouble and confusion which they refused to accept. The result was a search, conscious or unconscious, for some anodyne which should enable them to maintain their dreams. In the end both died tragically without having realised all their remarkable gifts. However wonderful the rewards may be which such a life of vision seems to offer to the poet, he seeks them at his peril unless he comes to terms with ordinary reality. This new issue was forced on Alberti in spite of himself, but his powerful intelligence told him what it meant, and with high courage he drew the full conclusions from it.

The issue which faced Alberti as a poet faced him also as a man. It is significant that after the publication of *Sobre los Ángeles* he not only tried to bring his work into a much closer relation with practical life but gave much of his time and energies to politics until he fought as an airman in the Spanish Civil War and at its disastrous close followed his friends into exile in the Argentine. The crisis through which he had passed was more than a crisis in his creative life: it was a hard process of adjustment to a mature view of existence. A few years later Lorca was to pass through a similar ordeal when he visited New York and was horrified by the realities of metropolitan life and especially by the hideous condition of the American negroes. This experience had a terrible effect on him, and he never quite recovered from it: at least he never regained the complete and balanced outlook in which he had written his *Romancero*. Though the 'twenties began with many hopes and ideals, it was not long before keener intellects saw that an apparent calm on the surface hid dark forces at work underneath. Alberti's realisation of this turned him to politics, but his political life was only a part of something wider, of his discovery that a tragic view of life was the only thing that could make sense of the universe as he now saw it. For a few years after the armistice of 1918 European civilisation had regained some of its old unity and singleness, but this was really no more than a respite after years of hideous effort. The new shape of things soon began to show itself and to break the conventions in which men had been content to live. Above all, the old sense of security was perishing. Just as Eliot in *The Waste Land* depicts the crisis of the modern spirit which has lost the dignity and style of the past, so Alberti is above all the poet of those who have been forced to recognise the imperfections of existence, but, instead of complaining about it, have decided to face it with courage and candour.

In *Sobre los Ángeles* Alberti shows how an experience which might seem to be depressing and devitalising can be turned into the highest poetry. No doubt part of this success comes from the fighting spirit which Alberti shows in his war with circumstances, but part also comes from his masterly management of a modern technique If this experience had been expressed in a more regular and more harmonious form, it would have lost its most essential qualities. Just because it is so chaotic and so devastating it falls perfectly into an art which responds exactly to disordered states of mind and soul. And more important than this is the way in which Alberti's technique enables him to extract the last drop of poetry from each moment in his crisis. Because he knows so well what poetry is and has so sure an instinct for finding it, he is able to annex territories which have never been entered before. At a time when a less courageous man might well have broken down under the shock of such a crisis, Alberti summoned all his powers and created a poetry with a most unusual concentration and intensity. The forces which seemed likely to destroy his confidence and happiness are turned into poetry and made to yield that special delight which it alone can give. In transcending his own crisis through the magic of his art Alberti not only solves his own private problem but enables others to face experiences like his own. The destructive powers which assail him in the very centre of his life become his instruments for a new, creative outlook on some most important problems and are brought into a harmonious scheme which their very nature at first seemed to deny. Modern poetry may often seem to be concerned with disintegrating and depressing emotions, but at times it shows that they too can be made into a means for a greater sense of order and a new kind of harmony. In the last resort the creative principle which works in such unexpected ways imposes its own discipline and dominion on the most intractable material.

By following his sure instinct for what is really poetry

Alberti gives its special splendour to *Sobre los Ángeles*, but hardly less important in the final result is the intellectual passion and passionate desire for the truth which accompanies the creative instinct. Through this Alberti both makes his poetry relevant to the experience of other men and gives to it a strength which nothing can shake. In every poem we feel this solid foundation of fact, this determination to portray experience as it really is, and not to make concessions to any romantic or sentimental outlooks. In this Alberti takes his place with the best poets of his time, whose special characteristic and claim is that they give to reality the same intense concentration that they give to their art and by this have redeemed the charge that poetry at the beginning of the century was becoming false to itself and to life. "We have forgotten", says Pasternak, "that it is in our power to do one thing, and that is not to distort the living voice of life." The poet's voice should be the voice of life. It is this which speaks through him with a greater force than through other men and passes from him to a whole society whose undiscovered feelings he illuminates and makes real. In their pursuit of a purer, more essential poetry modern poets have set themselves a hard task, but, when they have succeeded, it has been in a truly new way. For in their combination of creative intensity and a passionate concern for truth they have produced work in which we find not only the peculiar thrill which we demand from any imaginative experience, but the sense of security and permanence which comes from the conviction that this art is intimately related to the real world in which we live.

INDEX